"In *City Centre* Simon has successfully managed to capture the heady and intoxicating allure of top level rugby in the final years of the amateur era, through his varied experiences as a player.

Rugby's friendships, the selection highs and lows, the desperate struggle with the inevitability of injuries and trying to start a family and a career in the City are issues Simon deals with openly and honestly.

Simon is a thoroughly loyal, intelligent and talented individual. He is the right type of 'rugby' person to take the professional game forward and I would have loved to work with him at international rugby level."

Nick Mallett

CITY CENTRE

HIGH BALL TO HIGH FINANCE

SIMON HALLIDAY

Matador
9 Priory Business Park
Kibworth Beauchamp
Leicestershire LE8 0RX, UK
Tel: (+44) 116 279 2299
Fax: (+44) 116 279 2277
Email: books@troubador.co.uk
Web: www.troubador.co.uk/matador

ISBN 978 1783061 129

British Library Cataloguing in Publication Data.
A catalogue record for this book is available from the British Library.

Printed and bound in the UK by TJ International, Padstow, Cornwall
Typeset in 11pt Aldine401 BT Roman by Troubador Publishing Ltd, Leicester, UK

Matador is an imprint of Troubador Publishing Ltd

To my family
To all those who smile at adversity

Acknowledgements

My sincere thanks go to Sir Clive Woodward for his foreword; a man who personifies the undeniable links between business and sporting success.

To my dear friend, writer and journalist, David Llewellyn, who encouraged me along the way and provided critical and inspirational support.

Thanks are due to my old friend Nick Mallett for his comments. It was he who pushed me to make the most of myself at a time when it all could have gone the other way.

To David Norrie and Getty Images for access to their amazing store of photos

Contents

FOREWORD

By Sir Clive Woodward

It was back in 1983 that my international rugby playing career was almost at an end and I was thinking for the first time about things outside of playing for England. Simon Halliday had just arrived on the scene and was a favourite to take my spot and was clearly destined to play for England for a long period of time. Through our passion to see England win at the highest levels we got to know each other well over the years, particularly during the time leading up to our Rugby World Cup triumph in 2003. I went to have lunch with him on several occasions at Lehman's, not with any agenda but just to discuss everything and anything that was going on, especially in the politics of the RFU.

Simon was a free-spirited player, whether for Bath, Harlequins or England. His career spanned a time when the national team emerged from a lean period to achieve two Grand Slams and a World Cup Final, and his insights into the club and international scene are fascinating. He suffered from the rise to prominence of Will Carling and Jeremy Guscott, and was unfortunate to miss out on a lot of game time as a result. But his value was never in doubt. He was a true exponent of passing the ball out of the tackle and on merit found himself in a World Cup Final on the wing.

I have often wondered about the inner workings of the City's big investment banks. Simon brings them to life and speaks honestly about the pressures in his daily business life, though he clearly enjoyed his time in the industry, notwithstanding the highly personal account of the Lehman collapse.

As the England Head Coach, I regarded it as critical to understand who my leaders were and how their skills could always be improved and coached, and how my team worked with one another to become truly 'one team': the best in the world – all three of the banks Simon worked for seemed to be aiming for that pinnacle. The difference between success and failure can be a fine line, and self-interest often gets in the way. It comes across that certain characters passing through Simon's orbit held those characteristics of leadership, warrior spirit and a drive for success, but by no means all of them.

I am sure that Simon would say himself that he could have acted less on impulse at times. But he is that person, I can relate to his frustrations with the RFU, and what I do know is that Simon's agenda has always been rugby related and not self-interested. He was very supportive of everything I and the England coaching team were trying to achieve. The fact that he couldn't always deliver on what was needed undoubtedly pushed him into conflict with those who he perceived to be the most obstructive. People like Simon who do question the status quo are the lifeblood of the game but tend to be eventually quashed by the silent majority.

Simon supports two great charities: CRY and Help for Heroes. I am also a patron of CRY (Cardiac Risk in the Young) and totally empathise with his clear commitment. Saving young people from avoidable death from sudden heart failure is a fantastic objective. Simon gives free rein to his emotions on behalf of both.

I have often been quoted making the comparisons between business and sporting ethics, and how they helped the England team move forward and develop into World Cup winners. Simon's book takes us down a road where he tries to analyse how both of these impacted on his life, and Simon's heart is very much on his sleeve as he does so. This book is an interesting read for all rugby and business followers alike.

From a fellow centre, and from someone who shares many of Simon's rugby values, I offer my congratulations on an often light-hearted exposé of his many experiences. As he rightly said, he is very much an open book. With Simon, what you see is definitely what you get.

INTRODUCTION

Amateur or Professional

It would be tempting to assume that *City Centre* is a chronicle of my life, but that would be rather boring and I would be advising you to stop reading now!

No, this is a collection of thoughts and memories from a unique period for Rugby Union and International Finance, which covered my adult playing and business life. Whilst the book is deeply personal, there is much in my life which shall remain private. For example, all of my family are dear to me: my late father Gordon and my mother Margaret, brother Christopher and sister Deborah, my children Sophie and Alexander – but my life with them is very separate, which will become apparent as you read on.

I am frequently asked whether I would have preferred to play in the professional era, and my answer has always been the same – no. But then it's easy to say that, as I was lucky to work in an industry which paid me well, and the thought of being paid to play rugby has always been anathema. I wanted the right to say no, or to do something I preferred rather than just turn out for my club. I remember once when I was a current international opting to go on tour to France with Oxford University instead of playing for Bath. My reasons for this decision were twofold, firstly that I fancied a few days in Southern France, and secondly I was helping out Oxford who had been shorn of their international stars David Kirk (NZ), Troy Coker (Aus) and Brendan Mullin (Ire). Part of the tour had been financed with the promise of their participation. I actually scored two tries in our surprise win over Agen, the then French champions, so I suppose I earned my tour!

The very thought of a twenty-first century international being given the freedom to make such a decision is unconscionable.

In the two Help for Heroes' rugby matches which took place in 2008 and

2011, only one contracted player actually told his club that he was taking part no matter what they said. That was the Rugby World Cup hooker Mark Regan, and it was typical of the man. To be fair he wasn't playing regularly for Bristol, but nonetheless his commitment to the cause was unusual amongst his peers. The simple fact is that for a professional rugby player, this is now the day job, and sits sometimes uneasily with the ethos which has always existed in amateur Rugby Union. There is also the fear of incurring injury during so-called 'meaningless' matches.

The concept of the British and Irish Lions in a professional world is also a marvel, almost like competing businessmen suddenly joining forces after four years of being at each other's throats. You will not find a Lion alive (with the possible exception of Austin Healey) who denies the special attractions of wearing the iconic red shirt over almost any other. Just ask any of the forty members of the triumphant 2013 Lions. Of course the bonuses for winning are significant and no doubt well worth the effort. As a selector for the 2001 Lions' Tour of Australia, in the professional era, I was struck by the passion of all involved to maintain the integrity of the concept.

Some of the old values we used to associate with the game of rugby have changed. On-field you cannot really complain – no more punching, high tackles, stamping or raking which would invariably go unpunished in my amateur days. There were some truly awful injuries inflicted upon fellow human beings which were somehow legitimised under the auspices of the rough and tumble of our game: I was once raked on my chest and face and left with deep lacerations and stud marks – I could easily have lost my eye. It was while playing for England against the emerging Wallabies and there was a mass punch-up whilst I lay prostrate on the ground. I didn't go off but went a little crazy for the rest of the match, trying to exact my revenge through a combination of high and late tackles, much to the amusement of Carling and Guscott who knew me well and how I would react. The miscreant was penalised as well as beaten up in the ensuing fight, but should have been sent off. My team management claimed not to have seen the incident, even though my body was a total mess after the match and I couldn't see properly for three days. What a difference to the professional era, when the punishment would have been many weeks or even months of suspension and a heavy fine. Indeed on the recent Lions' tour the alleged stamping on the head of Alun Wyn-Jones caused huge debate and two separate disciplinary processes.

The two other big issues for professional rugby are leadership and employment, and in a way the two are interlinked. It's clear to me that when pro players are drafted into a club's academy they become physical specimens almost at the expense of anything else. They are given very few life skills when many of them could be at university or in further education. Many of the academy managers have no formal training to help these youngsters, which is unacceptable. The RFU and the clubs should make it mandatory that those in charge of our young talent have strong qualifications. The impact is also felt on the field. We wonder sometimes why teams lack leadership and there are multiple examples of this every weekend. Simply, players spend too much time doing what they are told and do not think for themselves enough. It means that some obvious decisions are fudged or not taken at all. I look back at the great teams of the Harlequins, Bath and England. Any number of those players could have been leaders or captains. I don't see many budding or actual leaders in this current England team for example.

We also see the effect when players consider post-career employment. Not all of them can turn into coaches and rugby directors – if they wish to make the transition into the business world, they must have some transferable skills. In fact Rugby is a classic sport for this to happen, but again the players must explore the demands of business and understand how they can integrate themselves, or they will find that in their mid-thirties they will be struggling to find a career for the rest of their working lives. This is even more the case for players whose rugby career ends prematurely due to injury, since they have their whole adult life in front of them. As someone who juggled two careers simultaneously, it leaves me worried. There has to be some initiatives put in place right away because, apart from anything else, as with luck the ensuing pages will show, you can have plenty of fun with twin ambitions!

Prologue

Sunday September 14th 2008 will forever be etched into the memory of every employee of Lehman Brothers. That was the day our employment ceased. It was the day that the US Treasury announced that Lehman Brothers had filed for bankruptcy.

The crisis meeting between the Treasury Secretary Hank Paulson and the major US banks had come to naught. All the pre-weekend optimism of the prospect of a last minute deal being hammered out had evaporated.

The financial world went into shock and awaited the impact when the markets reopened on the Monday.

The despair and disbelief in the London offices of Lehman Brothers was palpable. Faces were drained of colour; eyes were glued to plasma screens scattered around the floor, searching in vain for news that it was all a bad dream from which everyone would wake and then business would be resumed as normal.

But all the London staff could see were TV pictures of Lehman's US employees streaming out of the New York offices, heads bent in defeat, clutching their possessions. Their briefcases, rucksacks and coat pockets bulged with the accoutrements of their working life: computers, boxes, files, pens, as well as photographs of wives, families, girlfriends, partners.

To anyone just glancing at the TV screens it appeared as if everyone had just been given an hour's notice to get out of the building ahead of an earthquake, a hurricane or a tidal wave. And in some ways what had just hit New York and was headed for us in London was every bit as devastating as any of those natural disasters.

So this was it. The firm was bust. And, as a result, 25,000 people were out of a job. Around the world stock markets were plunging amid rumours of an approaching and uncontrollable global financial crisis, which was about to overwhelm us.

The scenes around me in London were those of desolation. It was carnage. Some people were holding their head in their hands, bemused, bewildered and utterly stunned by what they had just learned. Others were talking frenetically into their mobile phones; but many more were in a state of utter shock, catatonic, able only to stare blankly at nothing. Because that was the only thing left to them. No job. No income. No more doing the thing they loved.

It was difficult to know what to say to anyone. Lauren, my assistant, came over and searched my face for some hopeful signs. She knew that if there was a chance then I would say something. I said nothing but the look I gave her clearly told her all she needed to know and suddenly her eyes filled with tears.

She, among so many people at Lehmans, relied totally on her salary for all the basic essentials of life.

The media take on it focused on the fact that it was the end of the high life for the multi-million pound deal-makers, and there were certainly plenty of those, but ninety percent of all Lehman's London employees were anything but that.

One salesman smashed his phone against his desk and stormed out, red-faced and empty-handed, next to him another had already packed his belongings and was halfway out of the office, taking his cue from the awful scenes being shown on CNBC.

To this day I have never understood why the bosses were nowhere to be seen. I could appreciate that there were big decisions to be made, important meetings to hold, but there were 700 people on the London trading floor who needed their hands held, to hear anything at all. Instead, what they got was nothing. Not a word. Not one single word of comfort. No explanation. By the time someone finally picked up the microphone with an explanation too many grief-stricken people had already voted with their feet.

I went to the ground floor and viewed the scene outside. Press and television cameras were everywhere. There were also police in attendance, as well as nervous security men on the door to the building. All the cameras were focused on the steady stream of Lehman workers fleeing the building, some looking confused, others in tears, and all in shock.

I felt oddly calm inside, despite knowing that not only had I lost a considerable amount of money through the company's bankruptcy, but that life, specifically my life, would never be the same again. Somehow it was as if my experiences in international sport, as well as the many years I had spent subsequently managing teams and dealing with disappointment and defeat, had been preparing me for a disaster such as this. Except nothing could have prepared me for what was a surreal end to my working life in the top tier of global investment banking. Nor could it prepare me for the terrible, emotional scenes as people picked up their shattered careers and headed for the exit from what had been Lehman Brothers.

This was the end of something for sure, and it also held echoes of the final match of my rugby career, which had taken place some sixteen years earlier…

CHAPTER 1

The Curtain Falls

Twickenham, May 2nd 1992 was the date and the setting for my final bow. This, the staging of the twenty-first domestic knock-out cup final, was probably the greatest club clash between two of the mightiest teams that English – if not world – rugby, had ever seen. Two famous names, Bath and Harlequins, were going head-to-head, both eager – if not desperate – to lift the prize on offer: the Pilkington Cup.

It was my last senior game of rugby, bringing to a close a career in the top flight that had spanned thirteen years. Emotions and inevitable pangs of nostalgia were already running high. I had left Bath in 1990 – of which more later – and was playing for the Fancy Dans of London, Harlequins – 'Quins' – regarded as a club of City Slickers by the majority of rugby players outside the capital; complete with their multi-hued patchwork quilt of a strip that is instantly recognisable worldwide.

In an exercise of extreme provocation towards Bath, Harlequins had won the cup in my first year at The Stoop, a trophy which had been the preserve of the Bath club for the lion's share of the 1980s and a run which was to extend into the '90s. In fact, between the time of their first win in 1984 to 1996, Bath were to lift the trophy on all ten occasions that they had appeared in the final, a staggering record. At the time of the 1992 final it was still the premier competition for England's clubs, despite its rather anonymous beginnings – in 1972, the first year of the competition, it had been without a sponsor and was known at its inception, simply as 'The National Knock-out Cup'.

By this time, owing to their incredible run of success in the cup and the league, and their near-total dominance of the still powerful Welsh clubs, Bath had earned the unofficial title of being the world's best rugby club. Perhaps the Auckland Blues – not strictly a club – or Wigan, the world's best in Rugby League, could raise a disputing hand. Nevertheless, Bath's prowess and stature in the game was, and is, unprecedented.

So it was as if I had issued a personal challenge to my former clubmates, something which was bound to attract fearful retribution by moving to, *and* turning out for, the upstarts who had the temerity to attempt to wrest from Bath's clutches, something which they had come to regard as being rightfully theirs. Indeed, the open-top bus ride around the beautiful Georgian city had become almost an annual ritual, as season after season the club's players had celebrated victory.

Bath had won no trophies in 1991. What was even more painful for the West Country club was that their opponents, and Bath's most hated rivals, were arriving at Twickenham on that fateful day in May 1992, as the holders of the trophy – a fact that was even harder to take, and had players and supporters of Bath grinding and gnashing their teeth in envy, anger and affront. But if that was not enough, and just to rub some refined salt into that wounded pride, Simon Halliday, a former Bath man to the core, was playing against them today, indeed he had played for Harlequins the year before, and had had the effrontery to score the winning try. Such treachery, in Bath eyes at least, was not merely unacceptable: it was an insult. So, as far as everyone from Bath was concerned, Saturday May 2nd 1992 was pay-back time for Harlequins in general, and for Halliday in particular.

If I appear to have overstated the case, the neutrals were also licking their lips at the prospect of the upcoming match. Geoff Cooke, the then England manager, and proud mastermind of two back-to-back Grand Slams, described the contest in the dramatic aftermath, as having the intensity and atmosphere of a full international.

In some ways he was stating the obvious; without exception, every Bath player on the field that day had enjoyed international rugby for their country. The Harlequins had selected an all-international pack and midfield. Consequently, every position oozed confrontation: take the opposing centres for a start, Halliday and Carling versus Guscott and De Glanville, a quartet which held 200 international caps between them.

The game itself was a titanic struggle played out in gladiatorial fashion before a capacity crowd, most of them seemingly supporting Bath. It was comfortably one of the most physical games I had ever played in, accompanied by a lot of growling and 'in your face' play by both sides. The Quins went for the Bath forwards early on, which was a masterstroke and totally unexpected. Mickey Skinner and the late Richard Langhorn had been sent off in the semi-

Will did occasionally surprise us with his pace, although Jason Leonard is still keeping up.

final against Gloucester for over-zealous rucking, so we dragged former England lock Paul Ackford out of retirement. That decision was perceived as having left us fallible, however, the apparent weakness was proved a myth; Paul played a blinder, and the early Peter Winterbottom try was a direct result of ferocious forward play. The gauntlet had been flung down.

Meanwhile, I was getting my retaliation in first, and in today's rugby would have risked a yellow, if not a red card. But I knew that I was entering this match as a marked man, an impression confirmed by post-match conversations with the Bath team. The famous Rowell pep talks featured me in a major way, as I knew they would. Bath were far too disciplined and professional a unit to target a player at the expense of the game plan, but they were out to unsettle me, and I responded in kind. So much so, that late in the game when big Steve Ojomoh burst through the middle, I moved in to take him out, despite the screams of Will Carling for me to stay out wide and cover Phil De Glanville, who was lurking dangerously on the flanks. Will was spot-on, since the ball came back, and Phil squeezed over for a try despite my best efforts to cut him off. 'The King is dead, long live the King' was perhaps the line, as Phil, FEC (future England Capitan), shot me a triumphant glare.

3

And so the best clubs in the land were locked at 12-12, and not just for eighty minutes, but for a further thirty minutes of extra time. I allowed myself a self-indulgent glimpse of the perfect close of my career, surrounded by the supporters and players of the two clubs which I held most dear. What could be better than sharing the trophy at the home of rugby, and drifting off into the sunset with smiles all round? Alas, sport, and indeed life, is not like that, and for us there was a cruel sting in the tail.

Almost everyone in the Quins' back line except me had attempted a drop goal to edge ahead in the closing seconds, but without success. A tired Jonathan Webb, the Bath fullback, punted the ball downfield just to remove it from the danger area, and the last line-out of the game unfolded. Paul Ackford, one of rugby's great line-out exponents, had dragged his body around Twickenham in unbelievable fashion, and had given Nigel Redman, in Bath's second row, a torrid time. But, at length, more than 100 minutes of rugby took their toll on the ageing Ackford. And for only the second time in his rugby career, the legs finally went; famously, the previous Twickenham wobble experienced by Ackford had been when he was playing for England and was given a sucker punch by Federico Mendez against Argentina in 1990. On that occasion, when he was being helped off the pitch, his legs suddenly buckled under him, splaying, Bambi-like, in different directions. That particular video clip has been replayed to the boys many times since.

And so it was that the Ackford wobble reappeared at Twickenham; Nigel Redman palmed the line-out ball to the Bath scrum-half Richard Hill, and the scene was set for fly-half Stuart Barnes. I will say much more about Stuart later on, but suffice to say that the stocky, Napoleonic figure, who was Bath's captain, already knew precisely what he was going to do and from fully forty yards. The drop goal attempt, rather like Ackford's limbs, wobbled a little on its way, but, agonisingly for Harlequins and their supporters, it still somehow found its way over the bar, and the dream finale to my career was over. In a way, it was justice done, but it meant that a heroic Quins' effort went unrewarded.

They would never admit it, but I suspect the Bath lads knew they were a little lucky that day. But therein lies the secret of their success over the years. In the changing rooms afterwards, I wandered among my erstwhile team-mates and the bond was still there. It never goes of course, not once the connection has been made, although stresses and strains can be impactful, and I felt and saw the reserved attitude. But how could I explain anything to them? My wearing of a Harlequins' shirt was not exactly a come-on, an invitation for a sit-down to chew the fat with my one-time club-mates.

My career then, was over, played out among many of my closest rugby friends, and yet there was no end on which to sign off, since rugby friendships are unique. Such relationships endure throughout the game, the playing career and beyond, adding to the well of nostalgia that perpetually brings rugby people together. How many of us have been to rugby dinners and heard the opening lines "I remember when..."? The word 'raconteur' must have been coined by mediaeval French rugby players, given that most of us have, at one time or another, constructed lurid accounts of tour antics, exaggerated stories of late night revelry, and related tall tales of off and on-field shenanigans, all of which have subsequently shouldered their way into rugby folklore.

However, although the legs do eventually give way and the joints finally seize up, the capacity to enjoy the people and the memories is everlasting. I maintain that my experiences in rugby have helped to prepare me for most things in life, and have presented me with lesson after lesson in people skills, imbuing in me a regard and a respect for others. In many cases you learn the hard way, since this great game is unforgiving and intolerant of ego-based behaviour, and therefore represents one of the greatest levellers I have ever encountered. Somehow it is counter-intuitive that I ended up in investment banking, one of the most egocentric and self-centred industries known to man or woman.

Thus the very game that had helped to shape my life came directly into conflict with the place where I spent most of my waking hours – a gross over-exaggeration of course, but any business that kicks off at 6. 30am can get to feel like that.

I remember vividly in my first weeks at UBS Philips & Drew, one of the major investment banks in the City, the prophetic words of my then boss Denis Elliott: "Simon, here is the way that I see the order of things: health, family, work. Without the first you are good for nothing and nobody, without the second why bother with the third?" He was speaking to me as a family man, so it was easy to make the connection.

The way that we all lead our lives is dominated by our approach to people around us. Rugby taught me, among other things, humility, but the game also gave me confidence to express my views honestly and to stick to them. Sport makes you flexible, and at home and in the work-place I reckon that is pretty important.

And if honesty leads to unpalatable truths, then so be it, as we all have to look in the mirror and accept what is really there. It is only when you deny what is in front of you that the problems arise.

Yet another trophy. Barnes and Chilcott were key members of the Bath 'Family', not bad players either

CHAPTER 2

The Curtain Rises

As my playing days ended, so another opportunity presented itself – coaching. Suddenly there were invitations to visit schools, where I was asked to give pep talks to wide-eyed children, who could hardly believe that a real-life rugby international was sitting in front of them.

"Sir, did you really play with Carling and Guscott?" Despite myself I would find myself smiling at the inquiry, before conforming to their ideas of stardom.

But what, I asked myself, did those two, Carling and Guscott, know about centre play? They were still at school when I first started playing for England. Will Carling freely admitted that his dreams of playing for England seemed dimmer as he watched me play on the television and realised that he would be in his mid-twenties before I hit retiring age. But then, young people are often ignorant of their destiny, in Will's case that of becoming the most successful England Rugby Union captain of all time and the man most responsible, with Cooke, for the standards being set by current England teams.

The questions from the inquisitive pupils kept coming. "Mr Halliday, did you always know that you would play for England?" Ah, now there's a question, and one that has to be answered carefully. Destiny in a child is a fickle thing, and confidence is fragile. To destroy a dream, even inadvertently, especially a child's dream, has to be the cruellest act. So, with shining eyes I replied: "You can all do it, you know, if you really try, and never give up. Remember, rugby is a game for all shapes and sizes. " On spotting an undersized pupil in one corner, whose expression was eloquence itself as it screamed out, 'I'm too small'.

"After all boys, I was called the mighty midget (it's true!) at school, and look at me now, " I said, pointing to my already protruding stomach. And the truth is, I had absolutely no idea of my destiny until I left school and went up to Oxford University.

My pre-university career was indiscriminate, a random collection of sporting distractions. I was fanatical about all sports except football; perhaps that is why I am a Manchester City supporter, a true blue, although it is a shame that they play in light blue and not dark, which would have been my preference given the university I attended.

It was at Moor Park Prep School, Shropshire, where I went from 1969 until 1973, as a nine-year-old, that the foundations for my sporting life were laid. Unusually for a prep school, there were two headmasters, Hugo Watts and Derek Henderson. They had both played Oxbridge rugby and cricket, but most importantly, they were great men. The school they ran was a feeder for the likes of Downside, Ampleforth, Worth, and the occasional non-Catholic competition. My Catholic religion has always been important to me, and among many other things the two sports-mad academicians taught us how to mix work, sport and leisure time with a healthy love of God. Sin and forgiveness were often close behind one another, although accompanied by a painful reminder that corporal punishment was alive and well in the 1960s. I often found myself standing outside one of the two headmasters' rooms, awaiting the dreaded moment when some implement, often a mini cricket bat, would be brought to bear on a backside protected only by a pyjama bottom – not enough I can tell you.

As I ploughed into every available sport – boarding school and huge playing fields making everything possible – I suddenly found myself going down another path, equally exciting, if a little mystifying, and one which was to shadow my sporting life thereafter. For some unaccountable reason, I was exceptionally good at Latin – as my fellow rugby men would testify; that penchant for the language made me proficient at crosswords, but only the *Telegraph* version of course. *The Times* was positioned at a slightly more elevated intellectual level, at least for me and my crossword colleague, Rory Underwood. We would pore religiously over the clues every Saturday of an international weekend. It became a bit of a ritual for the two of us, and there would be worried faces on the bus *en route* to Twickenham if it was not at least half done before we arrived. Even Jason Leonard was known to offer his assistance when the need arose. Funny how people can become superstitious about such things.

My ability as a budding Latinist soon turned into something more serious.

Hugh Watts arrived in my geography class and summoned me without offering a reason. Every naughty ten-year-old immediately imagines that he is being rumbled for a recent act of stupidity. But no, it was to inform me that G stands for Greek, not geography. I dropped the study of the physical world and moved more deeply into the ancient world. My classics career was well and truly under way. Shortly afterwards, a promising music career was also cut short, this time primarily due to backyard cricket, while my French lessons were doubled up, another language in which I was also showing promise. Was there a trend here, as my maths and science teacher John Slevin appeared to give up on me? He confined himself in my school reports to the barest of comments: 'Simon is very poor at these subjects'. More importantly, he taught me cricket and how to play straight, as well as how not to lose my temper when I was dismissed. Ten years later I scored my maiden First Class century for Oxford University versus Kent, and although I cannot say I whispered a thank you to John as I raised my bat, he should definitely take credit for that hundred, just as he should have done for Stephen Henderson, another of his protégés and a fellow school friend of mine, who, on the same day, scored a double century for Cambridge University against Middlesex.

My parents, 2, 000 miles away in Turkey on a four-year naval posting, were looking on and taking a great interest in my progress, clearly unable to affect my academic development, but reassured by positive headmasterly comments. This was just as well, since the report which I carried out to Turkey every holiday with trepidation, was generally a mixture of brilliant term/exam results in the arts and severe criticism of over-exuberant behaviour, and desperate marks in maths, physics and chemistry. My father handed out warnings across the board but had to rely on my weekly letters to assess my progress.

At this point, aged eleven, I was playing rugby, at fly-half, and I was kicking goals, but frankly I was hardly breaking any records. Mike Thomas, who taught English and rugby, was convinced that I would be a centre, Lord knows why, but his words are in print so he was obviously a visionary. He was technically very meticulous, and such attention to detail was just as well for me; mind you, at the end of my career I still could not pass off my left hand! I had another major reason to thank Mike Thomas: when I returned to Moor Park to teach in my gap year between Downside School and Oxford, I started my senior rugby career in the 4th XV of Ludlow RFC and Mike was the appointed referee for my first match. I made a couple of darting breaks in the first half until one of the opposition forwards decided to take me out, and I was on the verge of being thumped when I screamed at Mike for assistance. He came racing over, blowing furiously on the whistle and pulled the thug off me, delivering a strong warning and saving a seventeen-year-old's full set of teeth and unscarred features. It was the only time in my rugby life that I had real reason to thank a referee for saving me from a physical battering.

Due to my ability in classics and languages, I was placed in the scholarship form, and duly got the top scholarship award to Downside School. Other than being terrifically proud and a little surprised, given the mixed nature of my school reports, my other main emotion was sadness that I had to wait so long to share my success with the rest of my family. At the end of the summer term I met up with brother Christopher and sister Deborah, boarded a BEA flight to Istanbul, a THY connection to Izmir, and had a minor celebration at our home in Buca, on the picturesque outskirts of the city. We soon forgot the reality of school life in England, and lost ourselves in the Turkish bazaars and minaret-strewn atmosphere of a stifling summer in Asia Minor. Suddenly the ruins of Ephesus, a mere hour's drive away, had relevance for me. Many hours poring over Latin books and early introductions to the history of Greece and Ancient Rome, allowed me to make some sense of the magnificent amphitheatre and the dilapidated yet still potent Temple of Artemis. Turkey as a place had a deep impact on the whole family, with its Ottoman history and tolerant Islamic culture. The people themselves loved children and, luckily for us, the English; they were not so keen on Americans for some reason, so we felt at home and I even learned some of the language. The word 'Inshallah' – God willing – summed up perfectly their attitude to life and remains a valuable lesson for the Western culture of stress and strain and hurry-up. We often looked on in amazement as whole families attempted to cross a busy highway with what seemed like all their household belongings, with no regard for their own safety or the blazing horns. Inshallah.

So it was that in the autumn of 1973 I said farewell to Moor Park. I have to say that for this particular bronzed teenager, after a ten-week Turkish delight, it was a rather mournful trek back to England to begin a Catholic public school education. There is no doubt that four years in the Middle East at such a formative time in my life had been a major influence on me. Being so far away from my family for protracted periods also taught me a certain degree of independence, but simultaneously made me very sensible of the emotions and feelings of others, including my own. I was always looking to see if people around me felt as I did. When I reflect on my highs, one of my greatest strengths was my ability to harness passion and emotion in others, and relate to them very intimately. The control of my own feelings was not always easy, as fellow rugby players will remember, although they never extended to violence.

My prep school had also prepared me well for Downside, and indeed for life. In saying that Hugh Watts and Derek Henderson, the Moor Park heads, were great men does not do them sufficient justice. They and their wives, Ursula and Ann, who were really house mistresses in all but name, were surrogate parents and moulders of young intellects. They gave me my priorities and taught me values which have stayed with me all my life – I am sure that countless former Moor Park schoolboys would stand up and say 'Aye' to that. In my farewell report they said things about me which will always remain private, as well as special, but it is my privilege to recognise publicly their contribution to my life.

Sadly, Hugh died some years ago, but his words of advice still ring in my ears. Derek Henderson lives quietly now – in Oxford, of course, as befits an old Blue – but sadly lost his wonderful wife Ann recently. His irreverent good humour and dry wit are qualities all young men aspired to emulate. Both he and Hugh were frequent visitors to Cornwall, and had summer houses nestling in Daymer Bay and Polzeath. The common feature was St Enodoc Golf Course, a truly magnificent location overlooking Rock Estuary, and well known for the Himalaya Bunker; if you went into it, you had to play out backwards, probably unique in golf other than the road hole at St Andrews!

Derek's acerbic wit came to the fore when I was playing with him, his son Stephen, and Hugh Woodcock, brother of *The Times*' former cricket correspondent John. I was almost decapitated by a flying golf ball, with not so much as a 'fore' in earshot. As I picked myself up off the ground, Derek bore down on the poor unfortunate and unleashed a volley of abuse, accusing him of nearly destroying England's championship aspirations that coming season by killing an important member of their team. A trifle over the top in my opinion, but typical of Derek.

On another occasion, Will Carling and I had just completed a round at St Enodoc – we often holidayed together pre-season in Cornwall – and Philip

Watts, Hugh's youngest son and a school contemporary of mine, wanted to introduce Will to his fearsome, but lovely mother, Ursula. "Mother, this is Will." Her reply was withering, "Will who? Does he have a surname?" A humbling moment for the young England captain.

But back once more to 1973. I headed to Downside, a proud top scholar, although not quite sure how. The fact that I had excelled in Latin, Greek and French must have offset weaknesses elsewhere. By far the best impact however was that most of my school fees were to be paid as a result. So my parents were happy enough!

Hugh Watts was himself a product of Downside, an Old Gregorian, and often talked to me about the school and what to expect. After a year in Junior House, compulsory for all new boys by way of gentle introduction to the rigours of boarding school life, I went straight into Smythe House, well known for its sport, but not for its academic prowess. As a top scholar, but someone who was also keen on sport, I was a little confused as to where my priorities should lie. It soon became apparent – Dom Martin Salmon, who had introduced both me and my brother to Moor Park, was a sports fanatic as well as being a strict disciplinarian. A Smythe boy was expected to perform strongly across the board, but it had to be said that school plays, operas and non-athletic interests were some way down the list. House sports days were sacrosanct, and I remember that every single member of the house was expected to participate in the boxing competition, since one point was awarded just for taking part, often leading to victory by numbers, if not by performance. But no-one cared, it was the winning that mattered. I was in heaven with wall-to-wall sport in an environment which suited me.

Mass was said daily at 7. 00am and I often assisted as a server to get into breakfast early, while Sunday mass was, of course, compulsory. So religion was part of my working day, and among many things it taught me the rudiments of humility and respect, preparing the way for what rugby would later do for me. Religion also made me stoical in adversity, since the Catholic faith is steeped in adversity and presents innumerable ways in how to deal with suffering (perhaps too much sometimes). I may not have realised it quite then, though, since we used to spend most of our time escaping with the bare minimum participation, rather than aspiring to monkhood. Owning up to playing hangman in the back of a hymn book in the abbey during a spiritual treatise was one of my less glorious moments.

The Benedictine philosophy *'Laborare est orare'* (to work is to pray) is essentially pragmatic and reveals an understanding of life's pressures. The ability to deal with, and respond to, any and all setbacks is not just confined to the sports world, as I discovered. However, despite acknowledging everything that Downside did for me, sadly I rarely go back there, although an occasional visit to the magnificent abbey, visible for miles around, is a peaceful and awesome experience in a pressured life

Downside in the '70s had a fearsome reputation on the rugby field, enjoying three unbeaten seasons on the trot. The entire school had to watch every home game, and every member of the First XV was hero-worshipped. They were nearly all prefects, wore school colours on everyday dress, and we juniors all wanted to be like them. An unhealthy, almost elitist set-up one may think, but what an identity it gave the school. When the unbeaten record finally went, versus Dulwich College, most of the team, and the school for that matter, were reduced to tears.

I was starting to appreciate the power and emotional force which, it seems to me, only the game of rugby can generate.

My unusual academic development gathered pace. Rather bemused, I traded history for ancient history and found myself debating the merits of Hannibal and his use of elephants in warfare as opposed to the tactics of Napoleon in the Battle of Waterloo. In those days we all wanted to continue with our best subjects, the ones we found came easily to us and history definitely qualified as one of my best subjects.

Maths and science could happily have been the casualties to my mind, but I wasn't going to argue with Dom Martin, who compounded the situation by also extracting me from any further biology. Presumably the thought process went something like this: he is going to do classics and languages and lots of sport so we had better construct a curriculum that reflects those priorities. Thus, my O levels, taken at the age of fourteen, were a curate's egg – excellence, matched with mediocrity and, in the case of physics and chemistry, failure.

Half the academic establishment at Downside had written me off, while the other half began a battle to keep me off the sports field and in the classroom. Molière, Voltaire, Homer and Horace were the order of the morning, and then my tutors would watch me career off to indulge myself. However, it was mainly cricket where my hopes lay. Some years on, in 1982, as I completed my maiden (and only) first class hundred against a top-class Kent bowling attack containing Kevin Jarvis, Graham Dilley, Bob Woolmer, Chris Cowdrey and Graham Johnson, I reminded myself of that fact, and felt somewhat vindicated. In other people's minds, my appearance in the 1979 Varsity Rugby match indicated that cricket was not my game. Yet, I harboured no thoughts of serious rugby commitment, and had every intention of making it as a cricketer.

When the time came for me to sit my A-levels in the summer of 1977, I was leading the cricket averages. My ability as a rugby player had been recognised and fly-half and full back were my two options. But I had neither enough power nor enough pace, so how my coaches decided I should be a wing was a mystery to me. And when the press contacted Downside to discuss my England selection, the head of rugby, Roger Smerden, revealed this fact, much to my surprise. Naturally, Roger will now describe himself as a visionary given that I filled the wing slot for England in the last two years of my career, and moreover in a World Cup Final. So he was the second rugby coach to have predicted accurately my playing position, albeit for different reasons.

When my A-level results came through in August 1977 it was a shock to my teachers that I got only two Bs and a C in Latin, Greek and French. Crisis discussions took place but they all pushed in the direction of an Oxbridge exam the following term, and I was advised to apply to Lincoln College where the 'Stearns exhibition' was available for students who had academic and sporting ability and applied for French and Latin. My place in the school as a top scholar had by now been fatally undermined and I was in for a further shock.

The Lincoln College master revealed in December 1977 that I was unsuited for an Oxford degree course. My entrance papers were unimpressive, my interviews humiliating and the sporting angle of the exhibition award was completely ignored. At seventeen and a half, I was too immature and narrow-minded to make the grade, and I was confused and bewildered, if not crushed: I had been trapped into thinking that my destiny was mapped out, and my first big failure, although in hindsight not very surprising, left me uninspired and rueful.

It was a major life lesson, and when I reflect on other defining moments in rugby, they have often emerged from disappointment and unpromising situations. The mental strength derived from coping with adversity makes you better equipped the next time around. For example, I was dropped three times in one year from the England rugby team; you need a sense of humour as well as mental strength to deal with that.

Downside, predictably, was furious and made a number of representations to the university, claiming everything from gross injustice to simple human error. Nonetheless there were no comebacks and the old boys' network kicked in. I found myself before Dom James, the Master of St Benet's Hall, Oxford, and it was clear that I had a chance of achieving a place after all. Intervention was the order of the day, no doubt some of it divine!

He talked about the family atmosphere, the importance of tolerating one another's company, of respect and friendship, that no women were allowed above the ground floor (neutral reactions to that one – come on Simon, don't blow it now!), and finally that I would indeed be studying French and Latin at Oxford University. What a feeling; despair turned to joy, and what had seemed like an intimidating, inaccessible walled fortress of learning, became the next four years of my life.

Nepotism can mean many things, and not all of them attractive or justified. Reading an account of my entrance to the Varsity – 'quite grotesque' if you believe Craven A (you need to know the song!) – it might appear that I benefited from a heavy degree of sponsorship – not an unreasonable conclusion.

Throughout my sporting life and career in financial services, there have been countless instances where you size up a situation or an individual and make the marginal call. Pure statistics may not always tell the story, and anyway here was an amazing opportunity and I took it with thanks.

To this day, when people ask me which college I went to, their faces glaze over when I mention St Benet's. Even Oxford undergraduates look blank until I remind them that it is positioned next to the Oxford and County Secretarial College. Breakfast at 8. 00am was worth getting up for every morning, just to survey the pavement outside heaving with nineteen-year-old girls on the loose in Oxford. Never mind the Puffas and pearls; the sleepy students were wide-eyed by the time lectures started.

The other great benefit of St Benet's Hall was its proximity to The Parks, where Oxford University played cricket. Being able to complete a couple of hours of study on the morning of a match, before slipping across to The Parks was invaluable to me. Moreover, it was also possible to pop back to the college to pick up a book, should I be out early in my innings, and purport to do some revision: fellow students will testify that academic work on the boundary's edge is a contradiction in terms, there being many passing distractions.

CHAPTER 3

The Blues Scene

It was an early evening meal at St Benet's which defined my rugby career. That may sound extreme but we all know about coincidence, destiny, right place right time, and my dinner seat opposite Edward Quist-Arcton was exactly that. 'Eddie Q-A' had been an under-graduate at Keble, and was studying a post-graduate course at Benet's. He was schooled at Taunton and brought up in Ghana, and yet to listen to his soft spoken, articulate voice, you would have thought he was an old Etonian. But the notable thing about him was the Oxford crown on his sweater. I was simultaneously entranced and overawed; a real life sporting Blue sitting opposite me. To digress briefly, further down the table sat Dom Anthony Sutch, prospective monk and future headmaster of Downside, as well as the eventual godfather to my daughter, Sophie. This was the man who many years later was rumoured to have been involved in the conversion of Lady Diana, the Princess of Wales, to Catholicism, such was his position and standing in the Catholic community. However, other than being one of the most impressive men I have ever met, he was also to become a close friend, and still is. It was probably just as well that this most persuasive of speakers was not sitting opposite me, or I might have ended up a man of the cloth myself.

Back at the action end of the table, Eddie was gently probing my rugby background, while I was declaring my avowed intention to be a cricketer. He nonetheless persuaded me to attend a Blues' rugby training session at which I could register for the freshers' – the first year students' – team. Even more impressive, another squad colleague enjoyed the use of a car and so one evening we made our way in a beaten up old Austin Maxi to Iffley Rd, home of Oxford Rugby, and tentatively, nervously, I entered the changing room of the revered Blues.

Eddie shepherded me towards a baby-faced character who was nonchalantly tossing a rugby ball from one hand to the other. You remember these little things

17

when they represent a big moment in your life. No doubt Tony Watkinson, the Oxford captain and cause of my jitters, will not remember any of this detail, although he does now take credit for my entire international career: "Taught you to pass, dummy, sidestep, run straight," his words echo in my head to this day. 'Watko' looked me up and down, briefly checked out my rugby kit and, I thought, rather condescendingly said, "We'll give you a go." Well, that was good enough for me and the freshers became my rugby life in that first momentous term.

It was rather fortunate that I was nowhere near good enough to make the Blues' team, since there was the small matter of first term exams, called prelims. For some unaccountable reason, a classics and modern languages course meant that I had to do a number of history papers. Luckily the authors I studied were Bede, Gibbon (the decline and fall of the Roman Empire) as well as De Tocqueville (French Revolution) and Macaulay; so three out of the four were at least relevant to me. However, the problem for all rugby players was that the exams took place on the morning of the Varsity Match. One famous example, Malcolm Moir, also a Catholic but an Amplefordian, missed his exams since he had been selected, and while scoring the winning try that year, was also being sent down. I am not aware that his career has suffered as a result, but the circumstances of my Oxford entrance were such that I only had one choice.

To my great relief, I passed, and a second door unlocked to a student life which I will not attempt to help you visualise, if only because much of the next few years was a blur of activity, ranging from constant partying through to frantic late night essay writing to meet deadlines. I came into contact with a huge number of people, more than I could have expected, and this was due largely to the fact St Benet's Hall was not big enough to run its own cricket or rugby team, and had no academic tutors of its own. Therefore I studied at New College, Lincoln College (by a quirk of fate) and St Edmund Hall, and played cricket for Trinity (where Christopher, my brother, was a student) and rugby for St Edmund Hall. Given that 'Teddy Hall' as it was known, was *the* sporting college in Oxford, there are no prizes for guessing where I spent most of my time.

The Buttery, as it was known, became synonymous with late night drinking, beer games and general revelry. However, my ability to participate was significantly enhanced due to the procurement of a back door key to St Benet's Hall, which allowed a late return to my college room without having to awaken

Father James, the Master, which would no doubt have tested his Benedictine tolerance.

It was Dom James who recognised, after my first year, that I simply could not live in Hall. All students were charged a college levy called 'Battels', covering general college expenses as well as food. This was a princely sum of nearly £500 a term, yet I mostly ate out of Hall due to my sporting commitments and therefore was even poorer than the penniless students we already were. I made an emotional, and successful, appeal to Dom James to be allowed to live out in my second year and, to the chagrin of my frustrated fellow students, packed my bags and the following September was sharing a flat in Norham Gardens with my brother Christopher and friend Simon Denehy, who promised Dom James that they would take care of me.

My new abode was only a few minutes' cycle ride from the college, so food was within easy range, an important fact given that no self-respecting student spent time in culinary pursuits, and I was no different. 'La Maison Francaise', the University French Institute was also just around the corner, where I would theoretically spend time studying for my French degree. So it was very convenient, and gave me freedom and flexibility. It wasn't just that women were not allowed above ground floor in Hall, not even relatives, but the whole restrictive atmosphere in St Benet's somehow didn't suit me. I was as diligent as anyone when essays had to be written. But my life was both full and hectic, and I needed space. My parents, aware that I was fleeing a place of some security and safety, disapproved heartily and a few feisty conversations ensued, but my freedom was beckoning, and I jumped at it. I remained very connected to the college and Father James himself had a big hold on me, not surprisingly since it was he who had given me my chance at Oxford. For myself and Eddie Q-A, we respected and delighted in his interest in us and our sport; Father James felt there was a real chance that St Benet's could provide the university with two Blues, unprecedented for a college of sixty students in a university of 12, 000.

The following winter, as our selection became a reality, the college was informed that Father James had incurable cancer and that as a consequence he had only months to live. This was obviously a bombshell for all of us. But he fixed his eyes on us and said: "I will be there to see you and Eddie play in the Varsity Match." He battled on with the sort of courage that beggared belief. Sadly, in the end, he didn't make it, and one week before the Varsity Match, we trekked up to his monastery at Ampleforth for the funeral to say

Centenary Varsity Rugby Match in the snow. The RFU refused to clear the pitch – senseless. We brought on buckets of hot water at half time.

goodbye to the man who had opened the door to the next piece of my life.

Eddie and I dedicated our Varsity appearance that year to Father James, took the field in his honour, and drank to him through an exceptionally long night, while celebrating a rather turgid (but who cares?) win over Cambridge, on the second Tuesday of December 1979. Father James may have missed a great moment, but he had already acknowledged the previous summer that I was likely to deliver my first Varsity sporting ambition, that of winning a cricket Blue. I had spent the summer playing cricket for the 'Authentics', the Oxford Second XI. For those who know Oxford, the geography doesn't need to be explained. But for those who don't know, this wonderful city is peppered with college cricket grounds, all picturesque and importantly within reach of pubs and drinks parties. It was mainly at these grounds that we would play our matches, which was just as well given that riding a bicycle with a cricket kit perched on the handlebars, limited the distance we could all travel.

With a bunch of players I still regard as close friends, I summered with a bat in hand, and paid scant attention to my academic studies. They were certainly important to me, as I wished to prove the admissions tutor wrong, and so I made sure to keep my head above water; even taking books along to all games, should my batting efforts come to naught. But things did not quite go as expected; the earnest academic intentions ceded place to sport as I plundered runs all summer, including two 50s in the second team Varsity Match, and 300 runs in four innings in the Universities Tournament, which followed; a competition which was contested by English, Welsh, Scottish and Irish counterparts. It was a halcyon year for me and as I returned to my native Dorset for the summer holidays, and continued to score heavily in the Minor Counties Championship, I was content with my lot, loving the people I was with and thankful for the opportunity which Father James had foreseen with a twinkle in his eyes.

The Rugby Varsity Match of 1979, which was won by Oxford, was a tactical struggle that was sometimes painful to watch, but it was my first experience of Twickenham and was certainly the biggest rugby match of my life. The North Stand echoed to the high-pitched squeals of many thousands of attendant schoolboys, screeching "Oxford-Cambridge" in one breath with indiscriminate enthusiasm. They cared not a fig for the result; this was a day out from school, in the home of English rugby, and a match of endeavour for them was a thrill.

For me, the game was technically an unmitigated disaster; I already knew that I could cope with the rigours of first class rugby as I had performed creditably against international performers such as Nick Preston (then playing for Richmond and England), as well as Dai Richards (Swansea and Wales), whom I had encountered in the traditional pre-Varsity game, the Stanley's Match at Iffley Road. But here at Twickenham, in front of 30,000 spectators, I hardly touched the ball. If I had any talent, you would not have guessed it. But in hindsight, this game and indeed season became important for me due to the presence and influence of a certain South African rugby man named Nick Mallett. He was in the middle of the back row in that match, was comfortably our best player and even kicked a long range penalty; an unusual skill for a No8. He is now of course a household name in world rugby. He had been capped twice by South Africa, then became the most successful coach the Springboks had ever had, winning seventeen games on the trot in the late 1990s; he then stepped down to club rugby and enjoyed success as coach of the star-studded

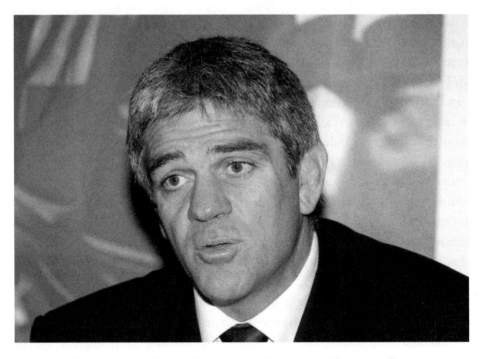

Nick Mallett, Blue, Springbok and International Coach. One of the main influences on my career.

Stade Francais, before returning to international rugby and taking charge of Italy, eventually guiding them in 2011 to a maiden Six Nations' victory over France. A few years ago, as he and I congregated for the pre-Varsity Match evening, the Vincents dinner, he pinned me with the notorious Mallett glare, declaring that I would have been so much better a player had I listened to his advice. The irony from the point of view of self-esteem is that he was probably right, even though I felt that my international career had not been that disappointing. The point was that Nick had arrived in my rugby career at a pretty important juncture.

Our lives are shaped by different people and the influences they have on us. Often we are happy for others to show leadership and dominate the agenda, and, as a fresh-faced nineteen-year-old, fazed and rather confused by a turbulent first year at Oxford, I was ready to be led. Nick was an infectious character. The whole squad was in awe of him, and it wasn't just his age and experience. He was 6ft 5in and a supreme athlete, and was well aware of his attributes as a player and as an opinion former. He totally dominated the Oxford team as a consummate ball player, and was as tough as teak in close quarters. He often played fly-half during matches, partly because we needed one (like me, Reg Clark the No10 was primarily a centre), and partly because he wanted to, so that he could dictate the play. Most set moves revolved around him given his 'impact' style of play, and when he deigned to pass (not often) there was always space to run.

Nick would have played for England many times, but in 1980, after being selected for the England trial, the selectors took him off after thirty minutes. He promptly informed them of his displeasure and deselected himself for good; shades of Stuart Barnes in 1987, and two players of similar ilk and ability. I sat between Nick and Stuart at the Vincents dinner in 2002 and the privilege was undoubtedly mine, for two of the most talented players of their generation not to have played enough for their country due to selectorial whim, was bordering on criminal. In Nick's case, this also refers to South Africa who confined him to two caps, when twenty would have been a fairer reflection of his ability and worth to the Springboks.

Oxford had, and still has, a strong connection with South Africa, as well as Australia and New Zealand, through the 'Rhodes Scholarship'. In many ways bringing 'Rhodes Scholars' and southern hemisphere graduates to the university was the Dark Blues' answer to Cambridge's Land Economy courses, which attracted a great number of experienced players from both hemispheres. Indeed it is a matter of record that Stuart Barnes was the last Oxford undergraduate to pull on an England Rugby shirt, and that was a decade or so ago. It was predictable that many southern hemisphere undergraduates would be able to cope with the rigours of first class rugby.

The universities needed the influx of talent and at Cambridge the likes of Gavin Hastings, Mark Bailey, Rob Andrew, Marcus Rose and Huw Davies all emanated from Durham way as postgraduates. At Oxford, the Macdonald brothers, Mallett himself, Phil Crowe, Troy Coker, David Kirk among others all graced the Varsity Match; and these 'mature' students, home bred or from the southern hemisphere, are vital to the lifeblood that still courses through the mainstream of university sporting life.

As Nick Mallett strode through the rugby fields of Europe (Oxford toured a lot), I realised that there was something more in me than Varsity rugby. He pushed, cajoled, criticised and praised me all in one sentence. I started to mix with the best in the land; Nick maintains that I was the first centre to challenge the Paul Dodge/Clive Woodward domination of the early 1980s. Indeed, I replaced Woodward in the England team in 1983, only to suffer a dislocated ankle almost immediately, which goes to show that Nick was spot-on, but then he mostly was.

So what was it that Nick had which was so special? It was that sense of being the best, believing in yourself, striving for more, never being satisfied, and a degree of arrogance, yes; an imposition of one's own psyche over the opposition, making them fearful and less confident. Nick's ability to pass on these attitudes helped me – and many others – realise that I could go a lot further in the game than I had previously dreamed possible. Nick's passion sometimes worked against him, as it did against me on occasion. But he would not have had it any other way, and nor would I.

His bravado knew no bounds. On the university rugby tour to France in 1979, an extremely hungover group of players was recovering at a '*bar terrasse*' the morning after a post-match banquet – place a group of students in front of endless quantities of '*vin de table*' and low grade *pastis*, and there can only be one outcome. We were admiring the fast-flowing Dordogne River some twenty yards to our left, when Mallett challenged us to a swimming race across the river. This was no mean feat to contemplate; the great French river was a good hundred yards wide or perhaps more, and was in spate, due to recent spring rains, and therefore flowing powerfully. However this did not deter Nick one jot. He was determined to make it across to the other side. He stripped off completely and plunged in; and while his four challengers soon lost heart, Nick carved his way across the stretch of water, all the while being pushed downstream. Sure enough, despite one or two worrying moments two thirds of the way over, he emerged triumphant on the other bank. There was, however, no way he was going to make the return journey, and to his horror – and our delight – the nearest bridge was a good mile away. The entire squad, hangovers forgotten, tracked the naked giant through the parkland and past horrified old ladies, whose plans for dog-walking had not included an encounter with a 6ft 5in South African loping breathlessly up the riverside in his birthday suit and in a state of constant apology. What good sport for the lads, and Mallett, although bashful, later turned the event into a tale of prowess and daring, of course.

Such a character could only have been created by, and thrived in, the game of rugby football. His record as South African coach is even more remarkable because of his position in society. As an England-born, therefore non-Afrikaaner, he had to develop a sense of unity in the squad, despite the ingrained suspicions of many. To have integrated the players so successfully, and to have developed in them a record-breaking winning streak, represents a feat that only insiders can truly appreciate. Many wise South African heads have been shaken to think that this asset could have been lost to the national team.

Miserably, in the year of Nick's Oxford captaincy, he tore knee ligaments and missed the Varsity Match. A season full of hope, courtesy of two or three good wins against top clubs, turned sour, and we went on to lose to Cambridge at Twickenham in the only match that really counted, in disappointing fashion. I saw plenty of ball, unlike the previous year, since I had to assume the fly-half position after an injury to Paul Jenkins, our diminutive Welshman. As things turned out Jenkins was merely keeping the berth warm for an even smaller person, a certain Welshman from Bassaleg School in Newport, called Stuart Barnes, who arrived at Oxford the following year.

My first forty minutes as a No10 were hardly auspicious, since we failed to create the tries which our possession deserved. Nevertheless, I feel that I became established as a Varsity sportsman, having gained my cricket Blue that summer. Nick, meanwhile, out of favour with the England selectors for no good reason other than selectorial pique, was destined to compete his way to a cricket Blue before returning to South Africa, where he clocked up a host of appearances for Western Province as well as too few appearances for his country.

His appetite for exploring his competitive edge knew no bounds and the cricket field was no exception. His clash with the great Ian Botham needs to be recorded to get the measure of these two likeminded individuals. Somerset had enjoyed two dominant days in the parks against the university when Mallett strode to the wicket to face Botham, who by now was experimenting with gentle off-spin. After a couple of circumspect forward defensives, Nick dispatched the ball over the rope with an agricultural swipe into the trees for six, following it with a triumphant "Fetch that one!" An animated conversation ensued; a heavyweight affair when you consider the two men involved. This resulted in Botham marking out his full run-up with predictable consequences – Nick's middle stump cart-wheeled out of the ground the very next ball. Both then impolitely invited Nick to depart to the pavilion. Many beers later Nick's famous shot was described in great detail, with the actual facts being stretched this way and that until the audience was left with the impression that the six-hit was a rather daring shot off a full pace Botham delivery.

Nick remains a larger than life character and a great friend.

Oxford University tour of France, 1980, where it all started.

CHAPTER 4

Tours de Force

Any rugby player will tell you that they live for 'the tour'. No matter which sport it is, rugby, hockey, cricket or football. No matter where it is. No matter when it is. No matter who it is. And there is one important element common to all tours, and that is the attitude. Fortunately it is a universal one. It is the 'back to school: Let's behave like kids, but win important matches' mentality; and let nobody disagree with me, you know I speak the truth!

The level of excitement engendered by a rugby tour is unimaginable; from ill-fitting blazers to indiscriminate airport lounge boozing, kangaroo courts, male bonding, sight-seeing and legendary team spirit. No wonder I went on five tours (one of them cricket) in two years.

Later in my career, when I was either too injured, too old, or too busy to tour, I had to make some tough decisions, but in the early 1980s I was fancy free and up for anything. And so it was to France, Japan, Italy, California and Romania in quick succession. These turned out to be essential building blocks to my laying claim to an international rugby berth, but at the time each one merely represented yet another experience of a lifetime, an opportunity to play hard on the pitch, and the freedom and collective intent of the whole tour party to play equally hard off the pitch. Most importantly, friendships made on tour are long-lasting and resilient, I still bump into former fellow tourists from twenty years ago, and within seconds we guffaw over some well-orchestrated wind-ups, or attempt to remember the words of some hastily constructed song.

As I have already alluded to, there was the annual university rugby tour to France, which tended to be a demanding exercise in staying vaguely sober enough for the matches, while still being able to enjoy the amazing hospitality of the various French towns where we were hosted. One of my earliest touring memories is a reception at the Pernod Ricard headquarters in Toulouse, followed by an introduction to the mayor later in the afternoon; the two events were also attended by the opposing team. So we felt it rude to decline the offer of a small number of Pernod shots, and thus found ourselves clinking glasses happily and with increasing frequency as the 'do' went on. I suppose that it was entirely predictable then, that on our arrival at the ground, the 'players' with whom we had just been imbibing Pernod were nowhere to be seen in the changing rooms, but had in fact turned into supporters, who waved at us from the stand, I would like to think, somewhat embarrassed, but more likely pleased that their job to nobble the *Rosbifs* was done and done well. Very well, as it turned out. We lost comfortably although we couldn't blame it all on the Pernod; we also fell foul of another traditional French habit of bringing on replacements. With twenty minutes to go, four or five impact players suddenly appeared on the pitch, with of course full co-operation from the local referee. Our sense of amazement (and injustice) at this unauthorised tactic was greeted with a Gallic shrug and an offer of more free beer.

Touring the great rugby bastions of Southwest France also brought me into contact with the great Serge Blanco, then playing for Biarritz. He was already well known locally as a wonder boy with a huge career ahead of him. We of course were totally ignorant of this, until he casually ran through half the team and scored under the posts with nonchalant ease and to what was clearly accustomed acclaim from the crowd. Luckily for Oxford, the great man was taken off at half time, and a major revival in the Oxford pack in the second half, accompanied by one or two huge fistfights (a common occurrence in those days, although as usual nobody got hurt), allowed us to record a famous victory. By the time I encountered Blanco as an England player, it was midway through the era where we had worked out how to beat the French – tackle on gain line, keep disciplined, oh, and... stop Blanco! Easy pickings, but to be fair England became masters of this tactic, and their reward was to win eight matches, home and away, against France on the trot between 1989 and 1995.

Blanco would have to be to be my all-time fullback choice in any World XV, although personally I would have loved to have played with Andy Irvine. The Scottish fullback's ability to see the space in front of him was legendary, and it was his misfortune to be playing in the JPR Williams era, when the latter's all-round skills, particularly against rough, tough teams like the All Blacks, won him many a close selection battle for the Barbarians and the Lions alike.

Possibly my best French touring moment came many years after I had left

Oxford. I was contacted in the late 1980s by the tour captain Rupert Vessey, who was in something of a panic. Oxford were due to play against Perpignan and Agen (much easier fixtures in my day!) that Easter. Their then rugby celebrities, David Kirk, Brendan Mullin and Troy Coker (New Zealand, Ireland and Australia internationals respectively, and an undeniably heavyweight gang of talent) had made themselves unavailable for a number of reasons. Rupert was desperate, surely not that desperate, I suggested flippantly, although I knew that Bath had a crucial Easter fixture against local rivals Bristol, which clashed with the tour. However I was able to enter into good-natured negotiation with Bath for my release, and the upshot was that I flew to Toulouse with my wife, Suzanne. We travelled to Perpignan via Carcassonne, that glorious medieval walled city *en route* and very much in the heart of the region where I had spent some happy months as a student. We had planned for one game followed by a few days in the Catalan region of Spain, where Suzanne's parents had an apartment. The game versus Perpignan was a cracker; they had some internationals on board, so I was appropriately fired up as a current England international. We played our socks off, but were twenty points off the pace, beaten by the sort of ball handling that English teams could only dream of at the time (not now of course). Nevertheless, for me a fabulous dinner in an old church inside the city was an ideal end to the day, washed down, as it was, with a few glasses of the local Vin du Pays. I should say it would have been the perfect end to a great day, because late on I suddenly found myself pinned to a wall with an impassioned plea that I *simply had to* turn out for Dark Blues against Agen. The French media had pre-marketed the international players, and the game would be a PR disaster if I didn't play. Sometimes not speaking the local language is a distinct advantage, but on this occasion the French word for 'please' seemed to have many variations. I wilted, with an understanding smile from Suzanne and our Catalan stay was cut short by a day, the trade-off being that I would be paid for an extra day of car rental. How easily pleased we were in those days; I wonder what the going rate would be now, what percentage of the gate? It would have been a respectable figure then, given the gate at Agen's home ground; at that time the club was the powerhouse of French rugby containing half a dozen of the then current France team, including Daniel Dubroca, the national team captain. Let us not forget that the cigar-smoking all powerful president of the FFR, Albert Ferrasse, was also there. It brought a smile to my face to see Suzanne, my wife, charming him with her St Paul's

Girls' School French at the post match reception, perfectly good enough for Albert!

There was a sense of irony in our meeting, as his national team had whipped England yet again in a game in what was then the Five Nations tournament. We should have won but for lack of finishing power. I was going through a period of being ignored by the selectors, a not infrequent event, and was wondering what to do. So, when I masterminded a rare home defeat for Agen, scoring a couple of long range tries in the process, Ferrasse shook his head in wonderment that the French view of English backs as uncreative may have been wrong. But if England couldn't pick their best players, well... I hasten to add that this is not a personal sideswipe, since the whole of the Bath Rugby Club felt persecuted at this point, in so far as Bath was probably the most powerful club side in the world, yet they were unable to have more than a few of their side selected for England. Much, much more of that elsewhere, but for now I had left my mark in another corner of France and returned happilyunconscionable to Bath, having dipped into the Oxford University culture once more, albeit briefly, where I was reminded of its fresh-faced unaffected attitude, as well as having been the place where I really learned my rugby.

When you consider the great rugby touring centres of the world, Japan does not necessarily spring to mind. But the England students' tour to Hong Kong and Japan in 1981 was possibly the best of all my touring memories, simply because of the quality of the team on and off the field and the environment in which we found ourselves. The playing statistics were overwhelming, but then Japan was hardly a bedrock of rugby excellence at that time, and even now is still developing. Nevertheless, when we played in Tokyo's Olympic Stadium in front of 80, 000 fanatical supporters, it was a new experience for everyone. We finished by beating their national team by forty points; as a footnote to that scoreline, I remember that, some years later, in 1986 in a non-cap match, the full England side at Twickenham was unable to do any better than we callow student tourists had managed.

As for myself, I was now flying as a player, and enjoying myself hugely. I was fit, and seemed able to break the line at will. This was in no small way due to Tony Watkinson, my old Oxford captain, who was still studying medicine, and his well-timed passes which gave me the time and space I needed, fulfilling the role that John Palmer was to do so effectively for me when I joined Bath;

Jeremy Guscott, probably one of the finest centres ever to play the game.

ultimately Watko showed me the way that I would need to provide for the great Jeremy Guscott.

All great centres operate in pairs, and on that tour I won the plaudits, but Tony was the initiator. He also took me under his wing as someone who needed counsel and wisdom, and while we laugh about it now, and gently rib each other, he was another character who gave me insight and maturity enough to realise my ability.

As a student I was given to bouts of uncontrolled naiveté as an individual, as my Oxford tutor had noticed, and I very nearly didn't complete the tour for disciplinary reasons. As we celebrated our exceptional victory over Japan, I was lured into a drinking contest with our left wing, Mark Bailey, who was to go on to play for Wasps and England. Mark was a northern lad, Cambridge University-educated, very bright, with a wicked sense of fun. I was easy meat for him; we were sitting in horseshoe formation at the evening reception, and he lifted a glass of sake at me, in an invitation to down it, which I duly did. Over the next half hour, I lost count of the communal toasts we enjoyed, except that when the speeches started I was out of control and Mark looked strangely sober. Only afterwards did I find out that he had substituted water for sake; not a difficult thing to do, since both liquids are colourless. My colleagues desperately tried to stop me embarrassing myself. Alan Grimsdell stood up to respond to the toast by the Japanese RFU. To this day, I maintain that he resembled a bald eagle, but neither he nor the other officials were impressed to be informed of that fact by a drunken student, and on more than one occasion during the meal.

I was hauled up in front of the tour management the next day – threatened with expulsion from the tour as well as being warned that this behaviour would be reported to the RFU. I didn't particularly care about the last bit as I was hardly featuring in selectorial considerations, but I was more circumspect about Mr Bailey's invitations thereafter.

In another unusual quirk of fate, I only toured at all because of the largesse of a Bath business man by the name of Cyril Beazer. After my disastrous masquerade as a Bath forward in a club trial during university holidays, the club made a more formal effort to persuade me to join, supported by the urgings of Derek Wyatt, their former England winger, who was at Oxford attending a one-year teaching course. Derek, the 'oldest swinger in town' as we called him, is a unique character, not least because he is now a Labour MP. He was a fine player, unfairly tagged as the player who cross kicked to Andy Irvine, in his one and only international, when England were on the attack and Scotland scored in the other corner as a result. Nonetheless he was a prolific try scorer for Bedford and Bath, the master of the interception and one of the game's true thinkers; unusual for wingers in those days. Derek persuaded me to give Bath another go, as they had a gaping hole at centre due to Mike Beese's retirement and injury to another player. I was obviously tempted, since the great John Horton was at fly-half, and a certain speedster on the wing called David Trick was attracting rave reviews wherever he played. I suppressed my indignation about the previous experience, and agreed to play for Bath whenever Oxford didn't have a game. So Derek (who had a car) and I travelled through Welsh valleys only to get slammed by most of the Welsh clubs we played. At this time, Bath had plenty of backs and a few hit men up front but no lasting power against the mammoth Welsh forwards. Remember, England were only halfway through their barren period against Wales, when we could hardly win against them at Twickenham, let alone in Cardiff.

Cyril Beazer had offered to fund half of the tour fee of £200 if I would commit myself to Bath after leaving Oxford. I suppose that this qualifies as

Youthful but bolchy at times in my early twenties, a good quality to have, it made me play better

bribery, or even a signing-on fee, but I was very grateful anyway. You see, 'penniless' really meant that at times in my early days. The Bath officials, to be fair, did not pressurise me and since my connections with the Harlequins had faded after playing for them whilst at Oxford, this was a natural decision for me to make. So when I returned from the tour, having survived a couple of dodgy moments in the red light district of Hong Kong on the way, I made a special point of bringing back some memorabilia to my kind sponsor Cyril Beazer. To my great sadness, he died very shortly afterwards, but I will always remember his generosity. He was a great rugby man and Bath supporter, even if the showers he installed in the changing rooms rarely worked.

Once again, a series of unlikely events had combined to push my rugby career to an important place, and my Japanese dalliance proved to me that Nick Mallett's conviction about my ability was not in fact South African blarney but a truth which was becoming more obvious to me and others in the corridors of rugby power.

It is undoubtedly the case that the England Under 23 tour of Italy in 1982 and Romania in 1983, sandwiched by a three-week rugby fun-fest in California for Lloyds Insurance RFC, were also major moments for a player, who by now couldn't get enough of rugby. Have boots, would travel, it seemed. I was playing fifty games a year, and as soon as the summer came, cricket studs were also tightened as I was by then a fully fledged minor counties cricketer for Dorset, averaging forty and facing down the likes of Joel Garner and Malcolm Marshall whenever Dorset qualified for the NatWest Trophy: cricket's national knock-out competition. If it seems as if everything was happening at breakneck speed, then it was, and for a while I was either recovering from one rugby or cricket tour, or preparing for another.

In addition, I was meeting people who would shape my career, on and off the pitch, at such an impressionable age that it was difficult for me not to be influenced. Not that I was complaining, since they were also the young cream of English rugby. Remember that England were fresh from their first Grand Slam in many years, and enthusiasm for the game was at a peak. Young

Simon Halliday passing out of tackle to Underwood: what people now call the offload, I developed into an art, even when airborne!

pretenders such as Rory Underwood, Stuart Barnes, Rob Andrew, Dean Richards and Brian Moore, all household names, were cutting their teeth and lining up to replace Grand Slam heroes of the likes of John Carlton, Peter Wheeler, Roger Uttley and John Horton. This was during the period when there was a growing understanding that English players simply had to get fitter. The statistics emanating from the All Blacks camp were awesome and awe-inspiring, and their 'aerobic' and 'anaerobic' fitness levels some thirty per cent higher than ours. This was hardly surprising since the 'beer and chips' culture was extremely vibrant through the entire rugby structure of not just the UK, but the entire northern hemisphere.

The first man who understood this was the then England U23 coach, Dick Greenwood. The year was 1983 and he was the incumbent national team coach, one of his first games being the famous win over the All Blacks at Twickenham. He reminded me on occasions of a moustachioed musketeer, and his wit was almost Gallic. But he was strongly of the opinion that English rugby was doomed to permanent underperformance because we simply had no gas for the first hour of a game, let alone the final twenty minutes. And it should be remembered that in those days the ball was only in play for a total of about a quarter of the match. However, Greenwood's early attempts to change the habits of a generation were decidedly primitive.

On one famous occasion, the squad had just landed in Bucharest, Romania, having manoeuvred our way through a nest of machine guns, which had been carefully positioned around the airport, as well as having negotiated a passage past some aggressive guards. After all, this was Ceausescu's regime and not too many outsiders were welcome, not even sportsmen. So we were feeling a little fragile, and not just due to the burning heat. Our arrival at the main city hotel was accompanied by a flurry of activity and the appearance of local cigarettes and currency (LEI – many thousands to the pound as I remember, due to devaluations aplenty) offered in exchange for well-known western brands, dollars, sterling or seemingly anything. Undeterred by the unusual environment, Dick ordered us out into the car park in the Romanian grit and choking dust, which was not my idea of a traditional welcome in what proved to be a stunning three-week tour. Mr Greenwood laid out his stall, and a tough one it was. The hard ground took its toll, and a number of players could testify to when shin-splints became a problem on that unforgiving, unyielding car park surface. The ground was like rock, and we trained on it for two and a half hours a day. Complaints and groans resulted in further physical punishment – the ultimate vicious circle. So we soon learned to grin and bear it. This was also the era when Vaseline was used as much between the legs as on the face due to excessive fattiness, particularly among the forwards (sorry boys). Kevin Murphy, the renowned England physiotherapist, revealed that the biggest impact of improving fitness levels was the fifty per cent decline in Vaseline orders.

Part of the horrendous training regime was driven by the fact that most of us were suffering from permanent hangovers. The heat and the lack of things to do – a trip downtown was usually made with an accompanying squad of the country's secret police – contributed to our drinking and although Dick was prepared to allow this, there was always a price to pay on the training ground the next day. Although I would not describe the cream of English youth rugby as a bunch of crazed alcoholics, it does demonstrate how far below the benchmark we really were at that time.

An even better example of this had occurred in Italy the previous year, when the U23s, on an oppressively hot evening in Treviso, were desperately seeking rehydration as much as a celebratory drink. For some reason there was absolutely nothing to drink until we got to the reception, where Asti was the only alcohol on offer – not a Peroni in sight. Enter Stuart Barnes, who decided to educate us in an Oxford/Newport drinking game. I had seen all this before at Oxford, but thirst was the overriding consideration, and I certainly did not hold back. By the end of the evening, my Latin degree was unnecessary in order to appreciate the literal meaning of the word 'spumante'. At least two thirds of the team were profoundly unwell, and Messrs Greenwood and Finlan, the management team, spent much of the night helping to clean up the resultant mess. At eight the next morning, we were all reminded sharply of our responsibilities to the country and one another, following which the real punishment started. It was not before the clock struck midday that an impossibly tired squad was permitted to rest aching limbs and bodies. Stuart Barnes' drinking games were regarded with a degree of suspicion from then onwards, and the national selectors at this stage were not quite sure what to make of this ebullient and influential young man. It was the start of a love/hate affair from which neither side emerged without a number of temporary and permanent scars. In spite of that, Stuart put his mark on both tours; he was a No10 of extraordinary talent, the like of which English rugby had rarely seen, perhaps unsurprising, considering that his rugby pedigree was distinctly Welsh.

In 1983 that proud rugby nation was very much among the top three in the world, and fly-half was the pivotal position, so this is no mean praise.

Touring helped create the bond which we all shared, through success and failure alike, and I firmly contend that the many weeks spent in the company of future England colleagues were invaluable. As each tour ended, there would be this feeling that we had grown up just a little more, had developed a deeper relationship on and off the field, and were setting a base for the future, which in hindsight was all about re-establishing England as a major force in world rugby. There were at least half a dozen of us who would go on to taste success as Grand Slam champions twice in a row, up until then an unimaginable achievement for the England rugby team.

CHAPTER 5

The Bath Phenomenon

Any traveller happening on Bath in the last 2000 years must have undergone a pleasant experience. Set, appropriately given its Roman roots, among seven hills, with the city centre at the foot of them, Bath has drawn people to it across two millennia: first as a Roman City, Aquae Sulis, whose hot springs (incidentally the only hot springs occurring naturally in Great Britain) have become known for their therapeutic qualities; after being granted city status by Queen Elizabeth I in the sixteenth century, it then emerged as a fashionable Georgian City, that Jane Austen found irresistible, so irresistible that she featured it in some of her novels; Beau Nash strutted his stuff there, as did many a Georgian and Regency Dandy. It was in these periods that the local mellow stone was used for the construction of the elegant residences to be found in Royal Crescent, and higher up on Lansdowne Hill, as well as in Lansdowne Crescent. Smaller houses inevitably followed, all of them in that buff yellow hue, lending the hills some delightful lines and gentle tones and contributing to the overriding impression that the city of Bath is a truly inspirational place prompting thoughts of beauty, restfulness and culture. From the historic Roman Baths and Pump Rooms up through the Circus into the Royal Crescent, where the opening of the Bath festival takes place every year, there is an air of comfort, a strong sense of history and an overwhelming feeling of West Country calm. It is a welcome antidote to the other West Country rugby giants, the more industrial cities of Bristol and Gloucester. Bath has attracted a large and consistent following because of the exploits and excellence of its rugby club, which was to become one of the most successful of the modern era.

As a youngster Bath had always been a no-go area for me, being ten miles from Downside school; the only times I visited it was on the odd school trip, and in my schooldays the one thing it most certainly was not was a hot-bed of rugby. The club had been founded in 1865, but had always been the poor relations of West Country rugby, although the view of the abbey and Pulteney Weir is one of the richest in Britain, unmatched by any other rugby venue around the country, if not in the world. Uniquely the clubhouse and ground are in the city centre, a stone's throw from shops, restaurants and museums, not to mention the River Avon, which on occasion has reached out and flooded The Recreation Ground.

Back in my schooldays there did not seem to be any likely set of circumstances which might propel this modest, unassuming city club into a name to be feared at home and abroad in the rugby world.

However, a glance back at major events and their underlying causes, reveals that there is invariably a confluence of circumstances, an unplanned gathering of key people, which then creates a momentum that becomes unstoppable. Simply put, that is pretty much how Bath became a phenomenon. Not that anyone foresaw that.

I certainly did not have some hidden insight, nor did I personally light the touch paper, which launched the club into orbit. But I was there, and what is more I saw, and shared in, the birth and the development, and I felt the power surge as it coursed through the city. And it was truly remarkable, this ascent to the top of rugby's tree, in the same way that the ensuing decline was brutal, unforgiving, but in many ways predictable.

There was no inkling of any special team in the making as I started to play regularly at centre, but this is not to say that we lacked talented players. I was part of a backline that contained John Horton, England's Grand Slam fly-half; David Trick, the lightning fast winger with international aspirations; and John Palmer, a little injury prone (I obviously caught that from him), but one of the most highly regarded centres in his position in the country. So there was plenty of talent in the three-quarter line, but we were regularly outgunned by the major Welsh teams and our West Country neighbours Bristol and Gloucester; we did, generally, see off London and Midland teams, so I got used to this trend and was happy enough, because when we backs did get the ball (which was not that often) we would run it with great intensity and passion, and no little skill, on the assumption that we may not see it again for a while.

This is not to say that our pack was not capable, or tough, or even at times extremely rough. In fact Bath had something of a reputation for being punchy and aggressive, although ultimately no heavyweight. Stuart Barnes has reminded me many times that his ability to launch a spiralling up-and-under was matched only by my offensive behaviour when it landed on a poor unfortunate fullback. As I got older, I tended to tap it back in order to retain possession, and frankly that was far more constructive. But in the early days, I went for the man, early or late, and often high. It was a tactic that Bath found themselves employing early in the game, partly to get the crowd going. It generally resulted in a fight, particularly against the Welsh, however the perpetrator (me) invariably slunk away, and was nowhere to be seen when the fists and the fur flew. I can vividly remember Terry Claxton, the truck-driving Harlequins' skipper, lecturing the multi-coloured toffs about their reluctance to 'mix it' at a game down on the Recreation Ground. But we lacked bulk and it would always count against us.

The mix was very exciting and somewhat unpredictable, even if we couldn't count ourselves at the top of the tree. Of course, I haven't even mentioned the North of England, which provided the bulk of the England team, mainly on the back of the North beating the All Blacks in 1979. This was the Beaumont era, with other great characters such as Tony Neary, Fran Cotton, Steve Smith and Mike Slemen, and the Leicester power base was always evident, such as Peter Wheeler, Paul Dodge, Clive Woodward and Dusty Hare. Compared to all of these regions and personalities, Bath was a pinprick.

What impressed me about Bath at first was the remarkable local spirit of the city and club. This was personified by an amazing character called Simon Jones. 'Jonesy' was a flyaway flanker and totally fearless; he needed to be, he was often five yards ahead of the next supporting forward, and he often lost the ball, when, inevitably, he was overpowered by multiple opposition forwards. But he was irrepressible and he never gave up. Off the field he had a wicked sense of humour which would often leave you the victim of some practical joke. He was a ladies man as the perpetual glint in his eye would testify. I learned to stay nearby in post-match entertainment since he was often at the centre of late night party ideas, and the pretty girls gravitated to him. No-one was quite sure whether to take him seriously, but equally it didn't matter much, particularly as his on-field commitment was absolute, so what he got up to off the field was interesting but entirely his affair. Simon carved the effort for Bath upfront in my first year, because he had pace and ambition and always led the way. The crowd loved him as a real 'son of Bath' and he would always respond to their enthusiasm. I had particular reason to thank him for his unbelievable commitment to me on the fateful day when I broke my ankle. Simon was not playing, it being the county championship cup semi-final between Somerset and Middlesex, which was being staged at Bridgewater, but he was watching and supporting Somerset from the stands.

I was carried off and placed on the clubhouse floor until the ambulance arrived, and Simon rushed down from his seat to offer help, and when it became clear that I was hospital-bound he came along for the ride. I will never forget his support and friendship in that hour of need.

It may seem strange for me to focus upon Simon as a central character in the emergence of Bath as a global force in club rugby. In the 'rogues' gallery' at the recreation ground, which carries portraits of Bath's many internationalists, there is no Simon Jones. His influence and contribution to the Bath rugby club is overlooked in the majority of books recounting the club's history, however there is one exception, and that is the second volume of Kevin Coughlan's excellent chronicle, *After The Lemons*. But in general his name would not spring readily to the lips of journalists, selectors, players, both past and present, were they to recall Bath's greatest moments. But I should like to pay tribute to his infectious enthusiasm, good humour, honesty and most importantly, his commitment to the Bath cause. By the time Bath started to win the knockout championship, then called the John Player Cup, he had long since been left out of the side; not only had age caught up with him by then, but the advent of future international characters such as Paul Simpson, John Hall, Andy Robinson and Dave Egerton made the Bath back row a very crowded place.

People will recall the famous moment when Willie John McBride applauded the Lions' replacements in South Africa after the 1974 series had been won. He was articulating an undeniable truth in rugby football, if not sport in general, namely that the obvious heroes sometimes mask the equal contribution of others not in the public eye, whose light may shine less brightly, but are nevertheless valuable, indeed essential, to the overall effort and achievement.

Simon was not a shrinking violet, and he did not shirk the public eye. His part in the play was not a walk-on one, and he should be proud of his role in creating momentum for the Bath chariot. The wheels of this particular chariot were not just assembled, attached and left to run unaided, but in the early days the chariot was rickety; sometimes worked but many times the wheels threatened to come off

I remember a particular day at St Helens, Swansea, which is a sand-based pitch and therefore guarantees a quick, pacey game. In the early '80s very few sides even threatened a win on Swansea's home ground, and this day was no exception. After an early punch-up and a couple of warnings, we were comprehensively dismantled and lost by forty points. As usual, Bath had given great value for money and were warmly applauded for their expansive attitude, but frankly this wasn't good enough anymore, and after results like this a number of old stalwarts were gradually eased out of the side, and some frighteningly good youngsters appeared on the scene. The transition was hastened by the impending return of two players who became synonymous with the club's image; they were probably two of the hardest men who ever played, and they were to propel the club into a position where we could at last dream of competing on a level playing field. This duo was Roger Spurrell and Gareth Chilcott.

The world of rugby has long appreciated the many skills and attributes of 'Coochie' Chilcott as Gareth was somewhat inappropriately nicknamed, for off the field he may have resembled a teddy bear or a 'West Country cheese' as famously recorded by John Reason (the former *Sunday Telegraph* rugby correspondent), but as an individual he is a diamond. The characteristic bullet-head, the confrontation and snarl, and the cheeky mischievous grin are all trademarks, almost of a registered variety. On the other hand, Roger Spurrell, rather like Simon Jones, is hardly a name that trips off the tongue; that is, if you don't know rugby.

I never really questioned Roger or his background, other than knowing about his Cornish roots and his time with the SAS; but that is probably sufficient to set the scene. More knowledgeable people describe him as the best uncapped loose forward ever to play in English rugby. In his prime I cannot remember him ever being outplayed, at least, not in those areas of the field which the forwards love to call 'the hard yards'. He was never happier than when the confrontations were at their fiercest, and I remember on numerous occasions being silently grateful when Roger and company were fighting our corner.

This physical approach was a key stage in our development as a credible rugby force, and Roger embodied the new attitude. When I first arrived at the club, he was recovering from a badly broken jaw – can't think how he got that – and Gareth Chilcott was in the middle of a one-year ban for head-butting, but while I heard their names often, and make no mistake, many Bath loyalists held them in awe, it wasn't until they resumed playing that I could really appreciate their influence.

Roger soon assumed captaincy and began the process of building a team to be reckoned with, alongside Jack Rowell, the Bath coach who had arrived from Gosforth in 1979 and was also the managing director of Lucas Ingredients, a major division of Dalgety. Believe me, this was an evil combination, and hugely effective. The blunt, hard-headed confrontational style of Spurrell, and his near-satanical sense of humour, combined with the quixotic, maverick and satirical Rowell psyche, generally caused an explosive reaction from an increasingly talented group of players. Jack deserves a special place in Bath and England's history and I do not wish to underestimate his contribution to the early days at Bath RFC. Indeed his uncanny ability to extract the best out of his players has been matched by very few, if any, coaches in club history. But he would be the first to admit that this was about the players, especially in the early '80s. In fact, he was quoted many times to this effect, and his pre-match entreaty to his assembled team often contained little more than various verbal exhortations to inspire key individuals on the day.

Once Jack had said his bit, Roger would take the lead. He would be the first to admit that his own pre-match routine was somewhat out of the ordinary, as he paced around like a caged lion, growling a combination of challenge and encouragement to his team. In the 'pit' (the home changing room), however, Roger took the lead. His last cigarette would be crushed out during the changing room warm-up, then he would take his forwards into the shower room for a final haranguing. This was a passionate affair, the three quarters on the outside of what seemed like a secret, inner circle. But occasionally the best laid plans do not work and even the pumped-up forwards had to laugh. In the midst of the final throes of one shower room special, with metal studs clattering on the floor, there was a sudden cacophony of swearing, shrieking and general noise. Nigel Redman, the young international lock, had leaned against the shower button by mistake and soaked the rest of his team-mates! It was an angrier bunch of forwards than usual which emerged to contest the game, and no doubt we performed rather better as a result.

I am sure that it was a myth that Roger removed the head of a budgerigar in a Cornish hotel foyer at the end of a particularly raucous post-match pub run, but it reinforces the image of a man who had a devilish streak from time to time. As the owner of the city's best known night-club, the 'Bog' Island Club – created out of former public toilets, which had been themselves on an island of sorts in the middle of the road – he was one of the better known figures among party goers, and a hard attitude on the door was definitely required.

Roger and I had a very competitive relationship, and while I hope I can claim a lasting friendship, in his eyes I always had to prove myself. After all, I was living and working in London when I began my proper playing career down at Bath, and there was an inherent suspicion that I was not really committed to the cause. Jack Rowell would often ask me, in front of the squad of course, "Hallers, we still don't know if you are one of us" and I would grin sheepishly as if accepting that I was still some kind of probationer.

However, there were times when I did feel hard done by, because I believed that I was doing my bit, but thought that it wasn't being recognised. I would catch a tea-time train from London, arriving at Bath just in time for training at 7. 15, followed by a mad rush for the last train back at 9. 40, no dinner of course, and the prospect of a very tiring following day. I was 'away' with Bath every weekend of the winter, except on the odd occasion when we came up to London; for the other midweek session I would go down to Dorking, a local Surrey club, with my housemate and Oxford friend, Tim Elliott.

Tim would drive me down to take part in their team training which was always much appreciated. A local Surrey club with a very friendly atmosphere, Dorking was a perfect reminder of the vibrancy and importance of junior club rugby. Other than that, I often ventured into the Clapham darkness and sprinted between the lampposts on Clapham Common, just down from the Windmill Pub, strangely, the only one within walking distance of my lodgings on Broomwood Road. When you consider the training methods of current aspiring internationals, it beggars belief that anyone could have been in position for international honours with such a schedule, but the only alternative for me was to move clubs, and that was hardly on the cards. So my rather strange existence, nomadic in many ways, continued for the whole of the 1982-83 season, but, at the age of twenty-two, and suddenly the centre of rugby attention, I was happy enough.

It was a simple fact of Bath rugby life, and quite clearly a differentiating factor, that no player could take anything for granted. We started to create a huge team spirit, driven mercilessly by characters such as Jones, Spurrell and Chilcott. By the turn of 1982, there was a great sense of optimism in the air, until we ventured to Leicester in the opening week of January. We were dismantled (well, 21-9, but it felt like dismantling) by a supremely well organised Leicester side, marshalled by Peter Wheeler, Les Cusworth and Dusty Hare, not to mention the illustrious Paul Dodge and Clive Woodward, apparently under threat from Halliday and Palmer. Well, not that day for sure. And predictors of a West Country phenomenon in the making down at the Recreation Ground had to put their thoughts on hold for the time being at least.

But one of the famous and ferocious post-match Rowell diatribes had a massive impact on us. I think that he was genuinely upset by how we had lost this particular match. So were we, of course, but Jack built up that particular defeat into a *'cause célèbre'*. We had been out-thought, and had not known how to respond; he spoke of the need to run into space, not to panic when under pressure, and to be mentally much stronger. He spoke of the extra level of commitment required to win these sorts of games, he encouraged us to feel the pain of this defeat and to allow it to recur. He wanted this game to be a turning point for the club and for the players in front of him. When I read the press reports, there were clear indications that we were being dismissed as a top-flight team; the equivalent of a shooting star, lighting up the odd game for a while but then fading into darkness.

But everyone was wrong. It was a masterstroke by Rowell and he had, perhaps inadvertently at the time, lit a touch paper which burned for the next decade with a strength and heat which was too intense for the domestic game. We did indeed carry the hurt of that defeat with us thereafter, and Bath became the scourge of Anglo-Welsh rugby as we completed a twenty-three-game unbeaten run against the best of British rugby. To this day, I can scarcely believe how we did it. I played every game, whether Wednesday night or Saturday afternoon, and it resembled the crest of a never-ending wave. The city was buzzing, and every home game was packed to the rafters; as our record developed we became the team to beat, and every away game was a titanic struggle as teams strove to break the unbeaten run.

To give an insight into the attitude of mind we had at that time is to understand how our success was crafted. We would watch the opposing team come into the ground, and we would rarely come out onto the pitch ourselves to warm up, eschewing common practice. The team would create amazing intensity in our pre-match build-up, and we would deliberately target weak spots but, more often than not, we would not attack their known strengths. Ironically, this was more effective; the opposition often lost heart when their best was shown up as being not good enough on the day. I look back at those great times and often wonder about the key to our performances; other than enjoying the benefits of a fantastically talented bunch of players, we did have an incredibly single-minded approach, and every big challenge seemed to bring out an even better response from the team.

In the latter part of my career, I remember practising this technique on a good mate of mine, international full-back Jon Webb. It was the semi-final of the cup and Bristol were at our place. We had discussed the threat of their backs, particularly Webb. I said I would take care of it. As we ran out onto the pitch, I went up to him and he smiled at me; after all I was giving him a lift to the national squad session after the game. He probably expected me to let him know the arrangements. Instead I glared at him, "First high ball, you're going to get it," I said calmly, but with certainty. He blanched a little, and looked unnerved. Five minutes later Stuart Barnes put up a wicked high ball, and I arrived at the same time as Webb collected it. I gave him my hardest hit and then held him down as the forwards arrived and kicked the living daylights out of him, starting a mass fight. Jon was very unhappy, but the job was done. He played an ineffectual game and we duly proceeded to the final. I apologised after the game, but not because I wouldn't do it again, it was our way.

The 1983 club record of consecutive wins is celebrated with a plaque affixed to the clubhouse wall. While not a great one for statistics, I believe that January to April run was worth recording.

It may seem inherently unfair to single out individuals when rugby is essentially a team game, but I think we all know that there are pivotal characters who have the priceless ability to provide the catalyst for others. I have referred to the growing credibility of our forwards who had historically been one of our weaknesses. The avalanche of points we started to score did not just happen, and among the many to whom I pay tribute is John Horton, probably one of the most talented fly-halves who played the game in England. A recent Grand Slam (1980) No10, he was hardly a novice, but he had several issues to deal with at Bath. He was surrounded by youngsters (with the exception of an aging Derek Wyatt) and had to harness all this enthusiasm, but he rarely panicked (unless a particularly large forward came running at him in open play – let's not forget, most self-respecting No10s in those days avoided tackling – talk to Phil Bennett and Naas Botha; tackling was an unnecessary chore which the flankers should be doing anyway) and invariably made the right call under pressure.

His ability to get a backline going was, and remains, unmatched by any fly-half in England since his time. He also set up the agenda for Bath's continuing success through the '80s. I will say no more – I can't pay a higher tribute than that.

The story of the legendary fly-half factory buried deep in Wales somewhere is well established through the words of the singer and entertainer Max Boyce. It was reinforced by the fact that at the start of every season there seemed to be another Welsh genius sporting the No10 shirt.

One of those names could easily have been Stuart Barnes. In true Welsh style, he was squat, quick off the mark and a very natural player. Having been selected for Wales Under 19s and a member of the full Welsh squad, it appeared that Stuart would follow in some illustrious footsteps. But you cannot deny your roots, and the Essex in the man (as well as the English) stepped forward proudly. By twenty-one, Stuart had committed to England, and the die was cast.

His first senior club was Bristol where real ale got the better of him – working for Whitbread didn't help. One of his nicknames was 'the barrel'.

I was down the road at Bath, and as an old Oxford mate of Stuart I was keen to join forces on the pitch again. But it wasn't until 1985 that Stuart came to Bath. This move was the first of many examples where recruitment/selection issues could have been handled better, considering the fact that John Horton was the incumbent No10. That he was at the end of his career, simply meant he deserved huge respect both as a person and a player. Unfortunately Bath rugby club wasn't great at dealing with such sensitivities; rather than indulge in gratuitous detail, let me just say that we all suffered over the years. Every player had their own almost ritualised tale of woe over some incident of selection or general mistreatment. Bath had already upset John Horton by selecting me at centre for my comeback game and moving John Palmer to fly-half. They claimed that John Horton was resting, attracting a stream of vitriol from him. It certainly took the gloss off my comeback, and this latest event simply hastened John's retirement.

The arrival of Barnes, however, did usher in a new era of Bath dominance. This is not to say that the club went through a wobbly period, but simply that it regenerated itself over the next twelve months, seemingly finding a reservoir of impossibly talented replacements for aged incumbents. How about this for a list: Guscott, Hill, Egerton, Hall, Sole, Cronin, Barnes, Redman, and Robinson – all household names in international rugby, who learned their trade at the Recreation Ground, and players who owed their careers to the environment of Bath rugby. And none of them played in the earliest glory days.

The legacy left to us by the likes of Roger Spurrell was exceptionally powerful. Simply put, we were never happy with our performances. Post-match analyses, even if we had won handsomely, always seemed to pick on weakness or mistakes, often embarrassing a player in public. This was a favourite game of Jack Rowell's, but the words were mostly very shrewdly chosen. He knew how to tease, to encourage and to motivate, depending on the player. He would leave you with a real sense of worth and belonging, qualities which were deeply embedded in the rugby club itself.

The other real driver from a coaching point of view was our fitness adviser, Tom Hudson, assisted by Dave Robson.

He strode into the club one evening, and presented us with a five-year plan. His opening gambit was that we were a bunch of losers, had no idea about fitness or how to look after ourselves, and this simply wasn't good enough. We were aghast, since we had a slightly higher opinion of ourselves than that. Nonetheless, we took it all in, and since Tom was obviously there to stay, we didn't have much option but to follow his strategy.

It was soon clear that we had become an extension of Tom's SAS unit from years back. His sessions were brutal, but always with a difference. He knew rugby and how rugby players worked so the fitness was never gratuitous where so many coaches can get it wrong. When your lungs were fit to burst, he would exhort you to ever greater heights, and his words would strike home. Did we want to be the best, not just in the club, or in England, but in the world? Strong words, but in the street fighting world of Anglo Welsh club rugby, that was our objective and we were producing results to match. Tom was never satisfied and would seek out players individually and demand answers to certain passages of play. The fact that we accepted his role was a measure of the respect we all had for him.

Tom's disciplined way of approaching his trade extended to the manner of his departure. Very few Bath rugby supporters, or Gloucester for that matter, will forget the sultry 1990 day in May when Bath won the Pilkington Cup by a record score of 48-6. For Tom, it was the culmination of his five-year plan. In his book, he had helped to create a multi-skilled, supremely mobile and totally committed group of players capable of international style rugby at club level. There was nothing left for him to do.

As the Bath team coach triumphantly cruised back to the West Country,

Tom turned to me and said somewhat emotionally: "I cannot do any more here. I need to move on." It was a strangely subdued way of saying farewell, for a man who was never short of a word. But having achieved so much for his club, perhaps it was appropriate.

As with so many stories of success, this is another name left in the shadows. Tom's pursuit of excellence had to be seen to be believed, and I doubt that we could have achieved all our success without him. I certainly owe him a huge debt of gratitude, for the way in which he inspired me as I recovered from my leg injury, both physically and psychologically. This is not to say that with Tom's departure, the team collapsed. It moved on and found a way to fill the gap he left. The strength of any organisation is respected by its strength in depth, and when I left, also after that game, in walked Phil de Granville. Need I say more?

If there was an enduring quality that both Tom and Jack had, it was their ability to think through the short-term. The whole rugby world will remember when Bath lost to Moseley in the 1988 John Player Cup; it was our first loss in

All conquering Bath Team – just fourteen internationals in this snapshot!

the cup for four years. The Bath team was packed to the gunnels with past, present and future internationals, and we were up against Moseley, a worthy enough team, but with few outstanding individuals, with the exception of John Goodwin, their winger. He was a fine player who deserved to play more at the highest level. When we proceeded to blow yet another scoring opportunity, we realised that somehow it was not to be our day. A 6-3 defeat tells you the nature of the game. The hysteria which greeted the final whistle was unprecedented, and the cheers in the rugby bars up and down the country resounded mercilessly. Bath may have been all-conquering, but we were hardly a popular club.

The atmosphere in the dressing room was murderous; we were stunned into silence. Eventually, Jack and Tom appeared, also seemingly speechless. Long moments followed, and then Jack got to work. His post match talk was very similar to the Leicester effort some four years earlier. He reminded us of how good we were, what the club meant to everyone, and how it was all about people dealing with adversity and disappointment. His tone was quiet but assured, and generated stirring emotions. I heard afterwards that he had spent the last ten minutes of the match outside the stand, unable to watch. Perhaps he knew, and was preparing himself for a rallying speech.

He made us promise to take this defeat out on every team we played in the foreseeable future; to take personal damage from the game away with us and use it to extract pay-back. None of this was spoken lightly, and the speech did not end until he made sure that we understood how seriously we were meant to take it.

At last we left the changing room, had the obligatory beer, and departed. Those of us in the England squad travelled to London for a training session on the Sunday, enduring hoots of derision and laughter. But instead of smiling sheepishly (well, at first we did), we absorbed the humiliation in order to turn it to our advantage. This was the Bath way; it was what set us apart, and it was how we drew our strength. That year, and the next, we won the league title. The following two years we won the knock-out cup. That was some speech from Rowell, and some reaction from us.

CHAPTER 6

Jack Rowell – The Coach, The Man

Now seems to be an appropriate point at which to single out the person who master-minded the transformation of a modestly ambitious West Country club, seemingly destined to remain in the shadows of its more illustrious neighbours, into the stunningly successful entity which was Bath.

From a purely personal point of view there was no doubt about it, in my mind Jack Rowell and Simon Halliday represented an unholy alliance.

"Are you one of us?" he used to ask me frequently, when I was a Bath player. I always used to squirm with embarrassment. On the face of it, it was a hurtful thing to say, it struck me right to the heart. The implication was: you don't really care, you're an outsider. You don't belong.

Jack Rowell was no ordinary coach. In fact he was a complete maverick, although he would no doubt retort: "Who cares – look at my record!" And a pretty good one it is too; nearly twenty years as Bath coach, a hatful of winners' medals, England coach (a Grand Slam), subsequently the director of rugby for a newly-rejuvenated Bath. He returned to take over when they were on the verge of relegation from the premiership, and the following year they won the league – coincidence? I hardly think so.

So why have I said, more than once, that Bath was in a way successful in spite of Jack, not because of him? Because I meant it, and it sounded very churlish then, as it does now. I simply felt that he often held us back, risking inferior teams coming close to us, and entertaining thoughts of an upset. When unleashed, the Bath team of the '80s was sensational and unstoppable. Well, perhaps I am both wrong and right.

Put simply, Jack was a wind-up merchant. He was like a latter-day warlord from *Lord of the Rings*; he created chaos and fuelled anger. Yet he always had control. He would preside over a shambles of a training session, until we were all shouting at each other, and the worse we trained, the better we played on a

Saturday, or so it seemed. Jack would revel in the unhappiness, and then act as a unifying force. Divide and rule was probably his motto, although I never challenged him on it.

Jack often showed me up in front of the team, but it was always genial and often very funny, though I say so myself. There were references to my status as ex-Harlequin, City pinstripe-suited player, public school privileged type, Oxford Blue, and being a little too fresh-faced for all this rugged, rough-house West Country rugby, and so it went on. But it did get the team laughing, and it wasn't malicious or vicious, so what the hell.

The 'Rowell way' was to keep everybody on edge, and he was inherently a nervous man, or at least he appeared to be so to me. Twitchy movements and an uncomfortable demeanour were all part of the training pitch banter and the pre-match team talks that he indulged in. But underlying this nervousness was

Roger Uttley and Jack Rowell, Patriarch of Bath Rugby, we were nothing before he arrived.

a profound knowledge of the game coupled with an astute understanding and appreciation of what made people tick. His sound-bites were as memorable as they were inimitable, while his sense of occasion was faultless; we rarely went out onto the pitch underdone.

He taught us how to win playing poorly – a rare ability. Yet his style of coaching often led to frustration, and in those days I was nothing if not impulsive – and it often showed. In a now infamous incident, I was within a month of my first (belated) cap in 1986 and the Southwest was facing London in the Divisional Championship. Most of the Bath backs, who had carried all before them so far that season, were on show, including me. For me this match represented the end of a long road to recovery, after the 1983 injury. So I was sensitive about having a decent game in front of the England selectors.

But Jack had decided that we were going to win the game in the forwards, which was a mish-mash of Bath, Bristol and Gloucester, all of whom hated each other, being local rivals. Imagine Mike Teague and John Hall playing for each other. In any event we lost the game comfortably, and I was predictably furious, having seen far too much of the London players and very little of the ball. I had also missed a few crucial tackles. My mood was dark.

As we trooped disconsolately off the pitch, I spotted Jack chatting amiably with the England selectors, and I admit, I completely lost it. Using language of which a West Country farmer would have been proud, I let rip, and a stream of invective reached both Jack and a number of the selectors, who looked at me rather bemused. Jack hurried down to remonstrate, but I was out of control, accusing him of destroying my career and other equally ridiculous statements. But I was convinced that his conservatism had cost us all dearly.

Jack informed me that he would never forgive the outburst, and my father wouldn't talk to me afterwards in the bar – a little tricky as we were visiting my prospective in-laws that evening. John Reason of the *Sunday Telegraph* even questioned my temperament in his report. All in all, it was not a happy episode. Fortunately we all got through it, and I went on to get capped by England that January.

Coaching, of course, goes hand-in-hand with selection. In the same way that Sir Clive Woodward had the pick of the litter of that era for the Rugby

World Cup 2003, so Jack presided over the most talented group of players in English club rugby – sorry Leicester.

Yet this sometimes led to selection issues. I remember vividly the Thursday before one particular Pilkington Cup Final. We were all gathered in the Bath changing room for our last training session. Jack was in full flow, and we were feeling good. One small problem: we had four back row players for three slots (John Hall, David Egerton, Andy Robinson and Paul Simpson – all of them England internationals), three wingers for two slots (Tony Swift and David Trick, both of them internationals, and Barry Trevaskis, a record try-scorer for Bath that year). Jack had failed to finalise selection. As he urged us to go out and train, this fact was pointed out to him. What on earth was going through his head?

He eventually singled out the unfortunate players who had been dropped (Paul Simpson and Barry Trevaskis), and ten minutes later the two disgusted players were seen leaving the ground. Jack could get away with that sort of thing at club level, but when he became England coach it had to be different. He needed to be more even-handed, and more cautious. The challenges which he laid down were at first novel; he challenged some players whom he thought were in a comfort zone, and he was probably right. He accused Jason Leonard of cap-counting and soon fell out with Will Carling who had been captain for so long he was probably complacent anyway.

Cooke's England had been built on qualities which surely resonated with Jack, but once in charge of the Red Rose side himself, he traded on uncertainty and it didn't go down well. The England boys were in no mood to discount his cynical witticisms. They were taken at face value, and sometimes they hurt.

It wasn't all bad of course. Under Jack, England won the Grand Slam in 1995, and beat Australia in an epic Rugby World Cup quarter final revenge match, perfect payback for defeat in the 1991 World Cup final. It couldn't last and didn't, sadly. In the 1995 semi-final against New Zealand they met their nemesis, Jonah Lomu. They were destroyed. Something or someone had to give, and it was Rowell, who quickly gave way to Clive Woodward.

Jack was an enigma; kind-hearted, yet cutting, humorous and angry at one and the same time; he was passionate to a fault, and he loved his players dearly. He created a monster of a rugby club through his genius and a single-minded desire to succeed. The world of rugby should salute him, as I certainly do. He once paid me the compliment of saying that I was the first name on the team-sheet (well, sometimes). Given the quality of my fellow players through the years, I feel very humble if that really was the case, although I would guess that it was said in order to flatter me.

But that was another quality of Jack's, he had the ability to make us all feel very special at any one time, I would hope that we repaid him for that on the field. Yet there was still that nagging sense of unfulfilment. Not because we didn't win enough, but rather because we only showed our true ability under pressure: Gloucester, 1990. That was nowhere near enough, given the resources at our disposal.

Who should one blame for that? We were all obsessed with winning, and we were rarely asked the sort of questions on the field that would force our hand and push to even greater heights. When a team really confronted us, such as Cardiff, Leicester, Llanelli, or Neath, we would respond fiercely, and the game would develop into a classic. But too often we would do just enough, satisfying ourselves with seeing off the challenge and saying 'look in the book'.

Although Jack, a 6ft 7in giant from Gosforth, loved to see us win in style, he was inherently conservative. I suspect he knew that the purists had issues with our approach. Indeed, I think he almost took pleasure in knowing that we had so much power and talent, but rarely displayed the qualities that befitted such a team.

As a postscript to this mini-tribute to Jack, I vividly recall the contrast between the years at Bath and my final two years spent at the Harlequins. The difference in intensity was staggering; the desire and hunger of the Bath players was legendary and distinct. The quality of a Harlequin side with a dozen internationals was undeniable, but somehow the heart wasn't quite there, the humility towards each other not real enough, and the caring and inter-dependence a little forced.

Bath was a family pure and simple, Jack was the Godfather and for fifteen years the club was a force in the land. Need I say more?

Further postscript: of course, he also had a life outside of rugby, as the managing director of Lucas Ingredients, a subsidiary of the giant food group, Dalgety. A highly successful businessman, it was always a mystery to the team why the Rowell wallet made so few appearances at the bar. Perhaps he suspected (and rightly) that the entire team would suddenly be on his shoulder to take advantage of an unexpected opportunity!

CHAPTER 7

A Brief Flirtation with England

There is no question that my experiences on those early tours to far-flung fields of play had helped bring me to the cusp of a full England cap. My form appeared irresistible and from January to June of 1983, I enjoyed a twenty-three-match unbeaten run with Bath, unprecedented in the club's history, as well as two unbeaten tours to California and Romania.

As the winter of 1983 approached, my name was on everyone's lips as a replacement for the ageing and increasingly injury-prone Clive Woodward. The press had been predicting my selection over the Tigers' centre, although Leicester folk may have been less impressed, since I would be breaking up their beloved triumvirate of Les Cusworth, Paul Dodge and Woodward, whilst of course at fullback there was yet another Tiger, the fullback 'Dusty' Hare.

The England side was rebuilding after the Beaumont Grand Slam exploits, and a young Peter Winterbottom was also making his mark on the team, in the back row, so there was change and anticipation in the air. I admired Clive hugely; a player who thought about the game as I did; who approached the game as I did, taking every chance to run freely, expressing himself and trying to fulfil his potential. Who can forget his great exploits in the 1980 Grand Slam season under Bill Beaumont?

In truth, England squad sessions intimidated me since the household names were all still there: Peter Wheeler, Mike Slemen, John Carleton, Maurice Colclough, Steve Smith, Dodge, Hare, to name just a few – and I was being regarded as the rising star. It didn't sit easily with me, consequently I was always relieved to go back to Bath, where I felt at home. But destiny was calling and I went with it.

I cannot quite remember my feelings and emotions as I learned of my selection for England's full side against Canada in October 1983. It was not a 'cap' game, as the younger nations in rugby had not yet earned that status in the eyes of the international rugby board. That has all changed now of course, with games such as these meriting the award of a full cap. For me, however, the lack of an official mark of my England debut was irrelevant, and I was brimming with nervous excitement.

This match against Canada was also a dress rehearsal for the major rugby event three weeks later – England versus the All Blacks, and logically my debut game. It would not be an understatement to say that the New Zealand All Blacks were the team to beat in world rugby, particularly with the famous *Haka* to confront in the lead-up to the match. So while the match versus Canada was important, everyone had one eye fixed firmly on the other date in mid-November. In the event, England won comfortably, 28-0, in sleeting rain. Not exactly the playing conditions I would have wished for, but I played solidly and did not commit any howlers, so all seemed set fair.

Dick Greenwood was the England coach, and had brought his Under-23 fitness views into the senior stage. So we were all instructed to be ready for a morning run in Hyde Park the following day, which was of course a stone's thrown from the Hilton hotel where the team was staying. I had forgotten to bring any trainers, and in any case had moved on from the official post-match function to another party so was suffering from a monster hangover. An executive decision swiftly followed, and I permitted myself a wry smile as I looked out on the scene from my room on the 23rd floor. The cooked breakfast had arrived at the same time as I spied the long line of rugby players winding through the park. I felt a momentary pang of guilt, but it did not last, and I continued to munch away whilst constructing a suitable letter of apology to Mr. Greenwood.

My flirtation with England came to an abrupt halt with a fracture-dislocation of my left ankle. It happened in a quarter final of the County Championship. I was playing for Somerset against Middlesex at Bridgwater. There was a counter attack from an unpromising position on the field and the ball was loose. I scooped the ball up on the run and began a curving run with my back still facing the Middlesex players. As I arced back up the field, I felt my shirt being pulled by a clutching hand and I was caught. In a flash of hindsight when so many things could have happened differently, I often wonder why I did not go to ground and accept that I could not escape. But no, I fought on until I had my right leg lifted and I was balancing on my left. I was stranded flamingo style, until help could come. And come it did, as opposition and team-mates alike swarmed around me, hunting the ball. I felt the pressure of more people on me bearing down on my left leg until it was too much to withstand. So down I went, under the weight of three or four players.

I was told by spectators and players that the sound of my ankle dislocating from the rest of my leg was akin to a rifle shot. I felt no pain, but as I lay on the ground I saw my foot at right angles and could scarcely believe it.

Meanwhile, a ferocious ruck formed a couple of yards away, and my first thought was to move away, and fast, shouting unintelligibly. Close to the action, David Trick had seen what had happened to me, and was bellowing at Roger Quittenton, the referee, to blow his whistle. Eventually, play stopped and the players looked on in horror as everyone contemplated my displaced foot. Thoughts at moments such as these can be confused but one thing was clear – my season was over, and the future was uncertain. But the question of medical attention loomed largest. I remember insisting that a cover be placed on my leg as I was being carried off for fear of people seeing; I knew that my parents were in the stand. Perhaps from a sense of shame that my injury was unsightly, perhaps just to have something to say.

Unfortunately, the day was about to get worse. The Bridgewater medical room was under renovation, the on-duty doctor was stuck in traffic, and this was before the era of ambulances on stand-by; not a good time to sustain a serious injury.

So I was laid to rest on the floor of the bar and a GP raced home to get some pain relief. My first concern was whether the skin was broken, as I had visions of protruding bones, and was much calmer when told that there was no external, visible damage. In retrospect, this was supremely irrelevant but it was all I cared about then. Meanwhile, people came and went, powerless to help, and grim discussions ensued around the lack of doctors and ambulances. The nearest casualty department was Taunton, but an executive decision was taken that I would return to Bath where a medical team had been placed on standby to receive me. This was relayed to me, together with a couple of morphine shots from the returning doctor. The shock was wearing off and I was beginning to struggle with the reality of what had happened to me, particularly as I saw Derek Morgan, the chairman of England selections in the background. I was in pole position for my first cap against the All Blacks two weeks hence. What could anyone say? We stared at each other, wordless, but we could read each other's minds. I finally drew a breath, "I will be back, I promise you." Derek nodded and replied, "Yes, I know you will". Our eyes met again and then he was gone, nothing left to say or do but to get myself fixed.

My father came down to see me and looked distraught and pale. He said a few supporting words: "Mother sends her love", "Be brave", "We will follow the ambulance", and I nodded numbly. Of course, non-medics in these situations can do so little. By now I was being entertained by Simon Jones, my Bath colleague who had rushed down from the stand to offer help. All the old jokes were dredged up and I was puffing furiously on a cigarette; anything to keep me occupied. Finally, the ambulance arrived and an argument started about where I was being taken, as Bath was out of county. To be fair to the ambulance men, they were only following instructions, but eventually they agreed to drive me to the Royal United Hospital in Bath.

At moments like this, time passes but becomes a blur. To begin with I was settled, listening vaguely to Simon's best efforts to entertain me and for a while it worked. But as luck would have it, the Glastonbury festival was in full flow, clogging the main roads and delaying even the flashing blue lights of an ambulance. Then, on arrival at Bath they were uncertain over the directions to the hospital, which added still more time. By now, the gas and air had run out and I was in trouble and starting to lose control. Yet, throughout all this, Simon was a rock of support.

Eventually I became aware of a huge amount of commotion. The ambulance doors swung open, and I was rushed through casualty towards the operating theatre. Consent forms were signed and a lot of interest shown about how my foot was to be re-aligned. I moved from a state of calm to one of near hysteria as the thought of major surgery loomed. As I started to protest, Simon pinned me down, a mask was clamped over my face and the world went black...

Trauma ward for me was a totally new experience. I came around in a haze of morphine and signs of severe injury all around me. My foot was straight, thank God, and open to view due to the massive swelling, preventing the application of a plaster. I was told that the doctor had inserted a plate for the broken leg, a screw through the joint for stability, and had repaired a number of ruptured ligaments. Not that I really knew what they were talking about.

The enormity of my situation was beginning to dawn on me and then the visitors started to arrive. I certainly would not have wished to visit me as my mood was black. I duly informed Jack Rowell, the Bath coach, that not only were my playing days over but that I might never walk properly again. His vain protests that the doctors were hopeful were pushed away, and he realised that supporting words were falling on deaf ears. I could hardly speak to my parents without becoming emotional. Others came and went and I lived for the three-hourly morphine fix.

What a great feeling as the throbbing pain gave way to a blurred haze; a quite amazing sensation and often enough to send you to sleep. They were the darkest hours and within us all is the capacity to feel sorry for oneself, so no apologies for that. But I was soon to understand what people meant when they say that there is always someone worse off than you.

The next day I saw a pretty girl come into the ward to visit her boyfriend. She was in a wheelchair and accompanied by her family. I could see that she had lost a leg, but she seemed remarkably cheerful, and was obviously trying to keep her boyfriend's spirits up; he was in a bed around the corner from me. She had noticed a group of Bath players who were visiting me at the same time and she seemed to become quite animated at the sight of them.

Some time after she had left the ward, her boyfriend came over to see me. To my horror, I realised that he had also lost a leg, the result of the same motorbike accident, which had cost his girlfriend her leg – she had been riding pillion when it happened. How unlucky can you be? I attempted to find some appropriate words but, instead, he launched into a tribute to me, my rugby and my terrible misfortune. I did not know where to put myself, except to admire the courage of this young man whose injuries were so much worse than mine. When he eventually returned to his bed, I lay there for many hours, resolving to generate something positive out of the mess. This stranger, who I never saw again, helped me to understand a little more about inner strength.

Two days later I was moved to a side room off the main ward with another motorcycle victim who had an open leg fracture. Thank God I only rode a Suzuki 125, I thought to myself on more than one occasion. We were both suffering a lot of pain, and would count down the minutes telling each other jokes, until we could alert a nurse for more pain killers. It was a grim game but it did help pass the time until our wounds were bearable. My roomie was at last moved out to undergo a skin graft and I graduated to Ward C, which was to be my home for the next two weeks.

Life was almost fun. Roger Spurrell and Simon Jones were frequent visitors, illegally shipping in bottles of wine and beer and even attempting a cigarette until thrown out.

David Lamb, the team secretary and now a lifelong friend, insisted that I come to live with him and his family, seeing that I was to spend three months in plaster. I was stunned by his offer; that was followed shortly thereafter by a job offer from John Downey, a local stockbroker and a Downside 'old boy'. I told him that I knew nothing about the stock market – a quarter of a century on and no change there then – but this did not seem to bother him at all. Giving a sensible response to these acts of kindness from my hospital bed was a real struggle, as I could hardly string any coherent thoughts together.

As it happened, the Lamb family were to become the closest friends and John Downey's job offer changed my professional life. How lucky I was, although it didn't feel like that the following weekend. It was England versus the All Blacks, my putative debut until the injury, and the boys had planned to take me by wheelchair to Lansdown Cricket club, across the road from the hospital, to watch the match in more convivial surroundings. The duty sister was very nearly talked into it without referral, until her sense of responsibility got the better of her. She called one of the consultants, who came storming down to the ward, ejected my rescue party and lectured me for ever imagining that this was a good idea. Eventually, I was allowed to watch the game, in a wheelchair with its tyres let down, just in case anyone came back to try again.

It was a tough moment for me as the England team came out on the pitch, the same side that had beaten Canada with the exception of Clive Woodward, who was back as my replacement. England won a famous victory 13-7, and although I was happy for them, I felt entirely desperate. The ward sensed my mood and so the banter was muted that day. As night fell, and the last rounds of pills come through, I sobbed into my pillow, wondering how anything could ever be the same again. The tears were as much from frustration as sadness, and were the first sign that I was trying to find a way back. I tried to visualise how I would have looked in an England shirt facing up to the *Haka*, after all I had told Derek Morgan, chairman of selections, that I would be back, hadn't I?

The very next day, the physio arrived. This was a big moment. "Come on, let's see how much you can move the ankle. "

"I can't. Surely ankles with screws in don't move!"

"Oh yes they do. "

She was a battleaxe, and sorted me out in five minutes. The foot had to be at right angles to fit in a plaster, non-negotiable. Perhaps they needed the bed, or it was all part of the ploy; whatever the reason, I was out of the hospital two days later, plastered and ready for… well, not much, but at least I was upright.

A full debut against the New Zealand All Blacks and the 1984 Five Nations Championship had not been the only things on my rugby agenda; the summer of 1984 was also scheduled for a tour to South Africa. As it happened, after that tour, rugby ties with the Republic were then cut for years, until the emotional day in 1992 at Twickenham when, under leaden skies, Johan De Klerk spoke in front of a hushed capacity crowd as the Springboks reintroduced themselves to the only game that really matters from Cape Town to the High Veldt; from the Atlantic coast to the Indian Ocean.

Back in 1984, for a young centre who had been on the brink of stardom, but was now laid-up, South Africa was more than a continent away. Medical bulletins periodically suggested that I might be fit. Hope springs eternal, but deep down I knew that it was a dream.

I don't wish to dwell on the next nine months as they were what anyone recovering from this sort of injury would expect: three months plaster, two more operations to remove metal, 6000 lengths (or more) in a swimming pool, and hours of weight-training and physiotherapy. One, there was no alternative; two, it seemed as if I would definitely play sport again. In fact during that summer I was to resume my cricket career, which turned into a huge personal triumph.

CHAPTER 8

The Gap Years

I enjoyed a few months of cricket in the Minor Counties competition, which proved to be a great form of rehabilitation, and the Dorset boys were a huge support to me. We were one of the better teams in the championship, and the games were ultra-competitive, but they all sensed that this, for me, was but a stepping-stone on my way back to pursuing an international rugby career.

Meanwhile a depleted England staggered out to the Rainbow Republic, short also of Paul Dodge who had broken a leg, and Clive Woodward, who had retired, as had been predicted. A sticking plaster midfield emerged from the wreckage, with one of many attempts to turn Huw Davies into a centre. Huw, a product of Cambridge and an old university adversary of mine, was a fine player and good enough to pass off as a centre. But against Danie Gerber, the great South African who was in his prime, there was no contest. For me, one of the saddest aspects of that tour was that this was the tour when John 'JP' Palmer, my Bath colleague, made his debut. He was undisputedly the most talented centre I played with or against, bar none, but his talent was frustratingly unfulfilled because of his propensity to pick up untimely injuries, consequently too few people, selectors included, ever saw what he was really capable of.

With John Horton on Palmer's inside and Huw Davies on his outside, the Green and Gold side swept past them all and JP was caught up in the rush. The nation and I watched in horror as England was dismantled by a rampant South African team; rumours drifted back to the UK of a fractured camp, and dissent in the ranks. How could a Grand Slam era have unravelled so fast? Especially at a time when the major force in the country was undoubtedly Bath, despatching all-takers with a refreshing style too good even for the powerful Welsh clubs.

The answer lay in structure and selection, for it seemed that the squad came together in an entirely random fashion, with decisions swayed by one-off performances, regional bias and current fashion. There was no strategic vision; the Red Rose was considered the highest accolade in the game, and no questions were asked. The privilege was all ours, and squad selection was an honour meant to be cherished. All of this was fine of course, and sealed by a formal letter which invited you to be a member of the team, or maybe a replacement. I have kept the letters to this day as reminders of my early England career, but when you think about the underlying message, it seemed untrusting and judgemental. That underlying message was of disorganisation and inconsistency of selection, whereby the sensibilities of young men would not be considered when they were picked for one match, then dropped for the next, perhaps never to be given another chance.

These were dark days indeed for the English game, and in denial as ever, England lurched into 1985 with confidence at a low ebb, but with the prospect of another tour, which I was destined to miss. Cruelly, the last tour in eight years to South Africa was followed by a final tour to New Zealand in the same period. This would, in normal circumstances, have been the ultimate challenge for a northern hemisphere team, particularly since England had beaten the All Blacks at Twickenham in 1983; a game that should have seen me make my

Who said I can't pass off my left hand. Eventual debut vs Wales in 1986

debut. But after a mediocre Five Nations effort, and a couple of changes of captain, England departed to the 'Land of the Long White Cloud' for a predictable beating, even though the All Blacks played so poorly in the first test that only Grant Fox's kicking saved them. We took a caning in the second test and full revenge was exacted for the reversal of two years earlier.

I was playing again by now, but under the dark shadow of speculation that I would never be the same player again. However, all that I cared about was that I was absent from the tours. My career should have peaked between twenty-three and twenty-six years; that sweet time when youth and experience combine seamlessly, and to play against the two best rugby nations in the world was all I wanted – to be the best, to realise my talent. Instead I had a long, slow road back to contention for an international place, all the while watching the Red Rose being tarnished and battered on foreign fields. It was painful.

My next chance came in 1987, the year of the inaugural World Cup, when I was at last back in the national team. Four years on, I had put aside many doubts, including my own, and was finally back where I belonged, and New Zealand beckoned for a World Cup, which was unexpected. In those days, northern and southern hemispheres rarely met in competition; in fact, the maximum number of internationals per year was five, if you were lucky, and of course many games were not deemed to be full internationals, especially against emerging countries such as Japan, the USA, or Canada. So there was huge excitement about a totally new experience, and England was full of optimism, having beaten the 'auld enemy', Scotland, at Twickenham in March of that year. Scotland, having panned us by thirty points the previous year, had come down to London to claim the Triple Crown, bristling with talent, experience and intent. England, in contrast, had lost all three previous matches in that year's tournament, and had banned half a dozen players for fighting in the ill-fated match against Wales in Cardiff. Worse still, Richard Hill, our captain, had been fired and Stuart Barnes, a reluctant bench man, like me, had resigned in disgust at his persistent non-selection. This was not a promising situation, but in true underdog style we sent Scotland packing in a game of rare passion and commitment, 'tae think again' as they were to do to us in 1990, the infamous Grand Slam year that never was.

Against this backdrop, very few people understood why I didn't tour that year, having fought back from the dark days of 1983. Surely this was an unmissable moment in time to fulfil my destiny? Mike Weston was very subdued when I informed him that I was unavailable for the World Cup. Somewhere in his tone was an air of disbelief, but he soon switched into action mode. How could he change my mind, which had been made up because of stockbroking commitments? My partner, John Downey, was a huge rugby fan and wanted me to go, but even he recognised the problem. It was the year of Margaret Thatcher's re-election, the market was on fire (until the October crash – lest one forgets) and volumes were sky high. I was self-employed, and entirely dependent on my own efforts to pay the mortgage. This was also the first year of my marriage to Suzanne, a trainee GP, so not ideal to be going away for up to two months.

Mike did his very best to make the tour happen, while I was regaled with offers from retired stockbrokers who were prepared to take my place while I was away, and in theory I was tempted. But anyone who is involved with client relationships will know that you cannot pass customers around like confetti. As I wriggled like an eel to escape the inevitable outcome, I reflected on a comeback which was hardly going to extend to the length of the word.

Finally, every avenue was exhausted and I ruefully looked on as Fran Clough, Kevin Simms and Jamie Salmon jousted for the England centre position in the highest profile tournament the rugby world had ever seen.

Yet I was at peace, even if filled with regret; my tortured return to health had tempered my ambitions, and my suffering gave me perspective. While I still wanted success, it didn't matter so much any more; at least, I was prepared to accept that fate had played a part in my life. I comforted myself that I had proved my skills as a player to the world and that my turn would come again, World Cup or not.

Fate continued to swing things my way when England delivered a woeful performance against Wales in the quarter-final and bombed out of the competition. I watched the match from a hotel in Cornwall, on tour with the Dorset Minor County Cricket team. I rubbed my eyes with disbelief because the action was dire and devoid of passion; the fact that we lost was inevitable. Of course, the RFU hierarchy were disgusted – a much longer antipodean sojourn had been planned – and promised wholesale retribution. The manager, coach and captain were removed and many players – including two of the three centres, Salmon and Clough – never played for England again. Although I am as patriotic as the next man, you will forgive me for feeling just a little happier that I could regain my England place in due course, subject to form and fitness.

And so it proved. England finished the 1988 championship the following year on a high with an incredible 35-3 win over Ireland, the match in which Nigel Melville suffered a fracture/dislocation of his left ankle and never played again. I was paired with an impossibly young Will Carling in that game. It seemed that all was well with our new manager, Geoff Cooke, a coaching team of Alan Davies and Roger Uttley, creative if somewhat maverick, and a solid if unspectacular captain, John Orwin, who took over from Melville. I even managed to share the 1988 Australian tour with Will, who had exams and could only complete the second half. So I came out for the first half of the tour, in which we were incredibly unlucky to lose the first test to some dead-eye kicking from Michael Lynagh, after we had led 13-0. Why did I only do a couple of weeks? The stock market crash had destroyed confidence and portfolios, not to mention stockbroker earnings. We were not being paid for these tours, and once when I attempted to calculate my lost earnings from rugby commitments

Geoff Cooke, England Head Coach, with his Lieutenant Roger Uttley. Geoff was the chief architect of England's longterm revival.

through the years, I gave up since it was a useless exercise and frankly, I would have given much more, and then much more again to go on rugby tours. No defensiveness then, but offered as defence to the charge of non-touring. I had choices and I made them, with no regrets, although the real test was still to come, one which was to change the course of my rugby career forever.

From the winter of 1988 through to the spring of 1989, English rugby was dragging itself out of the mire; the disbelief after the 'Swing Low, Sweet Chariot' procession against the Irish led by Chris Oti and his hat trick of tries had evolved into a modest sense of expectation. The night of the 35-3 triumph, Donal Lenihan quipped at the post-match banquet, "We were proud to be part of a six-try spectacular, the only problem was that we didn't score any of the tries!" We were past caring, since a Willie Anderson-induced drinking bout had reduced us all to drunken wrecks. But as the year progressed, culminating in a stunning autumn win over Australia in Will Carling's first game as captain, 'England expects' became more than mere wishful thinking. Indeed, we went to Cardiff looking for the championship in March 1989, unsuccessfully as it happened, but for the first time since 1982 we were chasing honours. On all of our minds was Lions' year, a tour to Australia for the cream of British rugby, where the Wallabies were waiting to exact revenge.

Widespread speculation on selection for the British and Irish Lions had many of the England team going, and the Halliday/Carling centre combination was a favourite for the Lions' midfield; Will and I had formed a close partnership on the field, and were close mates off it. Despite the pressures of captaincy, he was a real prankster and rather frivolous, with a well-rounded sense of humour for a twenty-two-year-old. So when he developed shin splints, nobody took him seriously, until he removed himself from consideration for the last England international game against Romania, and shortly after that the Lions' tour. For him, this was the start of a very tepid relationship with the Lions since there was a view that his loyalties lay with England first and foremost and this wound up some of the traditionalists. This sentiment was compounded when the 1993 tour of New Zealand saw him fail to make the test team, and this on a trip when a consensus of opinion would have had him as captain. He undoubtedly suffered for having identified himself so passionately with an English cause, because it caused a degree of Celtic resentment, and that is his only similarity to Margaret Thatcher, whose poll tax plan was of course to blame partly for our Grand Slam reverse in 1990 against the auld enemy! So when Gavin Hastings pipped him to the captaincy, England grimaced and the Celts sniggered, but the Lions failed to gel and factions developed, in fact leading to a team of disgruntled Scots who struggled to perform, although they were not the only ones.

But let me return to the Carling withdrawal from consideration for Australia 1989, since I was also under great pressure. Predictably, I was starting to feel discomfort in my left ankle and had undergone a course of cortisone injections to settle it down. My doctor, Mr Philip Bliss, who had performed the original operation, rolled his eyes at me when I complained of stiffness and pain, although not without some sympathy. He had warned me that the severity of the injury would curtail my career even if I looked after myself; and I had started taking regular strong anti-inflammatory tablets to kill the pain. My thoughts turned to the prospect of eight weeks down under, on hard ground and with constant training to meet the huge challenge of beating Australia in their own back yard. What mattered more, a short-term blast with the Lions, or extending my England career?

Meanwhile, I had a three-month-old baby daughter, a working wife and a depressed, unprofitable stock market still suffering from the 1987 crash. In fact 1988 had been a shocking year in the market. Private client volumes had collapsed, which meant fewer commissions and considerable financial pressure at a time when I could least afford it. In a way this was a role reversal from the problem of 1987, when we were so busy that taking time off was an impossibility. Now I was facing the problem of not enough business!

My partner, John Downey, kept his counsel because he knew it had to be my decision. So it was with a heavy heart that I called Clive Rowlands, the Lions' manager, to tell him that the 1989 Lions, already minus Carling, would also be without Halliday. My father penned a typically logical letter congratulating me on a brave decision, and confessing to concern over the potential long-term damage to my ankle, and how right he was. Roger Uttley also wrote, wearing his England hat despite being the Lions' coach, and expressed happiness that my availability for England as a result of my choice would be a source of great joy for England rugby supporters. It did not feel like it at the time, but I appreciated the gesture.

Now, when I sit and listen to tales of Lions' tours, I cannot escape the fact that I missed out on the biggest privilege that can be given to a rugby player from the four home unions. And I conclude that I should have toured. But that's another story.

England v Romania 1989. My last game as a selected England centre in my own right and just prior to my withdrawal from the Lions' Tour of Australia because of ankle concerns. Jerry scored three tries and Chris Oti scored four… I had my finest game that day as a distributor. Will Carling (injured) commentated that day, and expressed major concern about my hairstyle. Looks alright to me

That summer of 1989 also held a major surprise for me and the rugby world. Rumours were sweeping the press that a rebel tour of South Africa was being planned, selected from not only the four British countries, but also France. South Africa was firmly in isolation, and had been since the England tour of 1984. Nelson Mandela was still in prison, and there were plenty of horror stories of apartheid, so for the rugby authorities this was a potential bombshell.

No sport can tolerate discrimination of any sort, let alone rugby, and it has always confused me that a rugby nation as proud as South Africa was synonymous with apartheid. What a triumph that they have emerged out of those dark times, and ironically that a 'rebel' tour almost certainly helped in the process. But it is also ineffably sad that humble sportsmen are invariably made to carry the burden for such a fundamental issue, when politics and sport become entangled thus.

In the case of this 'rebel' tour, I was contacted by a mysterious South African, the name eludes me, who was based in a London hotel. He sketched the outline of the tour and listed the other players who had been approached, among them the cream of the French team; names such as Philippe Sella, Denis Charvet and Pierre Berbizier. They were among the best players in world rugby and I provisionally accepted the invitation extended to me, because for me, there was the thrill of a chance to play top rugby against a proud rugby nation, and the opportunity to rescue myself from the summer's wreckage.

Meanwhile, though, pressure was building on the authorities to act, and I duly got a call from Dudley Wood, the RFU secretary, and effectively the 'Mr Big' of English rugby at that time. Dudley was a toff, but he was still as hard as nails, and certainly intransigent. He politely informed me that my England career would be in jeopardy as this was an illegal tour. Equally politely, I replied that I would do precisely what I wanted when I wanted, and continued to talk happily in that vein until he delivered his trump card, "Oh and one more thing Simon, we know that you are being paid, and we will find proof, and that will certainly be the end of your career." That was not supposed to be part of the script, and I put the phone down.

This book is not a 'kiss-and-tell', since I did not tour, so I will not go any further down that road, except to say that I was somewhat envious of those who did tour. In reality I could not have gone because, having been declared unfit for the Lions, I could hardly then head off to South Africa, rand in hand. My decision, therefore, was pretty well made for me, even without Dudley Wood's intervention, however painful it was to me.

Rugby is about respect between those who play the game and watch it, and I was having trouble at that time, in reconciling my actions with this truth. It was of no little concern to me that some of the Bath side, my team-mates, were black – Steve Ojomoh, Victor Ubogu, Audley Lumsden and Jerry Guscott – and these were men with whom I shared my rugby life, and for whom I would go a long way. To their eternal credit, none of them breathed a word, but, at pre-season training following my decision to turn down the offer of a place on the rebel tour, I sensed that there was an even-stronger bond than had previously existed among us.

Yet another 'miss' then in the 'Halliday Tour Brochure', but it did end with a touch of humour. As I had withdrawn from the tour at very short notice, my name was still listed on the flight to Johannesburg. On the morning of the flight, I was in the office, gazing somewhat wistfully into space, when I was interrupted by a call from Terry O'Connor, then the chief rugby correspondent of the *Daily*

Mail and also a friend. He had somehow wormed the information out of a South African Airway's official that I was booked on the flight and he demanded to know why I was not at the airport.

I unsuccessfully inquired about the source of his information, then politely informed him that I had a client meeting due shortly, and had to terminate the conversation. Initially crestfallen, he realised that I was being genuine, and we both laughed like a drain, so he caught the plane and I had my meeting. Thus ended an exhausting summer of inactivity, but I felt uplifted that I had faced two big challenges and made the right decision each time.

CHAPTER 9

Headley Court – Proprioception and Rehabilitation

The word 'proprioception' was not one I had ever learned at school, but in the summer of 1984 it became my watchword. As all medics will know, it represents the communication between brain and limb and body movements; that instantaneous message which causes you to respond to changes in the terrain that may affect the balance of your body. I was playing a cricket match for Esher, the Surrey club with whom I was with the previous year. While batting I pushed my leg forward and collapsed for no reason, turning over my ankle.

I hobbled off and on my return to Bath I attempted to discover more about the problem. It turned out that there was some sort of a breakdown in communications between my limbs and my brain, the doctors suggested that I was unable to receive electronic messages quickly enough, and that I needed to seek specialist treatment to improve my internal communications. They recommended I go to RAF Headley Court, a rehabilitation centre based in Leatherhead, which deals with all kinds of physical disabilities and illnesses.

Headley Court was situated amongst the leafy glades of suburban Surrey, most unlikely surrounds for the kind of place it was. In 1984, it also contained a large number of servicemen who had been injured during the Falklands War and who mostly had long-term problems.

When I arrived, I was given a full medical and an explaination of how they were going to improve my reaction times, or 'proprioception'. For two weeks, I trained from 8am to 5pm, ranging from intensive physio to full work-outs in the grounds, on the roads or in the gym. I guess that it was not dissimilar to the everyday activities of an average professional rugby player in those times! At the beginning of the day, we had compulsory aerobics with the PT instructors. We all had to participate whether wheelchair-bound or able-bodied. It was a bonding session, and we felt like we were all in it together. The rest of the day, of course, was dramatically different for each of us.

It was here that I had another severe wake-up call. I was in a four-person dormitory and two were Falkland veterans. At night time we would lie in bed, trading stories. One of them, who had suffered a fracture/dislocation similar to mine, had an awesome story to tell. He had fallen into a pothole in no man's land on Goose Green, a scene of fierce fighting and many casualties during the war. He had dragged himself across rugged terrain for a number of hours, the battle raging overhead, until completely exhausted. As he lay there, he saw figures approaching out of the darkness. Not knowing whether they were friend or foe, he prepared for the worst, saying his goodbyes to family and friends. They were in fact British soldiers, a testament to his survival. I, along with my fellow patients, was stunned into silence at the amazing bravery of this man and I started to understand the immense courage and sacrifices undergone by the soldiers of the British Army.

Once again, I was reminded of my good fortune to be among such people. My instructors pushed me very hard that fortnight. Both were keen rugby men, and I pounded the Surrey roads and fields, as they urged me on, cajoled me and demanded more. It was the final piece in the 'jigsaw' and I finally saw that I was physically in shape to go to the next level – putting on a pair of rugby boots with real intent.

I left RAF Headley with hope in my heart, but importantly with confidence in my body. They will never understand just how important that fortnight was, for many reasons. Years on, when I am questioned about lost rugby opportunities by close friends, I sometimes tell the story of the Falklands' Major and it seems that no one needs to hear any more – and that's how I feel too.

Anyone who has suffered (haven't most of us) similarly will concur that you have to be philosophical about such things; injuries are a fact of life. However, as my rugby career wound down, game by game, I became more and more nervous that another terrible injury would befall me, particularly when trapped at the bottom of a ruck, pinned down by a mountain of heaving flesh, but thankfully I escaped further serious injury.

At about the same time that I injured my leg, an England B player called Francis Emeruwa suffered a similar fracture/dislocation injury to me during a sevens' tournament. 'Ema' was the rising star of English back-row forward play. He was tall, rangy and hard as nails; in fact very much what Bath would expect from their back-row players. I had toured with him to Japan with the

England students, when the New Zealand universities, playing against us in a triangular tournament, had tried to kick him off the park. He not only took the punishment, but handed some out as well – that was the measure of the man.

He was selected for the England 'B' game against Ireland that year, along with me. I was unfortunately suffering from a muscle injury, but this selection defined the 'next in line' for full England honours. Then he was injured in a sevens' tournament.

As we both languished in plaster, there could be no predicting the outcome. His wound suffered a severe infection, and he had to return to hospital for what amounted to emergency surgery. Many months of complications followed, but whereas I was able eventually to resume my playing career, he still suffered. Eventually, he attempted a comeback of sorts, and even played a game or two for Wasps, but to no avail. Thus one of England's brightest talents was lost to the game and I doubt that many people have heard of, or remember, Francis Emeruwa. The students and Under 23 teams of those days, containing the likes of Underwood, Moore, Andrew, Melville, Barnes and Richards to mention a few and which Emeruwa had been a part of, were to form the basis of the successful Grand Slam sides, and I would not have bet against Francis being part of it. Fate can be cruel.

There was another man who would undoubtedly have graced the playing fields of international rugby. He also happened to have been the most talented full back of Bath's modern era, with due apologies to Chris Martin, Jon Callard, Charlie Ralston, *inter alia*. His name was Audley Lumsden. He exploded onto the Bath rugby scene with very little warning in the late 1980s and introduced a new dimension to Bath back play. The midfield of Barnes, Halliday and Guscott, which disappointingly never once turned out for England, was in flying form, and suddenly there was a fourth leg to our attacking trio. I had managed to perfect – almost – my centre play to compliment Barnes and Guscott, by confining myself to creating opportunities. We couldn't all be the 'wide receivers' as it were, as I had enjoyed in my early days with John Palmer. Audley's performances in the 1998-89 season were stunning, and brought him to the verge of the England team. He and Jerry were cutting opposing defences to shreds on a regular basis; a real pleasure to watch. After six years at the club, it was incredibly rewarding for me to see how we had progressed, even though we were the regular crowned champions of either the Anglo or Welsh leagues as well as the knock-out cup, of course. Bath rugby seemed to have an unquenchable desire to improve.

For Audley, the dream of playing for his country was cruelly dashed by an innocuous tackle which proved to have major consequences. While playing an insignificant match against Plymouth, he went into a contact situation awkwardly, and came out of it with a broken neck. This was only diagnosed when he walked into the hospital for a check-up. Nevertheless, his season, and apparently his career, was over. Audley's head was fixed with a 'halo', a structure drilled into the head and intended to keep the neck perfectly still. We all applauded his bravery and breathed a huge sign of relief that he was not permanently damaged. His good cheer and humility were a lesson to everyone, particularly when one considers the price he was paying; England lost their finest prospect at full-back for many a year.

Audley quite remarkably made a comeback and played once more, this time in a Gloucester shirt. As Bath men, we could all forgive him that, given our joy to see him back playing. There will be many other instances of injury which will simultaneously depress the spirit and lift the heart; for every tale of disappointment and disability there will be a story of courage, rehabilitation and recovery, thank God.

As rugby players, we all know the risks of serious damage to our bodies. I for one underwent three separate operations to different parts of my body in the space of three years not so long ago. However, I have yet to meet a rugby man who regrets his commitment to the game. This is not to prove a point, but rather to acknowledge that sporting injuries go with the territory. One thing is certain – I have learned that the ability to conquer the debilitating effects of sporting injuries is a triumph of the heart and mind. The fact that we change our perspectives is also undeniable; that the narrow pursuit of sporting success is rendered irrelevant when one's health is threatened.

On a similar note, I was very struck by the strength of the bond developed by the England World Cup rugby team of 2003. This was not only because of the length of time they had spent together; there had been a number of personal tragedies in the previous two or three years which affected the whole squad and brought them much closer together. Some of the players seemed to have gained a sense of perspective on the importance of the game, which I am sure helped them relax under pressure, as well as being able to move on from adversity to turn the situations into something positive.

In the aftermath of the World Cup triumph, one of the great side benefits has been the huge contribution made to charities and good causes. We can never raise enough funds in aid of such support groups or forget that for every tale of heroic success there will be another story of sadness.

CHAPTER 10

Materia Medica

One of my favourite mottos, as befits a sporting classicist, is *'Mens sana in corpore sano'* as written by Juvenal in his satires: 'A healthy mind in a healthy body'. He was alluding to one of the great adages of sporting life: brain and brawn have to work together. Mental health is as important as physical well-being. You can't have one without the other.

It is something which Mike Tindall, the England centre who had built up his physique to amazing proportions, had learned to combine. In the early days of his career, the more physical the contact the better, but not unfortunately for his play. I am not altogether sure that in my day Mick 'The Munch' Skinner was too interested in the finer points of the game. As long as he was 'boshing' people, he was happy. Who will ever forget his great tackle on Marc Cecillon, the fearsome French flanker, during the 1991 World Cup? I certainly won't forget having to sit through endless replays of the famous hit featured on the Micky Skinner 'Greatest Hits' video.

On a serious note, the physical conditioning of the modern rugby player is a revelation. Hours of specialist advice ranging from psychological self-analysis to meticulous dietary planning; the professional player lacks for nothing. I can remember being told not to eat 'greasy, fat-filled food like fried bread', or to 'limit the number of roast potatoes for Sunday lunch'. That was about the sum of it.

I knew that times were changing when the England Grand Slam Team of 1992 was preparing for the decider against France in Paris. Despite the fact that we still had Wales to play in our last game, at Twickenham, no-one really thought we would lose against them. No disrespect to Wales, but they were on the verge of the bleakest period of international rugby in their history. Their club rugby was creaking, and the never-ending stream of quality players was drying up. The Dragons no longer held the fear and respect of nine years earlier, when I had embarked on my international rugby career.

So it was the French who held all the threat, particularly as it was a revenge match following the 1991 quarter final Rugby World Cup defeat they suffered at our hands in Paris.

Nonetheless, we were in a relaxed mood as we flew out on the Wednesday prior to the game and installed ourselves in the Trianon Palais Hotel, a touch-finder away from the Palace of Versailles itself, and a throw-back to the days when the Sun King Louis XIV and Marie-Antoinette had lived there some 250 years earlier. We revelled in the history of the place. That Wednesday evening, we assembled for dinner and out came the wine list. We had one or two wine buffs in the team, notably Paul Ackford and Paul Rendall. Their selections met with plenty of banter, and a number of us attempted to comment knowledgeably on the various vintages.

Amid all this frivolity, Geoff Cooke brought the room to order. He berated us for our apparent complacency in the lead-up to an important match, and complained that messing around with alcohol would detract from our performance. We pointed out, somewhat lamely, that it was only Wednesday and Cooke responded by banning all pre-match alcohol for future internationals, from the time we met up until after the game. So that was that; the wine was cleared away and out came the mineral water.

Again (some nine years earlier), I cast my mind back to the eve of my first international when I happily downed three pints of beer on the advice that it would help me sleep! Today technological and physiological analysis is proving beyond doubt that alcoholic consumption weakens physical performance. Yes, well, we've all heard that before... but perhaps it explains why the England football teams struggle to progress beyond the quarter-finals of main competitions... or am I being unfair?

Nevertheless, for English rugby players a sense of physical well-being was assuming greater and greater importance. This preamble is meant to offer a snapshot of the lifestyle and habits of players in the 1980s and '90s.

But what about the backroom boys? By that I mean the people who kept our bodies in one piece, the physiotherapists and the doctors, not to mention the sponge man!

Willie-John McBride was right to applaud the replacements in the stand at the grand finale of the Lions' Tour of South Africa in 1974. They played a huge part in the success of the tour, and undoubtedly, underwrote his status as a rugby legend. But the medical staff rarely get any plaudits. Yet behind the career of most players there is a defining medical moment, when their playing future is in the hands of medical and para-medical professionals.

Regrettably for me, the path to the physio's table or the operating theatre had become a well-trodden one, and people had begun to know better than to ask me the fateful question "How are you?" They generally got a *very* long answer. The point is I owe my entire career to the help of certain medics, and what an opportunity this is to thank them, as well as to acknowledge the many hours of treatment I have received from 'body healers' all around the world. I reckon I could have retired by now on the many pounds I spent in the pursuit of fitness, and BUPA would have been a lot less out of pocket as a result.

Philip Bliss was a Bath-based orthopaedic consultant. When I was wheeled into theatre for the correction of my dislocated ankle, I was just another name in a long list of players on whom he had operated. I first met him when he arrived for a post-operation assessment. A brilliant young surgeon by the name of Clayton Marsh had assisted him, and they professed themselves satisfied with their handiwork. Considering that I had visions of never walking again, their confidence was reassuring but seemed a little inflated.

I soon got to know Philip and developed a good relationship with him. He resembled a rather less portly Sir Lancelot Spratt out of *Carry on Doctor*. Most medical staff appeared to be terrified of him. In my early weeks and months of consultation with him, he took delight in embarrassing medical students by showing them my X-rays and asking for comment. In those moments you desperately wanted to help them out, sign language, or anything, as they stumbled through explanations. Mind you, my X-ray pictures were not recognisable as a foot, so the whole exercise was a little unfair.

Philip did not suffer fools, but was a brilliant and highly respected surgeon. As Bath became a force in the land, he linked himself to the club more closely and attended most games, acting as club doctor. He was the obvious choice of course as he had seen the inside of most of our bodies and was well-qualified to pass an opinion.

It was he who first realised that my ankle cartilages were going. He tried some cortisone, and later put me on a programme of Voltarol, a stomach-destroying anti-inflammatory, which was to last twelve years. In the summer of 1991 his advice was clear: on a ten-year view, never play again. In theory, that was it.

But, ever the negotiator and a sportsman who doesn't know when to stop, I asked for the short-term view. His eyes glinted, "Well, you'll probably manage twelve months or so…"

"Enough, " I cried, "it's a deal!" It certainly was; allowing me to enjoy two Grand Slams, a World Cup final and a knockout cup win with Harlequins.

As the years passed, our occasional meetings were brief and usually at rugby clubs or dinners. But little ever needs to be said. He was the reason I recovered to play for England, and he gave me the courage to keep going for the two great seasons of 1991 and 1992: it's as simple as that.

But day-to-day, or more correctly, match-to-match, it is the physios with whom players build a close relationship. It is they who keep you on the pitch, lie through their teeth about recovery prospects and tell you all the gossip.

In the early days, of course, they were only there for the odd massage, because I was super fit and had no additional needs. As West Country and Welsh rugby started to impact on my body, matters changed and I became a regular visitor to the physio's couch.

However it was not until the major injuries that I really began to appreciate their value, and the now-retired Gareth George deserves a standing ovation. He took it upon himself to help with my recuperation over a period of months for at least an hour a day and sometimes more. He was a bearded, pipe-smoking Welshman with a wicked sense of humour, and taught physiotherapy at Bath University. He was phlegmatic and unflappable, to a point at times where he seemed insensitive to cries for help.

How many times have you asked your physio whether you would make it for the big Saturday game? All the doubt: a pull, a strain, a tear, a tweak, would stubbornly stick around, and many were the times that a piece of supporting strap kept body and soul together.

Gareth dealt even-handedly with some of the best players in the country and was an integral part of Bath's success in the early to mid-1980s. I can still picture his enigmatic smile, and I now pay tribute to his commitment to the Bath cause; he never received the plaudits he should have, so here they are, from a grateful beneficiary.

As I moved into the senior echelons of the national team, it was my great privilege to spend time with the incomparable, pint-sized Kevin Murphy. He was the senior England physio for many years, then became the Lions' trainer, and was simply a legend. He had a wonderfully mad streak which ensured that he participated fully in all post-match entertainment. Funnily enough, it was a wild night on the England tour of Italy in 1982 which provides my first memory of him. I am sure that he treated me brilliantly throughout the trip, but on the last evening of the tour we saw the off-duty 'Murph' in action. He covered his curly black mop of hair with talcum powder, and went round banging people on the head with a tin sandwich tray. Many pints to the good, we all joined in the fun, and you can imagine the rest. Juvenile, yes, but it was harmless and great fun. Kevin became a good mate, and when I dislocated my ankle he supportively kept in touch.

In the years that followed, Murph kept me going through many stresses and strains. He just worked away quietly, never over-promising, and every problem was treated as seriously as the next. A thorough professional.

Yet, he was always up with the latest of us, and my wife Suzanne, also a late night party person, once famously smacked *him* on the head with a sandwich tray. Perhaps I told her the story…

When I eventually decided to call it a day, I wrote Kevin a letter of thanks, in acknowledgement of how much he had done to keep me afloat for so many years. He remains an inspiration, and wherever you are, hopefully in happy retirement, it was a privilege.

Back in sunny Bath, I saw out my career there under the watchful eye of Julie Bardner, a mother of three and a local physio. She ventured into the rough world of rugby and I have to say, appeared to be unfazed. Bad habits, and language, naked men everywhere (often filthy and smelly) crude jokes and imaginary groin injuries; she approached it all with a happy smile! As usual, I was her most regular visitor; by then there weren't many pieces of me that weren't creaking.

She will perhaps remember one particular session when I had suffered a very painful blow in the nether regions. She produced the latest piece of technology called a 'laser': a tubular piece of metal which transmitted rays. It was to be placed very near (about half an inch) from the damaged area for best effect. I go into such detail only so that you can imagine how I felt when I opened my legs so that the laser could be applied. I cannot recall who was more embarrassed, and from that time on I was always a little nonplussed whenever she smiled at me. Ah well, it was a choice between fitness and being needlessly modest in front of someone who has seen it all before.

I was first introduced to Alan Watson by the Bath and England scrum-half

Richard Hill. Alan had a reputation for his expertise in active recovery from injuries; in other words, more of a sports doctor. He was based in the Hogarth Clinic, in Chiswick, West London and operated out of a couple of defunct squash courts, under the name of BIMAL.

Over the years Alan has treated many of the best sportspeople in the UK, ranging from rugby union, rugby league and football to Olympic athletes. You can only do that consistently if you command the utmost respect for your methodology and implementation. Put simply, he knows how the body works and what it is capable of. This was exemplified perfectly when I was in the last few weeks of my career and approaching the biggest game of the then Five Nations' Championship against France in Paris in 1992. We were on course for the Grand Slam, a second successive one. It doesn't get much bigger than that.

Disastrously, I had strained a hamstring in the semi-final of the knockout cup the week before, for the Harlequins versus Wasps. I was attempting an outside break against an old rival, Fran Clough (Cambridge and England). In theory I was not having to run at great pace given that Fran was not the quickest, still, I felt the twang and off the pitch I went, immensely depressed. Hamstrings do not heal in a week, I had enough experience to know that.

Nevertheless, I had until the Wednesday night and so I sought out Alan Watson. His diagnosis was a muscle in spasm and that there was a chance that I could recover from it in time for the Paris date. His remedy was to lower his elbow into the damaged area to "Rub away the scar tissue!" as he put it. Wow! I lost more weight on that treatment table than I could have done in a sauna, and I decided thereafter that my pain threshold was definitely OK.

This happened three times, then on the Wednesday I was despatched to training with the hope of deferring a decision on my fitness until Thursday. No such luck; Geoff Cooke wanted me to prove myself then and there by not breaking down in training. It was definitely the worst hour of my season, but somehow the leg held.

On to the next day, with Alan's encouragement echoing in my ears. This was even worse; a running session on firm ground with the prospect of an afternoon flight to Paris. I was way off the pace – remember, playing on the wing – and Carling was furious. Dick Best didn't need to hand out verbal abuse; I was getting it from everyone else. I was disconsolate.

The session ended. "We are worried, will you be OK?" I reassured them that I had been holding back as a precaution, but deep inside my mind was made up. I would withdraw.

I decided to call Suzanne to tell her what I was about to do. She was not impressed: "Don't you dare cry off!" she screeched, "I have my dress all packed, the ferry leaves in three hours and I want to go to the Moulin Rouge on Saturday night, you'll be fine. " Incontrovertible female logic, I would say.

So, I stepped back from the brink, caught the plane, and the leg held. The 'Watson effect', I called it. And by the way, we won the game.

Alan also works on your mind; you have to be positive about any injury. You have to place it in context, and back yourself to recover. You have to lift the depression, and he is excellent at allowing the 'bad stuff' to come out. He absorbs it, and then turns it into a positive. A genius at work, and since my retirement he has seen me through years of treatment and post-operative therapy, often at impossibly late times of night. He will often do a thirteen-hour day, and even attended one of my operations so he could better understand how to treat me. All Alan's patients who happen to read this will subscribe to what I say.

Lastly, he is ambitious for your own hopes; and he has inspired me to start running again. It is a tough call, being a near-cripple after being one of the fitter and quicker players in English rugby. But if anyone can help me, it is Alan. A great man but such a humble one.

The tragedy of the death of another medical man, who I never got to know well enough, brought home to me how much we owe to others. It was a salutary reminder not only of how insignificant my own problems are, but also of how cruel life can be.

Paul Calvert was, I found out later, one of the world's top shoulder surgeons. He wrote many books and pioneered a number of techniques for dealing with what is a very complex joint. Believe me, I know.

I guess that playing centre places you in the middle of a very aggressive contact area, populated by back row forwards and the mobile members of the front five. Now of course, given new fitness levels, everyone can get there. I was certainly physical and did my fair share of tackling. I took plenty of hits like most people. So nothing out of the ordinary, and certainly no major shoulder injuries.

Therefore it came as a big surprise to me when I discovered that my right shoulder tendon had ruptured. Then, no sooner had I completed a lengthy recovery, my left shoulder went. Given my ankle problems, most of my friends and family had understandably given up on me by now; a total body replacement seemed to be the only option.

Paul was somewhat intrigued by me and had a perpetual smile on his face whenever he talked to me, either pre or post-operatively. I took it as a sign that he was confident about my prospects. People certainly kept telling me how good he was, and many months down the line I indeed made a great recovery.

It was shortly before the second operation that I heard that he was unwell, and noticed that he had lost weight. I then heard that he was suffering from terminal cancer, and had little time to live. I was stunned, and amazed to see his fortitude and stoicism in the face of such obvious bad news. I tried to persuade him to attend an international at Twickenham with me, but he felt too ill, and a few weeks later he passed away.

I am sure that I am one of hundreds who have benefited from Paul Calvert's brilliant surgical skills. In that sense, and on behalf of all of them, I salute him and mourn his passing, while living to fight another day on the tennis court and golf course.

I guess that medics see so much death and suffering around them that they subconsciously prepare themselves for the inevitable moment. My wife Suzanne, in the face of my multiple ailments, showed little sympathy. It is hardly surprising when she saw pain and suffering in her surgery many times worse than my own. Her reluctance to indulge me probably brought forward my recovery from operations by weeks at a time.

This eulogy to the medical profession could not be complete without reference to the venerable Mr John Angel, a celebrated ankle surgeon. When I first went to see him, he needed to get a view of the angle of my foot. So he rummaged around in his desk, and out came a yellow pages directory. He proceeded to open it at page 320, muttering, "There, that should do the trick, stand on there." I did as I was told but wondered whether I had walked into a mad house. When he declared his intent to operate, I was dubious, and Suzanne was against it. There was always the possibility of new technology. We both thought Mr Angel wanted to pass two screws through the joint and effect what is called a fusion.

So back I went to 300mg of Voltarol, powerful enough to rot the stomach, though somehow it never affected mine. Mr Angel would occasionally politely enquire, and I would decline with a grimace, ever closer to a decision. He even got a seventy-two-year-old man to call and tell me that following his operation he had been able to go on an Alpine walking holiday. Honestly.

But, finally, I made the call. Pain thresholds are all well and good, although my team-mates over the years may have struggled to think that I had one at all. Suffice it to say John Angel changed my life. The pain is gone, and out-of-control dancing has even become an option again. His only comments to me that I really remember were pre-operative: "Did I tell you that your ankle looks as if you jumped on it from three storeys up?" and, "You will wish that you had this operation three years ago." As for the former question, I defer to his ability to read X-rays, and in the case of the latter, he was right.

To have the power of healing is a stunning gift, and I both envy and admire medical professionals. They also make one's best drinking partners, as they have by far the best stories, as well as being prodigious drinkers, almost without exception. To all the great medics who have treated me or with whom I have been involved over the past twenty-five years, thank you for being so patient. To all those I am yet to meet, watch out!

CHAPTER 11

Centres of Attention

There is no disputing the privilege I felt from playing international rugby with Jerry Guscott and Will Carling, two of the finest centre three-quarters who ever played the game anywhere in the world, any time over the last 100 years. And for completely different reasons.

The privilege was matched by a whole range of emotions as their individual careers developed through the late 1980s and early 1990s. At the age of twenty-two, I was at the top of my rugby ladder, looking down on all pretenders to an international place. Unproven of course but with the excitement of international challenges ahead, six years on, older and wiser but no less ambitious, I had accumulated a miserable six caps as a result of my ankle injury, coupled to an inability to convince the selectors that I was worthy of a regular place.

As 1987 unfolded, I at last re-established my right (four years on) to a permanent berth in the centre, subject to form of course. My subsequent withdrawal from the 1987 World Cup seemed not to matter, as England blew up in the quarter final and many members of the team were widely discredited as a consequence and never again donned an England shirt. So I started the 1987/88 season as a core part of an England squad in severe need of rebuilding, under the stewardship of Geoff Cooke, newly appointed in place of Mike Weston the outgoing chairman of selectors.

Interestingly, and probably quite rightly, Geoff Cooke had no preconceived ideas about his new England squad, but he could hardly fail to be impressed by Bath's now traditional flying start to the season. Our superior fitness, teamwork and general skills were far too much for domestic club opposition. When Jack Rowell went public with the view that I was bound to start as the number one choice, there was a deafening silence from the new manager. We were slowly starting to understand that the new regime would make decisions when ready, and relay them directly to the affected individuals, rather than through the media.

It was in December that year that I first played against a young Will Carling, who was appearing for the North division against my divisional team, the Southwest. For West Country players, the divisional championship was an irrelevance and irritation. Understandable, given that Bath, Bristol and Gloucester players were more accustomed to knocking lumps out of each other, rather than bonding as a composite group. Nonetheless, the selectors regarded the competition as a very important yardstick for international selection. Many an undistinguished season was turned around by a good showing over the four games through December. For West Country folks, and particularly Bath players, this set of games represented a downside only, since early season form almost invariably placed them in pole position.

Thus it was that the Southwest lost to a fairly average North division, and Halliday had his first sight of Carling, of course aware of his growing reputation. His Durham background, not to mention Sedbergh, made him a natural target for a West Country roughing up. On the day he made a couple of decent breaks and I marked him down as an interesting challenge, but nothing more.

I sailed on serenely, as the Five Nations' Championship hove into view amidst much talk of an England revival, and my name was in the centre of the frame – until the dreaded hamstring strain, which was to become something of a feature of my fitness in the following years. This was undoubtedly due to the problematic ankle, leading to continual tightness in the back of the leg. The fact that I had to withdraw from the England squad was hugely disappointing, but then came the real shock. Geoff Cooke came to see me, and declared himself unhappy with my general fitness. "Return to Bath and get fit, play some games and we'll take it from there."

My trip back to Bath was a journey down a long dark tunnel. Since my delayed debut for the England side, I had been dropped three times over a period of one and a half years, before finally establishing myself as undisputed number one, and now this. I was incredibly down about it and even the traditional ability of the Bath lads to pull team-mates out of a depression, was ineffective.

I looked on as Carling and Kevin Simms, replacing John Buckton, who had also pulled a hamstring, opened the Five Nations versus France and promptly squandered a couple of chances to score a famous victory in the Parc des

Princes. I watched the game at home, simmering with rage, but powerless until I could prove my fitness.

Wales then came to Twickenham and departed with an improbable win, leaving an England revival still tryless and winless. Finally, the game I needed was in front of me – away at Leicester. The nation's press, plus selectors, came to watch what was always an almighty clash. As ever, it was a confrontation from start to finish, although played out on a dark, dank afternoon. I was fully fit and absolutely up for the contest, and I put myself about the pitch as if it was my last game. It was good enough, and Cooke signalled that he was at last ready to put me in his England side.

It heralded a couple of incredibly enjoyable seasons as England started to build real momentum, winning a number of impressive victories, notably the 'Oti' game versus Ireland at the end of that season. This was the first game that 'Swing low, sweet chariot' appeared on the singing agenda to celebrate Oti's amazing hat trick of tries. Remarkably, this was also the game when the strains

SH v Ireland. Now that is definitely a sidestep

of 'Jerusalem' echoed around Twickenham and England scored their – scarcely believable – fifth try. It was one of the most emotional days I remember at the great stadium.

In this first year my centre partner, Will, was unsure what to make of me. There I was, a committed Bath man, with an Oxford University education in classics and languages and a penchant for crosswords and the Carpenters; a stockbroker and a Catholic to boot – an unholy combination.

My recollection of Will is of an inordinately serious young man, who knew where he was going, but was possessed of a childlike sense of humour. A great mix, and I quickly struck up a close friendship with him. I knew he thought I was a maverick, but he also knew that I was deadly serious about fulfilling my potential in an England shirt.

The next big test of our partnership came the following October when it was clear that England needed a new captain, and finally a long-term appointment. There had been a whole host of short-term appointees: Micky Harrison, Nigel Melville, Richard Harding and John Orwin, all in the space of twelve months. Speculation circulated in the corridors of rugby, and Geoff Cooke yet again wasn't sharing his thoughts with anyone.

I was the only current England player who was a divisional captain; for some reason I had accepted the Southwest division captaincy, a poisoned chalice if ever there was one. I started to receive calls from the press: had I been sounded out by Cooke? What would I do if offered the captaincy? It would have been a huge honour and privilege, and I don't think I would have let England down. But my track record in terms of touring and fitness was hardly good, even if I qualified for the role based on all the other criteria. I was also somewhat volatile, and known for wearing my heart on my sleeve; not necessarily a negative quality, but probably not all that positive either, at least not for a leader.

As history shows, Will Carling became England's youngest ever captain and immediately carried off a famous victory against a strong Australian team. I even scored a try; one for the I-Spy book of my England career.

Ironically, it was the Southwest who enjoyed the most conclusive victory against the touring Australians that year, and it was my privilege to captain the side. To enjoy two great wins back-to-back was a great thrill. Partnering me in the centre for the Southwest was a youthful Jeremy Guscott, and not just youthful, but extremely ambitious. He was already hot property and my pleasure in being part of an increasingly successful England team was tempered by the thought of a threatening cloud.

Meantime, Will was building his England team with increasing intensity. It may surprise people to know that his style was deeply personal; he often wrote letters to players, and showed huge respect for the senior players in the squad. Perhaps he had no choice, as he had to win over some hard-bitten pros like Richards, Winterbottom, Teague and Dooley to name a few. There were many people who thought he would not last, but he and Cooke, together with Roger Uttley, introduced two essential qualities which had been lacking in English rugby: loyalty and trust.

They made it very clear that once selected, players would be given an extended chance. No one believed them of course, borne of bitter experience under previous regimes. So to experience a series of unchanged teams was not just a pleasant surprise but set the scene for a real sense of togetherness within the squad.

My personal relationship with Will continued to strengthen and we often shared brief holidays in Cornwall where Suzanne and I often went for summer or New Year breaks. Despite the increasing pressures of captaincy, Will was perfectly able to let off steam. A number of senior businessmen from the property world will remember a famous New Year's Eve when they scrummed down against a group of us from another table in the restaurant. Carling and Halliday were taught a severe scrummaging lesson on that drunken evening, but at least it served to confirm to us that Will and I were both playing in the right position on a rugby field.

In fact the friendships among the squad were very important in building what was to become the bedrock of a double Grand Slam squad. The likes of Rob Andrew, Rory Underwood, Jonathan Webb and Dewi Morris forged lasting friendships, as well as being high quality operators. Will was fiercely loyal to his players and backed them to the hilt in his efforts to create a group of players who would reciprocate his loyalty.

Of course you cannot take everyone with you on such a crusade. Notable cynics included the front row union, comprising Brian Moore (perhaps a frustrated captain?) and Jeff Probyn, who could never cope with Carling's high profile and all that came with it. Of course, Will himself had a healthy disrespect of the Bath club and all their achievements. He felt, not entirely without justification, that Bath had produced a whole string of 'nearly' internationals who had ideas above their station. Of course they dominated the club scene but that didn't mean they should be playing for England. This view was not shared by large groups of the rugby public and it clearly grated him.

Not surprisingly the England captain's relationship with his country champion club was somewhat strained. I wonder what he would have made of this England team: Webb, Adebayo, Halliday, Guscott, Swift, Barnes, Hill, Chilcott, Dawe, (Sole), Redman, (Cronin), Hall, Egerton, Robinson. I put Sole (born in Aylesbury and played for English Universities) and Cronin (born Germany and raised in London) up for selection as they are in fact as much English as I am Scottish! I have to say that for England never to pick a midfield of Barnes, Halliday and Guscott at any time had to be a travesty of sorts.

Enough regionalism and I do have my tongue somewhat in my cheek. It was certainly the case that despite Bath's often outrageous successes, we failed to display our full talents – until the destruction of Gloucester (48-6) in the sweltering heat of May 1990 (also my last game for Bath).

In any push towards greatness, there will be siren voices along the way preaching doom and gloom. Thankfully most of them were outside the England squad but there were plenty of them, mostly waiting for Carling to make a mistake. Nonetheless, as England approached the 1990 season, optimism was rife and also well-founded.

The squad was highly experienced with real pace outside the scrum as well as an embarrassment of riches in the back row. The 1989 Lions' team was packed full of Englishmen, although for me personally only one name mattered – Jeremy Guscott. Ironically, had Will and I been fit to tour, he would have stayed at home. But let's be clear, it was only delaying the inevitable. After all, I had seen his emergence at the closest of quarters down at Bath, and even in the rarified atmosphere of the best club in the land it was impressive.

I particularly remember his debut against Waterloo at Blundellsands in 1986. In those days Waterloo was one of the strongest sides in the North of England and fancied their chances at home to anybody. We arrived with an all international back line and Jerry Guscott as our debutant with me in the centre. We were all heavily marked as expected, while Jeremy stormed through the open spaces looking like a world beater. He even kicked a few conversions and penalties for good measure, one with the wrong foot. It was a stunning opener by any standard, even if he ruined it later that night by telling everyone that he was already rather better than the rest of us.

Humility is a prerequisite at Bath rugby club, or it was then, and David Trick took him to task for his public pronouncements. He continued to learn lessons along similar lines, all the while developing a formidable array of skills. His biggest problem was not so much his bad temper, but rather the fact that he was prone to petulance. On one occasion he took on Tom Hudson, the Bath fitness director, and must have wished he hadn't.

Tom was one of the most inspiring men with whom I have ever worked. He was an Olympic pentathlete, ex-SAS, and former director of rugby at Llanelli. He was as hard as nails and had a complete intolerance of mediocrity in any field of athletic endeavour. Such a combination set him apart from his peers; he once interviewed with England for a role in the training set-up and they were so frightened by what they saw they didn't have the courage to offer him a job – he was that good. England, of course, was not.

It was Tom who dragged Bath to their peak of fitness, and in truth when training in one of his sessions you just put your head down and prayed for the end. He definitely had a vicious streak in him; he is the only man I have met who will deliberately 'turn' during a squash match and beat the ball against you to gain the point while inflicting serious pain, usually in the back of the leg.

Jeremy chose to display his unhappiness about Tom's training methods one evening and Tom and he had a serious stand-up row much to the amusement of all. There would only be one winner of course – Tom decided he had had enough and sent Jeremy back to the changing rooms, effectively terminating his session. We were all gobsmacked. Jeremy had no option, current international or not, and off he went. I don't remember a repeat performance but Jeremy was not allowed to forget the incident for a very long time. He was no special case; we all went through our own individual tests as people and players. It was what made the club great. But he was special in every other way and his case for selection to the England team was fast becoming irresistible.

It was Will's assertion that I was a major reason why Jeremy was making mincemeat of the opposition and taking the lion's share of the glory and media spotlight. Therefore when the England selection came up he genuinely felt that the Carling-Halliday combination was the best for the country and for a while this view prevailed amongst the selectors. It was certainly true that Jerry and I dovetailed perfectly, and the team operated at its best when Stuart Barnes and I took on the opposing midfield in close quarters. We would always have Andy

Robinson there to keep the movement going, and the result would usually see Jerry into acres of open space.

In truth, however, I was perfectly positioned to know that my tenure as England centre would be short-lived. It was not just due to the spectacular try that Jerry scored for the 1989 British and Irish Lions against Australia in Brisbane. In training and playing alongside him as centre partner, I could see that his qualities were innate. I can identify four irreplaceable skills in him as a centre which were key to his position:

Pace – he had the long-run version which meant that once in a gap he would almost certainly score (for which he had a huge appetite) or create a score for someone else. He also possessed the 0-30 speed which the world now associates with Jason Robinson, but which was massively evident in Jerry.

Control of the ball – there was never a better handler/passer of the ball, with the honourable exception of Will Greenwood. When Jerry chose to pass (!) his sleight of hand was there for all to see, so to speak.

Decision-maker – the best centres in the world need to know the art of deception. When to run, pass, hold, kick, go to ground, seek a tackle, pass and loop. The man who can disguise his intentions holds the key. Here was such a man. I always used to say that the key to any game was the ability to open up a midfield (well I would; I was a centre), and Jerry lived and played in such a world, both for Bath and England.

Try-scoring – rather like Will Greenwood in the modern day, Jerry had an amazing nose for the tryline with his pace and awareness of the space around the line which made him prodigious for both club and country. He also loved scoring and was always uncannily on hand at the right moment. Many thought him selfish and undoubtedly there were times when he could have passed. But all great rugby predators can be accused of that, think of Gareth Edwards and Jonah Lomu.

Fittingly his last game for England featured a seventy-five-yard try, and although injury killed off his career earlier than he wanted, it was still an appropriate end. It may seem odd that I do not mention his defence. I jokingly suggested to my shoulder consultant that he send the bill to Jerry, as it was through doing all his tackling that I had incurred my problems. But in truth, Jerry was as good as the rest of us in defence. It was a chore for him, an evil necessity; he tackled when he had to. I do not blame him for that and I can rarely remember him shirking his duties. He might not always have been on hand but, I don't remember the teams he played in being noted for porous defence.

So, the major turning point in my career came that next year as England sought major success in the 1990 Five Nations' championship. As usual, warm weather training in Lanzarote was on the menu in early January and speculation was rife as to who England would pick in the centre. The team was due to be announced before the end of the trip.

Still captain of the Southwest, I had played out of my socks throughout the December championship. Geoff Cooke rebutted my observation that the rugby world was clamouring for Guscott's selection. To be fair to him, he always picked his own team rather than listen to popular opinion. He insisted that he had not made up his mind and that my form was very compelling. There was even speculation that Carling would be moved to fullback where we were slightly short on penetration. But Hodgkinson and Webb were both better and more reliable goal kickers than Rob Andrew, so that was never a realistic option.

We assembled as a squad and were given the itinerary for our trip to Club La Santos. Don Rutherford was clearly in a mischievous mood, as he had Will and me sharing a room. Eyebrows were raised and conclusions reached – "So they aren't picking Jerry then; Hallers has retained his place." It was no secret that Will wanted me in the team although I didn't see how the selectors could leave him out. Three days of ferocious training followed in perfect Canaries' conditions. We knew that we had a team which was on the verge of something special, and we would hit the ground running.

Meanwhile I happily roomed with Will and the issue of selection never came up. We both avoided the topic because there was nothing we could say to each other; I couldn't plead with him but he couldn't reassure me. The decision would be made and it would be for the best.

The third night, our one night off, we went out as a squad and got seriously drunk. Frivolity was top of the list. Merlene Ottey, the world famous Jamaican sprinter, was training at the Club La Santa and one of our props borrowed a leotard of hers from the washing line. It hardly fit of course but he made a good show of prancing around in it, like a latter day Linford Christie, never mind the lunchbox. She was certainly bemused by thirty grown men suppressing hysterical laughter the next day. As fate had it, she was wearing the very same leotard!

Back to the serious stuff. I eventually crashed out at 2. 00 am, but there was no sign of Will. It was selection night and I was vaguely aware of him coming in some time later. The next day we trained off the hangover with tension heavy in the air. As we wandered back to our room, Will broke the news to me that I had been dropped with a good degree of anguish. A conversation like that will always remain private but we both realised it was a personal thing, as well as the end of a happy and successful two seasons as centre partners.

I was philosophical. What choice was there? And Geoff Cooke took particular trouble to reflect the toughness of the decision; wishing that he could pick three centres. I shot him a sympathetic but slightly withering look – there is only so far you can go in letting someone down gently. Jerry and I had a long talk about the choice, and he confessed that he was far from certain he would get the nod. He was well aware that there was split opinion. But we were part of the squad, and team-mates at Bath. Life would go on.

And it did. It was a crushing blow, obviously, but this time I was just plain unlucky. What could be done about it? Well, play winger of course. The record shows that in 1990, 1991 and 1992, I played some of my best international rugby on the wing, so perhaps I was done a favour when fate stepped in to move me to another destiny, yet again.

As Will and Jerry stormed around the rugby fields of Europe, carving up the opposition, I was their conscience. They had to be on top form because I was right behind them, always pressurising. My personal form was never better and the press clamoured for me to be picked, anywhere, just get me on the field. Interesting because that was how I felt.

Will was like a rock throughout this period when I was either playing wing or warming my backside on the bench. For him, I was still an integral part of the squad and I valued that. I knew he felt bad as a friend that I was no longer playing. But as a captain he needed my help and support, just as he needed everyone else's. This in many ways was the secret of the success of the Will Carling Grand Slam team of 1991 and 1992. There was plenty of competition but very little friction; loyalty and trust were combined to achieve a common purpose.

Players may have queried some of Will's methods. At times he was uncannily calm and controlled, expecting the team to get on the same wavelength as him; it was almost a psychological war. The Friday before an international was captain's day and the agenda was set by Will. We assembled for a team meeting and were bantering furiously; a combination of nervous tension and friendship. We expected him to call us to order and start the meeting. But no, he just sat there and waited. One by one we lapsed into silence until the room was quiet and then he started. Whilst it seemed a little unnecessary, I could see that it was important for him that the squad take notice when he wanted them to. It was almost primeval. But it allowed him to set the agenda.

Of course he had an agenda as a player too. Few people can appreciate what he took on, back in 1988. Think of the facts: Will Carling inherited a perennially underperforming national team; a group of players with little self-respect or self-esteem, who hardly won back-to-back games; seven years without a championship; fractured selection policies; an administration totally divorced from reality with no proper connection to the team; and a history of five captains in twelve months. As well as turning round all of that baggage, he had to contribute on the field.

It seems strange to me that in the aftermath of Will's international career, commentators preferred to focus on controversies such as the 'old farts' episode, or his private life. And it still remains a mystery to me that England's most successful rugby captain with three Grand Slams and a World Cup final has yet to find recognition in England rugby's hall of fame. In fact, I would go further and call this a total disgrace, borne out of petty jealousy and ignorance. It is as though the hierarchy is too ashamed to let errors of the past be corrected and welcome this remarkable man back into the fold. I also hope that people will respect my ability to talk dispassionately on this topic, despite my closeness to Will as a friend.

It took me some time to appreciate how Will had contributed to the resurgence of English rugby. Remember I had come into the side in the aftermath of the 1980 Grand Slam and had seen eight years of underperformance. A year after Will's appointment we almost won the championship down in Cardiff. Then in 1990 came the famous Grand Slam that never was, followed by back-to-back Grand Slams and a World Cup final. Yet another Grand Slam was achieved in 1995 and a record number of England wins; these are just the highlighted achievements

The strategy followed by Cooke and Carling of establishing loyalty and trust, turned many individuals who collected significant numbers of awards and were recognised as England's very best, in some cases of all time, into household names: Underwood, Guscott, Andrew, Hill, Winterbottom, Richards, Ackford, Dooley, Moore, to name a few.

It seems churlish to deny Will Carling a place as catalyst in the resurgence of English rugby as a credible force. It is often said that the players were always there, and that he had the good fortune to be in the right slot at the right time. But this is exactly the point; these were the players who were struggling to win more than one or two matches in a row. Suddenly they metamorphosed, with one or two hiccups (Murrayfield 1990), into regular champions of the northern hemisphere.

And yet, English rugby fails to truly acknowledge the achievements of this man. His legacy was clearly damaged by the 'old farts' episode which led to his temporary removal from the captaincy. However the fact that the players themselves refused point blank to go to the 1995 World Cup without him as their leader speaks volumes. In Jack Rowell's words, Will may have been a 'prat', but he commanded huge respect.

Let us remember that this was a very experienced team with any number of replacement captains: Dean Richards, Rob Andrew and Brian Moore among others. They must have been shocked the following Saturday to hear a full house at Twickenham chant the name of the England captain. And to think that England had just won their third Grand Slam in five years under the leadership of the same man.

I have lost count of the times that I have been approached by people asking my views on Carling as a player, and my reluctance to comment is understandable. Not because I don't have views or am embarrassed to share them, but because I might be misinterpreted. After all, you could say that my career as an international centre was cut short as a direct result of Carling's captaincy, as much as to Guscott's irresistible claims to the other centre position. I could be forgiven for some bitterness, particularly after all my trials and tribulations. The truth is, however, very different.

Will had a very unconventional introduction to rugby. Not for him the drudgery of perpetual club training and stressful selection systems, where one bad game in front of the wrong person could put you back a whole year. Almost as soon as he left university, he was on a fast track. And his ability clearly warranted it, but the secret to understanding Will's contribution to the game as a player lies in a combination of ability and general structure. For the lion's share of his career, he was either captain, or the moral leader (e. g. Harlequins). You could not divorce the two.

In pure terms, he was an all-rounder. He had very few weaknesses, although I spotted a propensity for floating unpromising passes off his left hand; something of which I was also guilty. He had power and speed in equal measure; witness the 1990 try versus Wales, or his heroic second half exploits against the All Blacks in the 1995 World Cup semi-final. He assumed the role of midfield 'crash-man' when Guscott was at his peak, simply because Jerry was not interested in that essential role. Every team has to have such a person on board; the trick of course is to get yourself into the battleground of centres and flankers and then to do something constructive. Slipping the ball out of a tackle or multiple contact situation is a high-risk strategy. You need supreme confidence in yourself and in the running lines of those around you. From my perspective, many hours of practice at Bath with Andy Robinson (as a floater, on the inside) and Jerry Guscott (working on the outside) allowed me to indulge myself in this area. But you cannot 'just do it'.

England wanted Will to link with Peter Winterbottom or go in with the ball and set up the next phase for the broken field runners, Jerry and Rory. And it was mighty successful. Critics of Will's relationship with Jerry would do well to remember that although there were many scenes on the pitch, which showed Will and Jerry as less than symbiotic, Jerry often wouldn't come in for the ball and make it happen – perhaps I had spoilt him over the years – so it looked as if he was being ignored. But understandably, Will, as incumbent and captain, was hardly going to pander to Jerry's whims. The likely answer is that they were both jealous of each other; one was the leading centre and captain, and the other the young pretender.

And let us not forget Will's awesome defensive work. Very few teams ever went down the middle of the field during his time as captain. France, for example, hardly scored an open field try from set play for a number of years. I can safely say that missing a tackle was not on Will's agenda, and he made that demand of others in equal measure.

As kickers, none of us were frankly up to much. I in fact probably had the best left foot of the three of us, but Jerry had natural talent of course; his famous drop goal in 1997, as well as the 1989 grubber kick to score against the Australians, stand out in my rugby memory. But I may remind both of them that I kicked two penalties in the 1980 Varsity Match at Twickenham – neither of them easy – so there!

My lasting memory of Will was in 1992, my final season as a player. He was in sensational form, breaking the gain line, seemingly unshackled after the 1991 Grand Slam and the World Cup. He was very relaxed and it showed. I was also in superlative form, enjoying my best international season ever, on the wing. The tragedy was that the following year he got caught up in politics and spite. The war over the Lions' captaincy – Carling or Hastings – went beyond normal selection criteria. In swallowing his pride, as well as failing to make the test team, Will found a relationship with the tour party, by accepting his lot and committing himself to the mid-week team. He returned to England with an enhanced reputation, but I suspect somewhat bruised spiritually.

I suppose it must have hurt that Jerry had made it into the test line-up. But Will and Jerry were such different players that no comparison was really fair. In fact the only similarity was their pride and in many ways their inability to achieve even more than they did was down to that. I often wondered, whether they had set up a pre-match pact not to give each other the ball!

So where does Will sit amongst the all time greats? He rarely makes the lists of respected commentators despite having overseen his team during a phenomenal period of success; in large part due to the Carling/Guscott partnership. Some even go so far as to say that he held England back through conservative play. Fanciful stuff, based on envy.

The answer is an unusual one, I think. He occupies a unique position as the single biggest influence on English rugby in a generation. He made England the team to beat, as well as the one to hate. He returned pride, integrity, loyalty and trust to the rugby dictionary. I know, because they were absent before. He faced down the rugby world off the field, to his long-term detriment. But I believe he had his eyes open when he did it. England benefited as a rugby nation when moving into the professional era. Will suffered, and remains castigated. Such is the fate of those who effect unpopular change.

These are a few other captains, besides Will, who warrant similar accolades: Nick Farr-Jones (Australian), Sean Fitzpatrick (NZ), Francois Pienaar (SA), Willie John McBride (Ireland), Colin Meads (NZ), Martin Johnson (England), Mervyn Davies (Wales). Captains all, and legends. Over the top? I can hear the gasps of disbelief, but very few people know how hard it was on the inside of the English game when Will came along. I do, because I was living it on a daily basis and I saw the change. I also know about the pain and sacrifice endured through the process, largely personal, of course. The opening up of heart and soul to a cause has a downside. People pick at the flaws and anticipate weaknesses.

At twenty-two, the youngest England captain ever, he had his life laid open for all to see. There is almost a fatal attraction which wraps you up in the whole process; you are inexorably drawn in and become part of the machine that eventually grinds you up and spits you out. Will undoubtedly regrets many well-publicised comments throughout his captaincy. But I am equally sure that if he turned the clock back he would have said them all again. That is the acid test.

Love him or hate him, the Carling package is not easy to fathom. The captain was in the player, and the player in the captain. His legacy endures and is undeniable. Period. For the record, my top ten centres, in no particular order, are: Ray Gravell (Wales), Jerry Guscott, Will Carling, John Palmer (all England), David Johnston (Scotland), Philippe Sella, Denis Charvet (both France), Clive Woodward (England), Tim Horan (Australia), Danie Gerber (South Africa).

There is no conclusion to the Carling-Guscott chapter, as they remain deeply enmeshed in the fabric of English rugby. They may not have won a World Cup but their position at the top of rugby's tree is undisputed in my view. Complex individuals, both of them, but that goes with the territory. It was simply my privilege to be there when they were weaving their magic.

CHAPTER 12

Farewell to a Slam – and Bath

It was not the fact that David Sole walked out onto the Murrayfield, followed by his team, in what resembled a slow march. Nor the fact that the crowd roared its approval, thus setting the scene for a ferocious encounter. To be quite frank, none of us had even noticed the funereal march on to the Murrayfield pitch by the Scots, although I do remember wondering why there was more noise than usual from the stands. But we were exceptionally focused on the job in hand. The popular view that we were fazed by this slow walk was well wide of the mark.

The thing that did bother me, however, was the fact that all the Scottish players knew the words to 'O Flower of Scotland', their somewhat outdated anthem, which is decidedly anti-English. Even recent Anglo imports such as Damian Cronin were blasting out every word with venomous feeling. Of course, this was the year of the poll tax and Maggie Thatcher was even more unpopular in Scotland than she was in France. So feelings were running high. It should not be forgotten that England had carried all before them with three imperious victories on the way to this winner-takes-all showdown in Edinburgh, and we were now seemingly on the cusp of what many were regarding as an inevitable Grand Slam. However, most of the world seemed to have forgotten that Scotland had also won three games out of three in the build-up, albeit with a huge slice of good fortune. The press however had written them off, despite home advantage, which would have been red rag to a bull where the Scots were concerned.

Furthermore this was probably the best Scotland team ever to pull on the Blue Jersey, including among its number the Hastings brothers, Gary Armstrong, Finlay Calder, John Jeffrey, David Sole, Tony Stanger, just to mention a few. And people thought we just had to turn up to win? Think again!

Wind back the clock twenty-four hours, to the picturesque town of Peebles, on the Scottish border. This was where we had chosen to prepare for the biggest match of our lives. Peebles is one of the prettiest towns you could imagine, dominated by the hotel, much like a stately home, where we were staying. Phenomenal hospitality and an 'oldie-worldie' feel to it. In a way it could be considered as the calm before the storm. Perhaps, in retrospect, somewhere a little closer to the hostilities would have been a more appropriate base for us. Nevertheless, while we had confidence because of our performances that year, we were certainly not complacent. Indeed, the late Bill McLaren, the peerless Scottish BBC television rugby commentator who was doing the match that Saturday, described our Friday training session as 'near perfect', and 'awesome' – his words. But of course you don't win a match on the training field and a good Friday session is not necessarily a guide to a big Saturday performance. However, all Bath players, of my vintage anyway, will remember that the worse our Thursday training session went, the better we would play on the Saturday. Where is the logic in that?

A slight sense of unease, however, had insinuated itself into our preparations, especially when some of Rory Underwood's squadron did a mini-fly-over after training. The gesture looked a little too much like a premature victory salute. And one or two pre-match interviews took place which seemed like poor judgment by those players.

Nevertheless, as the game unfolded, in bright sunshine, England seemed to have diluted the Scottish aggression. Jerry Guscott scored a try out of the top drawer midway through the first half and we were ahead despite playing into a strong wind.

Is there a more contentious issue in international rugby than the decision to scrum down rather than kick a penalty in England versus Scotland 1990? Brian Moore versus Will Carling? What rubbish! There was a very clear option: kick against the wind for a possible three points, or take a major step towards winning the game with a try. Had we turned round at half-time two scores ahead with such a strong wind at our backs, that would surely have been game over. But as we all know we failed to score, and the Mike Teague knock-on at the beginning of the second half at a midfield scrum proved our undoing

From the ensuing scrum, the Scotland scrum-half Gary Armstrong broke right, chipped ahead and Tony Stanger beat Underwood to the touchdown. How we didn't score in the second half I will never know. The Scottish tackling was awesome to be fair to them, and at the final whistle the roof was in danger of blowing off the stand as the crowd celebrated the win.

That night the emotion from the likes of Paul Rendall, the England prop, was something to see. Paul had become a bit of a legend, working his way up from humble beginnings before finally becoming a fixture in the England front row. He was not only as hard as nails, but also extremely stoical – not much could faze him. But the events that day at Murrayfield, coupled with England's failure to exploit a number of scrums on the Scottish line, were too much for him to bear. He was inconsolable, ranting that the Scots had deliberately collapsed the scrums to stop England scoring a try. It should be remembered that David Sole had cut his shirtsleeves so short, that his opposite number Jeff Probyn had nothing on which to grip. So the Scots were clearly fearful of our power in this area. Part of the emotion stemmed from the fact that we had opted for a scrum rather than a penalty, not twice but three times. Pundits accused Brian Moore of hijacking Carling's decision, but the truth was simpler.

There is no time on an international pitch for argument; the front five felt they had the moment, and Carling gave it to them. Had we scored the try which was warranted, the Grand Slam would probably have been ours. Put bluntly,

Jeff Probyn, Brian 'The Pitbull' Moore, Gareth 'Coochie' Chilcott. An England front row not to be messed with.

Will (and by extension the rest of us) was let down by possibly the strongest front five to represent England for many years: Rendall, Moore, Probyn, Ackford, Dooley. Not to mention Winterbottom, Skinner and Teague in the back row.

In the early hours of that Sunday morning, tears were shed for that lost moment, as well as the stunning Scottish try which sealed our fate. The morning papers were razor sharp, condemning English complacency and muddled thinking. Anyone who has played in games of such intensity, will know that results can hinge on one or two key moments. Having described what these were, I also pay tribute to the mental strength and will to win displayed by Scotland, who after all carried off the Grand Slam themselves, and carried one of the all-time great wins into Scottish history.

While some English spectators have described it as one of the most gut-wrenching games they have ever watched – at least until the 1991 World Cup final – most people who watched the match will remember it as a highly charged and momentous occasion. Although I was on the wrong side of the result, I still marvel at the incredible scenes of joy in the Murrayfield stadium, in stark contrast to the look of utter desolation and anguish on the faces of the England players. In what is one of the greatest theatres of sport in the UK it is something special and all sportsmen treasure these moments. As I said in the aftermath of the shock Bath cup defeat, the measure of a group of players is their reaction to adversity. Losing a Grand Slam chance to beat the 'auld enemy' is about as bad as it gets in test rugby.

A look at the statistics following that defeat tells an interesting tale. England went on to win three Grand Slams in five years under Will Carling's captaincy, we participated in a World Cup final (beating Scotland in the semi-finals away, in the process), and confined Scotland to two wins since, in 2000 and 2006, with the two countries drawing in 2010.

But this tells only part of the story. There was much soul-searching among the England players following this defeat, and many of them absorbed this huge setback, letting it hurt them deeply, before, in the process, converting it into a positive force. I was quite certain that famous away wins in Cardiff, Lansdowne Road, Paris and Edinburgh (the following two years) were built on a platform of payback, of never wishing to feel so wretched ever again.

In the short term, the season fell flat and the disappointment of Murrayfield was compounded by the fact that I would be leaving Bath and moving to

London to take up a new job. I was also having to deal with the continued deterioration of my left ankle. And I genuinely felt that 1990 would be my last season.

The doctors were grumbling about the state of my ankle, despite my best efforts to preserve it (such as being a perennial non-tourist). I had determined to have an operation at the end of the season to establish the extent and severity of the damage, knowing there was a strong likelihood that I may not return.

So despite the Grand Slam disappointment, the pleasure of such a great Pilkington Cup win, when we hammered West Country rivals Gloucester 48-6, seemed as appropriate a finishing point to my career as any, after so many years of success at what can only be described as a unique club.

On a personal level it was bittersweet, my career had been so disrupted, but I had come to terms with that. I had also been lucky enough to survive a nasty injury and enjoy club and international rugby. On the announcement of my intended retirement I received a letter from an eminent rugby scribe paying tribute to me and my time on the rugby field. He regretted my retirement and wrote, 'Carling is Carling and Guscott is Guscott, but I know who I would want to play for my life'. I rightfully lived in their shadows for many years, but this was a moment for me, those words meant a lot. It was only one person's view of course, not the majority. But I felt deeply moved by the sentiment and have kept his letter to this day.

The post cup final celebrations were emotionally charged. It had produced a record win against old rivals, but also possibly marked the end of an era. Stuart Barnes, the captain, made an uncharacteristic speech in the Bath Pump Rooms at the civic reception held in our honour. He was very nostalgic, almost reticent, and made some touching references to me. We went back a long way, ten years on the rugby field to be precise and many drunken hours off it, and were well established friends. He knew we were unlikely to play again in each others' company, and this was reflected in his words.

Imagine his shock then, when I showed up at his building society office in Quiet Street, Bath, the following October to tell him that not only was I leaving Bath to return to London, but that I was planning to resume my rugby career – with the Harlequins.

This was to be a two-stage process. Stuart tried to work out how I might stay working in Bath, but I informed him that I was joining UBS, the Swiss investment bank, and the decision had been made. That no one else knew about this was a measure of my respect for Stuart. My rugby-based assessment was that the imminent arrival of Phil de Glanville from Oxford made it logical that I leave Bath. Stuart disagreed with this: "He goes nowhere near the first team unless on merit" – fair enough, but I knew that travelling down to Bath as a twenty-one-year-old was fine, but at thirty-one the mind and the flesh were less willing. In addition my father-in-law had offered Suzanne a medical partnership in London. A two-year stint with the Harlequins (if I remained fit) seemed a good way to finish.

But it appeared that I was betraying a whole city. Why would anyone leave a club like Bath, and at such a peak in their fortunes, a club the like of which would probably never be seen again? Why indeed, if not for the reasons above? At best, people were confused, and at worst they displayed outright resentment. Of course, it was impossible to go round and talk to everyone individually. A sense of helplessness beset me, hardly enhanced by one or two regional press articles which attempted to let me have my say.

Two decades later I feel that it probably wasn't so much my leaving Bath which hurt; it was more the sudden announcement that I would play for Harlequins – Will Carling's exhortations that I should come back and play with England for a year or two were compelling. After all I had missed the 1987 World Cup, and the next one was due to take place in England the following year. Surely this time we would complete a Grand Slam, after Murrayfield 1990. In theory it was great; I just had to get fit, and that was a tall order.

In truth my ankle was in a degenerative state. But the consultant reckoned that he had bought me a year or two, if I was lucky, with the help of a few anti-inflammatory tablets.

I still spent weeks agonising over all these major decisions with my wife. Many long evenings and empty wine bottles were the result, and in the end the path was clear. Nevertheless, it was with a heavy heart that my love affair with Bath came temporarily to an end. Some years later, on my return to the Recreation Ground, as coach to the Harlequins, I was approached by a life-long Bath supporter. Expecting a verbal lashing, I shied away. Instead, he put his arm around me and said affectionately "Welcome back, Simon. This is your real home you know." And of course he was right.

I am happy to say that after twelve months of difficult relationships with former colleagues, most of the Bath lads became firm friends once more. Stuart Barnes and I were still struggling a couple of years later, but finally mended broken fences one New Year's Eve when respective wives were also getting tired of the animosity. I still believe that it is the uniqueness of rugby friendship that causes great heartache. Stuart sent me his book as a peace offering with the words 'An end to enmity', inside. To once again be friends with the mighty man means a lot.

So what was it about Bath? There has to be something special at work for a regional rugby club to have dominated the national scene (and sometimes Europe) for more than a decade. To perpetuate this success, to foster the ability of so many individuals to such great effect; how was it done?

I can put forward a few suggestions, which could possibly explain the secrets to more than just rugby success. First, we were a family. Jack Rowell often referred to the 'Bath family' and what he really meant was that we looked after each other, both on and off the field. There were very few secrets among the players, because the club culture almost would not allow them. This bred huge levels of honesty, but could also create flashpoints. In one post-match debrief, I alluded to the fact that we had struggled to impose any pattern on the game because the line-out was a shambles!

That was dangerous talk, in front of a set of forwards who prided themselves in their performances in the line-out. One by one all the jumpers defended their individual statistics in the line-out; it seemed as if everyone had played a blinder. I ventured, "Strange then, that we did not get any ball…" and various amounts of cursing ensued until Jack Rowell called everyone to order, and in a less confrontational way, agreed with my analysis of the problem.

But the damage was done; my name was mud, at least for the evening. John Hall even threatened to 'sort me out' before the night was over. I watched my back throughout the session, but did not back down. You cannot venture into the war zone only to look for an escape route. The session was ferocious, because in their hearts the forwards knew they had played poorly. Pride had prevented them from admitting it, but we all knew the truth, families often squabble but the unit is close and committed to one another, and will move on from minor issues. The strength of the unit is key, and so it was with Bath.

We had an insatiable desire for success. There was some inner strength which coursed through the veins of Bath's total being. Every player who joined the club had to achieve it. But first they had to endure the statutory vigorous examination of character. This would happen over a period of time; as individuals we perpetually challenged each other, on and off the pitch.

I don't think in my case that I escaped any of this – in many ways, due to my sometimes maverick behaviour, I was singled out for treatment. It did not help when Jack Rowell presented me with a cravat along with my England cap (a belated presentation as I was late for the original some two years earlier and the selectors handed it to someone else with none to spare). Thus was created one of my many nick names, 'The Cravat Kid'. I was also often called 'Johnny', after the French rock star Johnny Hallyday. But other than my French-speaking ability (very average), there were thankfully no other similarities.

And as I've said, we were never satisfied with our own performances. We couldn't bear to lose to anyone, we hated conceding tries. I remember a game against London Welsh when we were leading by forty points with fifteen minutes to go. They were threatening our line and we spent ten minutes tackling everything that moved. It simply wasn't in our make-up to let them cross the line, and they didn't.

Our preparation was supreme despite the odd shambles of a Thursday when all Jack Rowell wanted to do was back-row moves. All three-quarter options were practised until perfect, counter attack skills could sometimes take up a full hour. Fitness sessions were brutal, and non-attendance was not tolerated; you would simply be left out of the side. Most importantly we talked everything through; each member of the squad had a voice, no one was ignored.

Does any of this sound familiar? Well, read Clive Woodward's book. But years before the publication of that particular set of theories, Bath was already engaging in an early form of his philosophy in the early 1980s. What a pity that English rugby was too arrogant to take it on board until the arrival of Geoff Cooke, when planning and preparation became the watchwords.

Nobody who was associated with this special time in rugby will ever forget the successes, nor what lay behind them.

Yet, those same forces that created this monster conspired to bring it to its knees with the advent of professionalism, which caused massive division as money became the driver and people sought to cash in on their efforts. It all went wrong, and the saddest commentary has to be the 'fly-on-the-wall' series that was made for television. The sight of John Hall delivering criticism about Jerry Guscott's lack of punctuality defied belief. John was a giant of the game; one of the finest international back rowers who ever played, albeit briefly. But he was a doer, not an administrator, and personnel management was not his skill. This is no disrespect to John. Many other big names came and went for the same reasons. It was sad to see a club tearing itself apart and in so doing destroying many of the relationships that had helped to make it great.

The return of Andy Robinson restored some sanity, and the club promptly won the European cup, with a little help from Clive Woodward. Andy, as a thinker about the game, was an obvious choice, as he subsequently proved to be for England and latterly Scotland.

After his departure the club lurched again, and indeed was almost relegated, due chiefly to a disastrous recruitment policy. So it took the second coming of Jack Rowell to spark something of a revival. Some things never change.

Despite the 'family' philosophy that was one of the driving forces behind our success, oddly there has never once been a reunion of this incredible bunch of players. Many of us have to pay to get into the ground to watch matches. Some players stay away on principle, and so have rarely visited the place where they won so many plaudits and gave so much. Let us hope that this scandalous situation will one day be righted. If the reunion ever happens, one thing is certain, it will create the biggest hangover ever experienced in the West Country.

But back to May 1990 when to all intents and purposes the curtain fell on my playing career. The ankle was so stiff after matches that anti-inflammatory drugs and painkillers were proving ineffectual. So when Will Carling took an inexperienced team to Argentina in the summer of 1990, I was on crutches in sunny Bath, having had my ankle partly excavated and 'reconstructed'. The doctors described the cartilage as looking like 'the surface of the moon' and they added that it was in a state of chronic deterioration. Not a cheering diagnosis, nor indeed prognosis, although Mr Bliss felt I could be active for a while longer. But give a sportsman an inch, and he will take a mile; all was apparently not lost, and consequently I felt bullish about running around again, even though there was no design or intention; simply a need to know that I would not be crippled at the age of thirty.

Meanwhile, the British Bulldogs had choked on Argentinean Beef, and Will, by now more accustomed to success than failure, returned home from South America in disgust after losing the series to the Pumas, and trailing behind him a number of young hopefuls, who had failed to make the England grade. He contacted me directly on his return, and I commiserated for a while, until he turned his attention to my general health. I knew that his inquiries were hardly medically-based and therefore waited for the punch-line. He explained that many of the England hopefuls were not ready to come through, there was no alternative,

I had to make a comeback, and anyway didn't I feel that there was unfinished business, like a certain day in March 1990 when a Grand Slam dream had gone up in flames; this was payback year and surely I wanted to be part of it?

Will was, and indeed still is, very persuasive, particularly when he has worked out a strategy and is ready to implement it. As England captain for two years, he had learnt so fast that he bridged any gap there might have been between him and his senior players. A great achievement, when you consider that as a twenty-two-year-old with but a few caps to his name he was suddenly handed the reins for a job which involved looking after a squad of highly experienced, yet underachieving, cynical, international players – even if they all wanted success.

The record shows that I came out of retirement, and that it was Will who persuaded me. But the deal was perfectly clear, it was subject to my fitness and form.

So I left Bath to join up with the Fancy Dans of London rugby, Harlequins.

The comparisons between Bath and Harlequins were striking. If there is one global brand in world rugby, then Harlequins are it. There are even associate clubs in South Africa and Australia, and the multi-coloured shirt is probably the most recognisable in the world.

Other characteristics of the club included: a strong connection with the city; it is home to many Oxbridge players (previously an advantage, though not so much now); players and members traditionally have enjoyed post-match entertainment at top London nightspots; it is also closely associated with Twickenham's corridors of power

Some of these statements may be a little dated, since the professional game has removed some of these traditions. However, if you had to make a comparison, Quins would still be the 'Cavaliers' when set alongside the new model army of dedicated professional 'Roundheads' equivalent to Leicester, Northampton, Gloucester or Saracens.

Nobody will ever forget the Harlequin description of Orrell RFC, then the pride of Northern England rugby, as a 'layby off the M6', before a big cup match. Quins then compounded that gaffe by losing the tie.

I started and finished my career at the club with the long spell at Bath in between, and was well placed to see the inside of this venerable club. Having joined Harlequins while still at Oxford, I soon found that on the field the club was a combination of rough heads and travelling Antipodeans, sprinkled with

Varsity players for variation. This motley bunch somehow socialised with the distinctly superior class of supporter off the field. Many of the key Harlequin officials were either on the RFU committee or were serious players in the city.

I will never forget the time when the team was given a tray of gin and tonics after a match as a special treat. On another occasion, a well-meaning official offered us a case of champagne in return for a win. No rugby player would ever turn down quality alcohol, of course, but gin and champagne tended to be on the menu well after beer-drinking, and not before we had left the dressing-room. My personal experience at the Quins was mixed, being unable to maintain a first-team place in the early days. My prompt departure to Bath was a logical outcome, and I soon developed a healthy dislike for my old club. There was never any shortage of talent but they lacked a team ethic or any corporate identity. As a Bath player, I am proud to say that I was never on the losing side versus the Harlequins – and it mattered to me!

In early 1992, however, we were joint top of the league, a pretty amazing situation, and we were playing Bath at the Stoop Memorial Ground. During this grudge match (my first game against the Bath lads for my new club), while we were comfortably ahead, Will Carling mistakenly kicked me in the eye as he was tackled. The entire crowd, and me, thought that I had been 'done in' by the Bath forwards. General outrage followed, as I was led from the field bleeding profusely with one eye shut. The match video finally showed the truth. We managed an 18-18 draw, having been 18-3 up at one stage; then of course we went on to lose the famous '92 final in extra time. So this maverick club at last gained Bath's respect and indeed was able to put a dozen internationals out on the pitch at one stage, most of them were English.

Besides myself, there was one other person who was synonymous with both eras – Dick Best. As a player, he suffered from a lack of specialist position in the forwards. So while he enjoyed a long career, he never held down a regular first team place but emerged as the captain of the sevens team. In those days, we were one of the best around and I was, believe it or not, one of the 'fliers'; as a twenty-one-year-old, the more rugby the better, and it wasn't until I got to Bath that the idea of sevens became a chore, mainly caused by the fact that Bath had no interest.

Admittedly, there was one great benefit for me in that early contact with Dick. When he eventually became coach of Harlequins and England, he brought with him a fearsome reputation as a taskmaster, with an acerbic, acid wit to match the best, something which earned him the sobriquet of 'Sulphuric'. The victims of his ritual humiliation sessions will never forget the experience, and although he was extremely amusing, there was also a ruthless streak to him. In anticipation of this, I had already sidled up to him for a quiet conversation, which went something along the lines of: "Don't mess with me, I've got the pictures, and I won't hesitate to use them." What I really meant of course, was that he and I went back a long way, and I was well capable of responding in kind if I were set upon verbally. Dick was very intense as a coach and demanded high standards. But he was well aware of the difficulty of changing the habits of a generation and for some reason the club could never quite get to grips with issues of loyalty and commitment.

One particular incident encapsulated this perfectly. It happened this way: despite me sporting a colourful black eye and stitches, the big game the following week was against Northampton. We were league leaders and so I was up for it, until Will Carling revealed that he, Peter Winterbottom and Jason Leonard all had 'troublesome injuries', ranging from a damaged finger to a bruised eyelash. Therefore, it was suggested, we should all withdraw from the league match against Saints, as England had a big game versus Scotland the following week. I assumed that this was a joke until Dick Best (the England coach as well of course) confirmed that this was the right strategy. Old West Country habits die hard, I guess, and I had to remind myself that this was London rugby. So we all pulled out, Harlequins lost, and we never saw the lead again that season.

Perhaps the withdrawal was justified, however, because England trashed Scotland the following week in a record away win.

CHAPTER 13

Dealing with the Twin Imposters

When I decided to move to the City of London in 1991, it had been a toss-up between James Capel and UBS Philips + Drew. Warburgs had decided not to proceed with my application (seven years later, they carefully reminded me of the fact), but UBS Philips + Drew seemed to want to offer me a role and JC was uncertain. I had played rugby for the stock exchange and I got to know a number of the traders; great market characters, such as Steve Dalby, Dick Hine, Adrian Faure and Ian Thomas. They ensured that I was introduced to the ex-Harlequin Head of Sales, Denis Elliott. Despite the fact that I had been a member of the stock exchange for four years, my knowledge of the institutional market was close to zero.

It is amazing what you can do if you nod sagely for a while over a business discussion, interspersed with a healthy dose of rugby chat. Believe me, I was incredibly nervous, but my future was at stake and I needed a job offer. So I was majorly focused on making a good impression. Various interviews ensued.

Eventually, the moment came. I had to meet the boss, a man no older than me, by the name of Hector Sants. Now one of the best known managers in the City (UBS, DLJ and Crédit Suisse followed by the FSA), he was at the time the youngest Head of Equities in any London-based investment bank.

I was taken to his office via a back route, to preserve my anonymity. Simply put, I was a current 'rugby international' based in Bath for both job and sport. A move to London may not have been of interest to page three of *The Sun*, but to rugby followers it was news. My potential move could not leak out, for obvious reasons. Of course, City banks are used to this, as they go around poaching rivals. So my paranoia was greeted with near indifference; a 'we've seen it all before' attitude.

Hector petrified me, partly due to his (obviously) awesome intellect. For me this was the moment of truth, when they would realise that I was a humble private client stockbroker, who knew precious little. So I sat there, in anticipation of a string of unanswerable questions.

Perhaps Hector knew that it wasn't worth putting me to the test. The questions never came, and I found myself treated to a monologue, to the greater glory of UBS Philips + Drew. He had an amazing capacity to talk for what seemed like an eternity before drawing breath; a latter day John Inverdale, perhaps, only not quite as fluent.

He threw the odd inquiry my way, possibly to check that I was still awake. Nonetheless, it was very clear that I was sitting in front of one of the City's stars; by the time UBS and SBC Warburg got together in 1996, Hector was effectively running UBS International Equities, in his mid-thirties. He was also a casualty of the merger, but he always had options. Once the City identified an individual's quality, there were never any shortages of opportunity. Then the gravy train would chug along, and good luck to the passengers. Investment banks take their pound of flesh – sixty hours a week, and twenty-five days holiday, with summary dismissal a real possibility, for a multitude of reasons. But don't expect sympathy – too much money is being earned for that.

Hector was certainly committed; he had a prodigious capacity to take on board the workings of the financial markets. He also spent an inordinate amount of time talking to people, although his main skill was not people management. He impressed with his mastery of the facts in many stock market disciplines. His knowledge base was legendary; he was one of the very few who could out-faze the Swiss and as a result they generally left us alone. He was undoubtedly a brilliant man in my opinion; he could work people out, and he backed winners. I marvelled at the fact that after the break-up of UBS, many of his departed protégés ended up in positions of senior responsibility elsewhere in the City. A clear effect of his legacy.

My performance in front of Hector was average – I sat and listened and nodded. But it was enough – he probably thought I could do little damage. After all I was to be away for twelve weeks of year one for the Rugby World Cup. So he could hardly be expecting miracles!

He was obviously interested in my rugby ambitions, and not just because he was Scottish. Remember the year was 1991, and the Scots were Grand Slam champions, although for not much longer. Most Scots were still wallowing in their achievements until the rude awakening of the English response in that very year, by way of our first Grand Slam since Billy Beaumont.

Just as well, since my knowledge of institutional broking could be written on the back of a postage stamp. Dealing with pension fund managers was just a touch different from showing Granny Smith that the moth eaten document she had was in fact a Glaxo Certificate, worth a considerable amount of money!

Luckily for me, very few of my early clients put me to the test. They obviously thought that I knew what I was doing. In addition, they were always keen to talk about the weekend's rugby first, and the forthcoming match. They hardly allowed me to sell to them – or perhaps they knew I was green.

Nonetheless, I gradually got to know my new colleagues – all 700 of them, compared with just four in my Bath office. Quite a culture shock. And what a diverse bunch they were – the Cockney fast trader, sharp as nails, and the old Etonian, charming but possibly rather dim, sharing the same platform. Then there was the bespectacled academic rubbing shoulders with the enthusiastic, teamy type, who seemed to get by with equal amounts of bluster and half-truths. In all honesty, I was undoubtedly in the last group. How else could I survive, a classics and modern linguist, in a Swiss Bank, trying to give advice on companies about which I knew precious little?

But all eyes were on the World Cup, so no one cared too much. And Will Carling had made it clear to me that the World Cup in that October was not open to people who chose not to go on the tour to Australia and Fiji in the summer. Luckily I had warned both work and home that this was a precondition. The Halliday predilection for staying at home was about to be challenged, and I began a four-month span where nothing seemed to matter except World Cup success.

The five-week tour to Australia and Fiji in the lead-up to the World Cup had the rest of the England party sitting in the plane ready to depart, with no-one quite believing I was going to tour until I was actually on board.

This final tour, unless you count the six weeks of the World Cup itself, when we were on tour but in our own country, was hugely enjoyable and exciting. We all knew there was a reckoning in sight for us; we had indeed avenged our disappointments of 1990, and were now the Grand Slam champions. Our closeness as a group of people was unparalleled in the eight years in which I had been involved, and friendships became very tight and important to us. We all knew that there was a major task ahead, and were preparing each other for it. So there was always an undercurrent of tension.

The tour itself was a little disappointing. We lost the test heavily against

Australia despite breaking them open out wide on numerous occasions, a feat which was to determine some of our tactics in the World Cup final some months later. Chris Oti's defensive weaknesses were shown up by David Campese, who scored three tries, and there was more than one occasion when I wished I was on the field instead of him.

I was still suffering from a horrendous stamping at the hands of one of the Emerging Wallaby props during a mid-week game. His studs had ripped my shirt as well as my back, and he had lacerated my eye for good measure. I stayed on however, and proceeded to go around hunting Aussie heads with high tackles as a form of revenge, much to the amusement of Carling and Guscott on the bench.

Perhaps the referee let it go, because he knew that he should have sent the miscreant off and didn't mind a dose of indignant English payback. There was a storm of media protest after the game and in today's world there would have been a citing and a ban for many months. We, however, refused to complain and moved on. Had I lost an eye – a distinct possibility – perhaps the reactions would have been a little different.

During this tour, we spent four days in Fiji, playing two matches including a test match. We saw first-hand the poverty of that proud nation, as many kids played rugby barefoot in villages without some of the most basic amenities. Meantime we stayed in a luxurious Sheraton Hotel – it made you stop and think, but then tourism is one of the major industries on the island. The people there were so happy and welcoming – they made a great impression on all of us, and I was sad to leave.

I was glad to sign off my fractured touring record with such an experience. All rugby players live for the tour and the 'craic' – as we called it then, although there may be other connotations these days. I was no different, just unlucky to have missed out on some amazing opportunities. However, I was pretty happy with my lot, particularly given that the frequent absences worked in my favour on many occasions.

My UBS mates were incredibly supportive over this period, and I always knew that they were there in the background. They cared so much they even sent the company research to the hotels at which I stayed. This was highly amusing for the lads, who would be perusing the local rags when a consignment of mail would hit the table, addressed to me with the heading 'Remember the day job'.

Having returned from Australia, there were a series of trial matches before the World Cup kicked off for real, against Russia, Gloucester and the England Students. I was in sparkling form, and people were talking about a change in the midfield combination, with me finding a starting slot. Given that I had missed my first cap against the All Blacks, and hadn't played against them since, this was a big deal for me.

But it didn't happen, instead I stayed on the bench and watched us lose the first match in a very disappointing, stuttering affair. We seemed to freeze, and so were condemned to a tough away draw (Scotland and France) if we wished to progress to the final.

We were on a huge adventure, as we approached the quarter final crunch match in France. It crossed my mind that I had a good chance of being selected but once again no, and I took it out on myself in a massive sprint session after the last training session. I felt fit and strong, and frustrated.

Even more so, when, in the heat of the match, Serge Blanco and Eric Champ, the hit man flanker, punched our wing Nigel Heslop repeatedly and effectively knocked him out. I was waiting to come on, and believe me I was ready. But Heslop refused to come off and when he missed a key tackle five minutes later which conceded a try, there was much upset in the selectors' seats. They had wanted to replace Heslop, and staying on did him no good.

When the game finished, Roger Uttley the England coach whispered in my ear, "Don't get too drunk tonight..." I looked at him, shocked, this was ritual, and we had won a big game, and another week in the competition against Scotland away in the semi-final. But the Crazy Horse was the designated party venue for our Paris celebrations and there was no way I was going to miss the festivities – I guess that I toned things down a smidge, but no more than that.

And as we focused on the Edinburgh clash to determine one of the World Cup Finalists, I was told that the selectors had decided I would play on the wing as the only change from the victorious quarter-final team. Although a centre, I had of course played on the wing the previous year, so I had no qualms at all.

Nigel Heslop was incredibly gracious, and we had a conversation which will remain private but, suffice it to say, I was humbled by it, and I hope if I had been the one missing out that I would have been so understanding. After all, he knew that if we beat Scotland, that he would miss out on the final as well.

Tension was heavy all week – this was our first visit since the trauma of the failed Murrayfield Grand Slam bid, and they basically had the same side. But we knew this was our time, and in a grimly intense eighty minutes, I think we would have found a way to win even if Gavin Hastings hadn't missed a very straightforward kick late in the game to square the score.

As the final whistle went, the look of relief on Carling's face was tangible. We had gone to the two most difficult places in the northern hemisphere and won – remember we had punctured Welsh invincibility over the last two years. So surely we weren't to be denied our destiny on our own ground in our own final?

Fast forwarding twelve years and looking back ten…

Who could ever forget that wet November evening in Sydney, in 2003, when England became World Rugby Champions? People who were there still describe it as the top sporting event of their lives. The Football World Cup in 1966, or latterly the Steven Redgrave Olympic rowing gold medals haul would be valid competition, I suppose, together with the odd Ashes test match in 1981, or again in 2005.

Frustratingly I was stuck in the office that week, and watched the match at home with my son Alexander and godson Matthew Luddington, plus his father Richard; a select gathering. It was fantastic to see the looks on the boys' faces at the moment they will always remember, the moment when their hero Jonny Wilkinson landed the winning drop-goal.

Text messages came through thick and fast from mates of mine who were in the stadium, and later on I had a few words with Andy Robinson, who berated me for not being there. He briefly described the scene: "Here I am at Manly Beach, which is covered with thousands of drunken English rugby supporters either in the surf or barbecuing. What a sight!" I was mildly gutted to say the least.

Those were moments of a lifetime, and brought back memories of that cold November day in 1991 when we contested the World Cup final against Australia. Most of my clients were there, as were work colleagues, one of them a steward dressed up in fluorescent yellow and marshalling the crowds, not because he couldn't get a ticket, of course. Someone did an analysis once of stewards' professions, and came up with all kinds of business pursuits, from dustmen and labourers to doctors and solicitors. But who cared? They were happy to be there and had one thing in common – rugby.

Despite a valiant effort England just failed to conquer possibly the best (prospective) Australian team ever to take the field, boasting the likes of David Campese, Nick Farr-Jones, Michael Lynagh, Tim Horan and Jason Little, not a bad quintet for starters. That said there is no excuse for losing a game we should have won.

The Australian dressing room in the immediate aftermath resembled the finishing line of a 10,000 metre race with people strewn around the floor in a state of exhaustion. Notwithstanding the cynical play of Campese, when he had deliberately knocked the ball on to prevent us from scoring, the game had been a heroic piece of Australian defence. They grabbed an early lead, and then simply hung on. Nick Farr-Jones was their extra defender in the back line, instead of in his usual position around the fringes. He, like the rest of the world, spotted that we were suddenly playing an expansive game, whereas in the lead-up to the tournament (away games in France and Scotland), and indeed in the 1991 Grand Slam season, England had played tight, controlled rugby. So why the big change? And did it account for our failure to go down in history?

Some well-known figures thought so. Disgracefully, Brian Moore, Peter Winterbottom, Mike Teague and Jeff Probyn have all pointed the finger in their own way, criticising England's tactics. And I thought rugby was a team game. More importantly, all four of these English heroes were never short of a word on, or off, the pitch, and they had been an integral part of everything we had achieved. It was collective will which had taken us from being an underachieving bunch of no-hopers to the crest of world domination.

I once read in a sporting book: 'The gap between accepting things the way they are and wishing them to be otherwise is the 1/10 of an inch of difference between heaven and hell.' Quite.

The passing up of a great opportunity – on home ground – still feels unacceptable after all these years. It is particularly hard to take when considering the incredible scenes of jubilation surrounding the 2003 triumph. In comparison, being described as a participant in the 1991 Rugby World Cup Final reeks of failure. And of course that's what it was.

But was all the criticism from within justified? Were all the senior players disenfranchised and as powerless to effect change as they have intimated? Were they the victim of a conspiracy of events, i.e no plan B, Will Carling's leadership, intransigence, the halfbacks who wouldn't mix the game up etc, etc?

I think that my version of events may just clear up some points of 'confusion'.

In the week leading up to the final, we had talked for hours about the best way to beat Australia, a side with a near-perfect mix of youth and experience, in some ways more talented than us. It should be remembered that we had played them in Sydney that July, and we had been roundly beaten. I was on the bench that day, to see Campese give Chris Oti the complete run-around. As a result the scoreline was one to make an Englishman wince, turning defeat into a rout.

But the video showed that England had cut open the Aussies whenever they moved it wide, Guscott, Webb and Underwood had all looked like world-beaters. Time and again the outside gaps would appear, whereas we were getting no reward from the exchanges up-front.

It was this experience that caused Geoff Cooke and Roger Uttley to consider a tactical shift. I say 'shift', because the previous year England was the most attractive side to watch in Europe: a record away win in France, a record home win against Wales. We knew how to do it. We had chosen to play tight through 1991 and two big away games in the World Cup at hostile grounds kept it that way, not surprisingly.

The stakes were high. Could we win a World Cup playing ten-man rugby? Everyone asked the same question and the answer was 'no'. So there we were: '*Olea jacta est* [The die is cast]' (Caesar crossing the Rubicon). We all bought into it, we practised it all week, and we went out to execute the strategy.

But we failed. Our execution was poor and, incredibly, Carling's and Guscott's passing was just not good enough on the day. Rob Andrew and Richard Hill were seemingly bewildered by all the possession, so much so that they forgot all about flexibility. The back-row played like headless chickens (I always thought Mick 'The Munch' Skinner had chicken legs), and had to take their share of the blame along with the halfbacks. I felt sorry for the front five because they did all that was asked of them. They even ran about in the loose: Ackford and Dooley on the rampage, to great effect.

And Australia? John Eales, a second-row forward no less, caught Andrew from behind in full flight. Rob Andrew was no Rory Underwood, but the adrenalin coursing through the young Aussie lock must have been incredible. Otherwise how else could he have done that? According to Jeff Probyn, Will Carling was urged to change tactics at half time. Well, not the game in which I was playing. Perhaps Jeff was talking to the Carling voodoo doll he carried around with him, pins sticking out from most places. Yes, they got on that well.

I am not exonerating Will Carling. He was the captain, and he could have shouted the odds at the most experienced English side that had ever taken the field. Perhaps it was a bridge too far for the twenty-five-year-old, who had melded together an improbable bunch of players into a great team. Maybe there was a lack of tactical experience in a man who had played just fifty-sixty first class games in his entire career at that point, despite three years as England captain. But I would challenge anyone to have made themselves heard in the heat of this particular battle. My conclusion is that, no, it was not Will's fault. He had brought us to the brink of glory.

It is said that 'a leader needs the wisdom to serve and follow', as well as to lead. On a day when none of us could hear each other speak, the self-appointed critics might do better to look within. What I do know is that it was the greatest rugby adventure, a glorious, typically English failure, but we were a world force, a permanent fixture with a rightful place at the top table.

The baton was passed on to the 1995 team, until Jonah Lomu came along, then, in 1999, they were thwarted by drop goal machine Jannie De Beer; before, finally, the payback from Jonny Wilkinson – and in Australia's own backyard. Sweet!

But back in November 1991, when the nation awoke on the Sunday, the reality was that England had fallen at the last hurdle. The team had failed to exorcise twenty-five years of sporting underachievement since the 1966 football World Cup final. One client later revealed to me that in the aftermath of defeat, he simply gazed at the ground, unable to speak, he was so gutted. It meant that much to everyone, supporters and players alike, all left with a feeling just as empty as the Grand Slam defeat against Scotland the previous year.

Suzanne and I returned to our Putney home, reunited with Sophie, our two-year-old daughter, and clutching a loser's medal. The story goes that Brian Moore threw his in the river in disgust – well, mine is framed on my bedroom wall. And why not? It was a great adventure, and we had still made a nation proud. I will never forget the crowd, as we left the Rose Room at Twickenham to go to the post match reception. There were hundreds of them waiting for us outside, and they broke into song as we boarded the bus. I recollect they gave us a rendition of 'Jerusalem' – perhaps I am wrong, but it doesn't matter much. What did matter was that they were there, acknowledging us and offering us all a sense of companionship. Our disappointment was mutual, but they understood that being there was a huge support.

Can anyone imagine my feelings on the Monday morning at 6. 45, when I arrived back at UBS? I was greeted on the steps by Sky TV cameras. "How do you feel?" My eyes must have glazed over. Dream over, back to reality, life goes on – how many clichés ran through my head. I certainly muttered something entirely predictable, before making my excuses and stumbling into the bank.

I often wonder how long the party in the City might have lasted had we won. Most City people are rugby mad. They have to be – otherwise why else would they all keep coming to the Varsity Match for example?

Instead, there was sympathy and supportive cries of: "We should have won! And, "Yes, of course – it was all Campese's fault."

But in the financial world, we discount events and move on. The entire game had been dissected by coffee time on Monday morning – yet the impression of the tournament was long-lasting and indelible. Football-mad market-makers found their sons wanting to take up mini-rugby. The Five Nations' tournament became a persistent topic, and days out to Paris, Dublin, Edinburgh and Cardiff were feverishly planned.

My 'team leader' took me into a meeting room and discussed my return to work. His name was Ed Knox, one of those rare breeds in broking who was bright enough to be a fund manager – which is where he ended up! I was reasonably scared of him, because he was so demanding, and didn't tolerate fools. So I was surprised at what he then said: "…Take your time getting back into it, you must feel gutted, we all are… what a traumatic experience, don't worry if you don't feel like working." I was nonplussed, and had no idea how to react. He was very emotional, and reality suddenly dawned on me. Even hardened City men realised that we had been on the verge of something special – and felt the disappointment themselves. My boss, Denis Elliott, even suggested that I take another two weeks' holiday to recover. What, after twelve weeks away? My immediate colleagues would have been well impressed! I politely declined.

The emotion soon wore off – bonus discussions were imminent – that discretionary award over and above the salary on which City folk rely. To hell with the emotion around a rugby match; try telling an employee they haven't had as great a year as they thought they had, and watch the fur fly! People's idea of their self-worth has to be heard to believed, and the game is a deadly one; poor management of expectations will result in deep unhappiness and possible resignation; not good news if it's one of your stars.

No such luck for a losing World Cup finalist. Not only did my long absence from the office fail to bring back the World Cup, it also provided an excuse to say I couldn't possibly expect a bonus having been away for three months of the year – fair, I suppose, but still depressing! On a serious note, it grated on me that I was losing out financially while playing to full houses all around the country. Nobody ever did the sums on how much revenue was being collected by the rugby union. All I knew was that it certainly failed to come in my direction. In hindsight, the 1991 World Cup signalled the start of an uneasy move towards professionalism.

It is fascinating to reflect that four years on Dudley Wood would still be suggesting that it would never happen – not exactly a visionary of this time; more of a King Canute.

Throughout this period, the England players looked on, while the Kiwis drove round in their brand new sponsored cars or French clubs went on strike over pay packages. Blatant professionalism was in our faces. I can remember being offered £30,000 by a club in France as far back as the 1980s, for example. The same amount of money was on offer for the Rebel Tour of South Africa in 1989. Yet no action was taken. You can understand why the likes of Brian Moore were hopping mad. The situation couldn't last.

In the meantime I was living a surreal life as an investment banker (in the making) while holding down an international rugby position.

Being recognised as a top rugby player is certainly something you expect, particularly in the City – although I cannot pretend that I had the pulling power of a Carling or a Guscott. Nonetheless, there were plenty of embarrassing moments.

I once accompanied the CEO of a major French company to one of our top clients for a meeting. Normally, as a broker, you fit quietly into a corner. Imagine my embarrassment, and the irritation of my client, when the first five minutes were spent discussing the potential result of the upcoming England-France match with me.

On another occasion, I fell foul of the Smith & Nephew management. They had heard about my problem left ankle, and announced during a major presentation that they were working on an artificial cartilage. This would probably sort out the ankle joint, but only if I was prepared to go to the US for six months – thanks!

Sir Ian, now Lord, MacLaurin of Tesco was a Corporate Head whom I knew reasonably well, mainly through his son, Neil. UBS was the Corporate Broker to Tesco, and had advised on a French acquisition. MacLaurin therefore arrived at our offices first thing in the morning to discuss the deal. Unfortunately, I had overslept and was trying to join the packed meeting as discreetly as possible. I sidled in through the entrance, but could not avoid passing in full view of Sir Ian. He interrupted his presentation, greeted me warmly and informed me that he was now a grandfather, due to the recent birth of a baby grand-daughter. I smiled warmly, muttered something unintelligible and scuttled to the back of the room. A look of thunder on the faces of the UBS Bankers said it all.

CHAPTER 14

The City Bites Back

The year 1991 was a different time for all English rugby players. A Grand Slam followed by failure to win the ultimate prize, the Rugby World Cup – what next? Well, another Grand Slam in 1992 was the answer. England was irresistible, winning all four games comfortably.

I was playing through my last season, and had a real swansong. Getting into the England side for the final stages of the World Cup had given me a boost, and with it my form had never been better. And this despite an increasingly chronic ankle condition, but I simply increased the dosage of anti-inflammatories and carried on.

Of course, my City career could hardly progress until I retired, simply due to the time commitment. The whole thing was becoming ridiculous; every weekend away, often including Friday nights, two other nights training, constant gym work, three days off before each international; and that excludes time with the physio if you were injured. Oh, and don't forget summer tours and warm weather training; all of this after a fifty-hour week! By now, Suzanne was a GP in Fulham, and I had a young daughter Sophie and another on the way (Alexander). Trying to combine all these commitments was simply a losing battle. I had promised UBS, and my wife, that 1992 would be my last season, and in all honesty I was happy to go. Despite enjoying a second Grand Slam – in which I played – the writing was on the wall, because the rugby-work overlap was becoming unsustainable, although there were still plenty of light-hearted moments.

One Monday morning, in January 1992, I came into the office after England had given Scotland a thumping 25-7 victory, and England's highest winning margin at Murrayfield. We were all on cloud nine, and on our way, although we did not know it, to completing a second successive Grand Slam. At Murrayfield I had had one of my best games for England. In fact as a result of it, plus a couple of decent club showings, I carried off the player of the month award at the venerable age of thirty-one.

I was also nursing a spectacular weekend hangover after a big celebration, so didn't really concentrate on what happened next. I picked up a flashing line at 9. 00am or so, two hours into the day. "*Times City Diary* here," said the voice. Very unusual, I thought, particularly if it was me they wished to contact. "Great win over the weekend – how does it feel to be back at work, etc …" they rattled on. "I just wondered whether clients mention it to you?"

"Yes of course," I replied. The reality was that it was all clients wanted to talk about; if we had a big investment story to tell the market, they didn't want to hear it from me. Nothing I could do about it, of course. Clients are difficult enough to talk to at the best of times, so better not to upset them if they want to chat about the weekend's rugby; at least they are not talking to a competitor broker!

"So do they give you congratulatory orders?"

"Of course not," I spluttered, professional dignity hugely offended. "Rugby is rugby, and then we talk business. If we deserve orders on the quality of our advice, then so be it. " My interviewer sounded mildly amused, congratulated me again, and was gone.

It wasn't until the next day that I realised my naiveté. 'All tales, but no sales at UBS' screamed the headlines. Although, with tongue firmly in cheek, the article implied I was slightly miffed not to have received a string of orders to celebrate the crushing victory.

Other than being the laughing stock of the office, the clients who had traded that morning were as indignant as were those who hadn't because the article suggested they should. I couldn't win either way – oh well, a lesson learned. Even at that age I hadn't learnt to keep my mouth shut.

Eventually though we reached the season's end marked by the sensational Cup Final of 1992 which was to be my last game of competitive rugby anywhere in the world. That is not as obvious as it sounds, since many retired rugby players are talked back into a pair of boots, just as I had been in 1990 by Will Carling, shortly after the original announcement of my retirement. A dislocated ankle some seven years earlier was finally turning arthritic, and the medics were wagging their fingers at me disapprovingly. Some years on, and many operations later, I now know why, but at the time it was tough to accept. So, having been talked back into a last two years with Harlequins, in which England won two

Grand Slams and reached a World Cup final, and in which Harlequins contested two knockout finals, winning one, there was finally no going back.

Jonathan Webb, England's full back and resident medic, had a little go at making me stay on. "Just think, Hallers, three Grand Slams if we do it again next year; in the history books for ever!" I snorted, then felt wistful, but knew it was a pipedream, and so it proved when England got old and blew up in 1993, and Webby regretted not following me out of the door.

Even Geoff Cooke, well-named since he often mixed a fair concoction of different and contrasting rugby ingredients – some of them dodgy – attempted to snare me for another year. "You are on a high, do one more year. Remember, it's South Africa in November." The Rainbow Nation was out of isolation, what an event; the last appearance of Danie Gerber, the prince of centres, a player who had destroyed defences over the years; and surely it would be the final hurrah for the legendary Naas Botha. How could I say no? Yet how could I start the season, play a signature game then cynically close the book? Sadly, therefore, I shook off the friendly arm around the shoulder and walked away. I had played first class rugby since 1978, straddled two Grand Slam eras, seen a World Cup final slip through my fingers, and played for two of the best known clubs in world rugby. Enough, perhaps, but I still shed tears unashamedly as I struggled to disentangle myself from the tentacles which had wrapped themselves tightly around me.

You see, rugby does that to you; the memories, the nostalgia, the life-defining moments, the euphoria of success followed by the despair of defeat, all washed down with a gallon of ale and the odd gin and tonic. You cannot just walk away, and actually you never do, as any president of your local rugby club, or retired executive will testify. They have a pint or two, and the eyes become watery as cobwebs are brushed away and memories return, albeit briefly.

But the real world and my career outside rugby was not going to stand idly by waiting for me to give my full attention.

It so happened that UBS was making great strides to break into the premier league, which was dominated at the time by James Capel, NatWest, SBC Warburg and Merrill Lynch. But we lacked creativity and vision, not a problem for the Swiss perhaps, but a block to getting the equities business moving forward.

Now in some ways my greatest strength was my greatest weakness. I was simply incapable of suppressing my opinion, particularly if I was passionate about something. This led to my first major confrontation.

The research department initially suffered a garrotting at the hands of Terry Smith, who was the Head of Research, but was more often referred to as the 'Grim Reaper from Chingford'. He first fired swathes of people. Then he part hijacked his colleagues' ideas and published *Accounting for Growth* (a famous and controversial publication concerning accounting practices), making his reputation and a fortune simultaneously. Finally, he was fired and launched a lawsuit to boot, fleeing the bank with a considerable sum of money. Not bad going!

Terry had star quality, and is far too bright for the industry. He was always interesting and very hard-hitting. He never gave me a hard time, but you could not ignore the record of the man.

UBS needed some stability and found it in Malcom Maclachlan and Mike Drozd, a couple of safe pairs of hands. They were great process people, but had no creative ideas, and we were in desperate need of inspiration and leadership.

Step forward Luke Wiseman, a Pan European salesperson and possibly one of the most remarkable men I have ever met.

He came to UBS from ABN Amro, and formed an effective sales partnership with Jamie Netherthorpe, a brilliant salesperson himself and also a Lord (hereditary). They were both hugely understated – rather unusual in this world of financial egos – but masters in their roles. However, Luke was a frustrated analyst and had a desire to get involved. We had the great idea to turn him into the 'creative director' of research, furnishing us with innovation and driving his department to produce interesting pieces of analysis. There was only one problem – how to get it done? We couldn't propose the changes through any committee process, as both research heads sat on all the committees.

So myself and Jamie, together with two other sales heads, decided to go straight to Hector Sants, our all-powerful Head of Equities. There were nerves and tension. Subverting the process in a Swiss bank was a high-risk strategy. But I knew that the whole sales desk wanted it to happen and as the Head of Sales I didn't fancy losing any staff through disillusionment.

Hector's face was as dark as thunder. He listened in silence as the four of us pushed for the change. It was a challenge to his management team, and he was apoplectic that we had acted so precipitously. "Is this a lynch mob?" he fumed. I suppose it was, and he, for one, had failed to realise the depth of unhappiness at the low quality of our research offering.

However, he did see merit in our suggestion, and Luke Wiseman found his niche, although the announcement of his appointment was carefully articulated. As for me, I found out later that I was within minutes of being fired at a meeting of the executive, for being the ringleader. Sometimes you have to take a risk in order to achieve; a philosophy of my rugby days. But it was a little too close for comfort.

Back to Luke, who is a very special person in many ways. He had only just recovered from an unbelievable accident some two years earlier, and was incredibly lucky to be alive. He had fallen asleep on the M40 while driving back to London, and careered into a field. Very unluckily, his car smashed into the side of a wooden fence. The sharp end of a stake went straight through the windscreen and buried itself in his head.

In a critical condition, he was taken to the John Radcliffe where coincidentally Jonathan Webb, the England full-back, was based. Jonathan told me that he had never seen facial injuries like the ones which Luke had sustained. It was touch and go for some time.

The doctors had to remove the skin from his face, and reconstruct the bones and shape of his skull. He lost an eye, and was terribly scarred, but he came through. He, however, never lost his optimism and desire for recovery.

I remember sitting with him in a pub, and watching him puff on a cigarette, while being fed through his stomach. His bravery was immense and incomparable.

Luke became a good friend, as well as a valuable asset to UBS. His heroism (strong word, but appropriate) taught us all some lessons; his cheerfulness in adversity was something that we almost took for granted. Such was the pioneering nature of the reconstruction he had undergone, that he became a feature on the BBC television programme *Tomorrow's World*. There's fame for you! But to him it was all a lot of fuss. And even today, some years on, as a colleague once again, he still sounds surprised if someone makes anything of his experiences. But that is the nature of the man.

As we progressed through the '90s, UBS became a stronger and stronger force in investment banking generally, and equities in particular. Inevitably, the process started to take over and many new initiatives began to be put in place in order to improve ourselves.

Team building and interpersonal relationships became core objectives. It was the age of McKinsey. Consultants crawled all over businesses with new ways of doing things, peddling expensive jargon. We often had to listen to pep talks from senior managers who returned from off-sites full of catchphrases and meaningless expressions. As a consequence we often played bullshit bingo. This involved counting up a number of these comments until you had reached a certain level which allowed you to claim bingo. Phrases such as 'think outside the box!', 'stretch the envelope' and 'go to the next level' all qualified. Poking fun at corporate jargon must be a habitual pastime for many people, and UBS' ability in this area was no different to its peers. So it was no surprise when a number of equities' managers were invited to a stately home in Oxfordshire for a few days' training course.

We were to undergo a series of analyses to find out what sort of people we were, whether we could work together, and how we could improve ourselves. I have to admit that I was extremely cynical about this. After all, I had been through fifteen years or so of exactly what they were trying to teach me. Rugby is a great leveller; you have to cooperate with each other, and submit to the will of the majority without losing your individuality. And the difference between good teams and great teams is the degree to which they are willing to surrender the 'me' for the 'we'. Selflessness, compassion and the desire to improve the weakest link are all important parts of the process.

That is anathema to many people in banking, not because they are not able to learn, it is just that they aren't used to it. Senior managers pay you on your productivity and profitability, not your teamwork; you get no credit for sharing the success. Book it yourself, and damn everyone else. I knew some people who were afraid to go out to lunch in case they missed some business, and it goes down under another name as a consequence. It is a real 'dog-eat-dog' world, which breeds arrogance and defensiveness at the same time. You try that attitude on a rugby field and you would be lucky if someone didn't land one on you. So I was well versed in how to run with a team approach, in fact, it was all I knew.

There was a lot of nervousness as we all assembled on the first day. The course organisers split us into teams and had us building bridges out of pieces of rope, or working out solutions to some complicated dilemmas. It was all recorded on video, with the express intention of establishing who could work in a team, who dominated and who held back. Not surprisingly many of us regarded the weekend as a great opportunity to get drunk on expenses – mind you, half the exercise was to bond more closely so that was not a bad thing.

However there were some occasions when emotions ran high. Tim Brown, a senior UBS figure, had been at the centre of the Blue Arrow scandal. Briefly, there had been a major fraud involving senior corporate and City figures. A number of people were either fired or sued. Initially Tim had been implicated, although he was eventually cleared, but he was understandably extremely sensitive to accusations of improbity. So when Mike Parker, a derivatives salesman, accused him of being untruthful in one of the many tests we had been set, there was almost a fight. Tim was in tears, not exactly the sort of example that should be set by one of our leading figures. But maybe it was a case of 'no smoke without fire'. I must admit though I was much more concerned on that course when my car was broken into (along with everyone else's) and I lost my mobile phone.

Investment banking had suddenly discovered off-sites, bonding and teamwork. It was all in vogue and no expenses were spared. A year later, I was flown off to Wolfsberg, the UBS corporate training centre; an imposing fortress-like castle in northern Switzerland. It stood proudly on the top of a hill, surrounded by thick forest; ideal country for running and cycling. In between lectures and seminars, we were encouraged to take exercise. In reality, there was no option and we had to take exercise, and it did at least relieve the boredom, as well as help to work off the massive meals we were expected to consume.

As with all things Swiss, the schedule was extremely regimented. UBS colleagues from all over the world were herded together to make us understand that teamwork was critical to our success. The funny thing was that all the presentations seemed to be aimed towards proving UBS superiority over Crédit Suisse and SBC, our two main competitors. This arrogance was breathtaking as well as amusing.

We split into groups one day to discuss corporate culture and I let rip. I have a very simple view of management and leaders in any walk of life. They have to be listeners as well as decision-makers, must be visible, and spend time with their people. I have seen the effect of a senior figure passing on congratulations to an employee. The sense of pride is tangible, and makes the person feel valued and their efforts worthwhile. Can anyone really disagree that it is fundamental to a successful team?

Imagine then the horror of my colleagues when I revealed that my boss, Matthias Cabiavietta, had not set foot on the UBS trading floor in the five years that I had been working there. Or put it this way, I had never seen him. We boasted a floor the size of a rugby pitch (at least), with 700-800 people. It was a statement that to me said he was just a cardboard cut-out.

When one of our groups made a presentation to a member of the group executive who had flown in from Zurich, and mentioned this fact, the ex-general spluttered his amazement and incredulity and flatly refused to believe it. Luckily, I was not named as the person who dared to make such an observation.

Two years later, Cabiavietta fell on his sword during the UBS/SBC merger when he took responsibility for the £1billion derivatives loss which UBS incurred. For sure, we were out of control. Each year, Hector Sants had applauded the big dividends we received from the derivatives group, pushing aside worried questions. He berated us for our scepticism, suggesting that this money allowed us to be paid bonuses, and that we should be thankful.

But you had to be nervous. Screen after screen was piled on top of each other until you couldn't see any of the whiz kids weaving their magic. Exotic deals came thick and fast. I was asked to bid my largest client for twelve per cent of Pilkington shares (the glass company) in return for a derivative. Come again? That was £200million! We marvelled at crazy price moves for which we were apparently responsible. It was scary, and nobody understood it, except that some people on the UBS floor were being paid multi-millions. One of the senior players was called the Six Million Dollar Man, and not because he looked like Steve Austin, TV's bionic man. Before the department blew up, he had mysteriously left, and his colleague was suspended for suspected serial drug abuse.

The SBC Head of Trading, Chris Salter, asked me during the merger process whether I knew what was going on. I shook my head and he simply observed, "Your trading book can be described as toxic waste!" Hmm. It remains my view that this is why UBS rolled over when SBC came knocking on the door, and sold us all down the river.

I don't blame Hector Sants who could not fully have understood the implications. Let's hope he does now, given his important position at the FSA and now at Barclays. Perhaps we should reflect on the fact that the head of this derivatives garbage can was an Israeli ex-tank commander named Ramy Goldstein – perhaps he was out of the loop as well.

Whatever the reason, as mentioned earlier, the demise of UBS was one of the City's greatest scandals, the majority of a top bank simply dismembered, and why? Because they could be. Never to be forgotten, an open sore in my mind because there was so much disrespect for good people.

CHAPTER 15

Dark Days in the City

He sat across the table from me, hands slightly quivering and eyes watery. I flashed a warning glance to the Head of Human Resources, with whom I was sharing the redundancy meeting. I had prepared her for an unpredictable outcome given the nature of the person opposite me. We already had standard measures in place including security personnel on stand-by for the worst case scenario, and counselling and outplacement consultants at the other end of the spectrum. You can never be too well-prepared.

Normally, it would be up to the manager to kick off the meeting, in the event of someone being made redundant. But this was no ordinary situation. Gordon was one of the most senior salesmen at UBS, and had been there for twenty-five years. He had formerly been at Philips + Drew, a London brokerage house, and was about to take an emotional farewell. UBS and SBC were merging. He was a casualty.

By way of background, the mega bank from Switzerland had decided to move into the London market in the late 1980s and Philips + Drew was the target. It probably could have been anyone; it was simply important to establish a platform. For a number of years following, UBS had crossed swords with the other national champions SBC and Crédit Suisse, as well as with other global investment banks such as Goldman Sachs and Morgan Stanley. This was not to ignore the grimfaced competition from the ailing British giants such as Barclays, NatWest, Kleinwort Benson and Hoave Govett.

I could mention many more names but the simple fact is there were too many players in the market. Something had to give…

Hence in December 1997, UBS and SBC agreed terms to merge their businesses globally. But as far as the London investment banking business was concerned, there was a little matter of 5,000 people (2 x 2, 500) all doing the same job. The rule of thumb in such a circumstance is that $1 + 1 = 1.25$, given the duplication of resources across all the business lines.

The other 'given' is that the bank in charge, in this case SBC, tends to make decisions vis-à-vis platform and personnel. At the human level, this means that a meritocratic approach is thrown out of the window. The best people do not necessarily end up in the best seats, but rather those whose faces fit invariably will, and where there is a marginal call, the vote will always run with the dominant party.

Without wishing at this point to pronounce judgement, I simply describe the facts as they were, which accounted for the presence of Gordon opposite me. He had clearly come to make a statement, and had no intention of allowing me to go through the standard script. He removed a piece of paper from his pocket, unfolded it and fixed me with a stare: "Simon, we have known each other long enough [seven years], for you not to patronise me. I am aware what this meeting is about, but if you don't mind, I wish to read a statement." I looked across to my HR colleague, by now looking a little nervous, who indicated that this was within his rights.

So I nodded and Gordon proceeded to deliver a deeply emotional tribute to the bank which was dismissing him; how much he had enjoyed himself in an environment full of great people; how much he owed to the bank as a whole; how he admired his managers, particularly Hector Sants (Head of London Equities); and how sad he would be to leave. There was more, but I was close to losing my own composure and wasn't taking it all in. For me, it was ever more poignant because on entry to UBS P+D in 1990, Gordon had been my mentor. He had taught me about market discipline, client behaviour, codes of conduct, and basically anything which had relevance to or meaning in stock markets. His influence on me had been fundamental to my success in the City.

As he spoke, I reflected on all this, wondering why we had failed to get him a role in the new organisation. Unfortunately, as far as UBS Warburg was concerned, he was too much of a 'loose cannon', too unpredictable, and not a 'face that would fit'. So they declined him a position. The galling thing was that I, as his manager, had to make him redundant. If that wasn't bad enough, it was made far worse by the fact that I knew in my heart that he was better than swathes of rather average 'Warburgians'. In fact, at UBS he ran the 'small client unit', a recently established group which looked after smaller, yet valuable, institutions, and he was extremely good at it. UBS Warburg had nothing like it, and I painstakingly explained the detail of the concept, and how we had implemented it. This was with the explicit aim of injecting the 'SCU' into the SBC business. In the event, they bought the concept all right, but populated it with their own staff, which was nepotistic to say the least, and the direct reason for Gordon's redundancy.

In due course, he finished and I congratulated him on what he had said. I quickly covered the technical ground as I had to, and then wished him well for the future in as kind-hearted a way as I could manage.

It had been my fear that the meeting could get out of control, but I had misunderstood the pride and the honour which was innate in Gordon's character. The problem may have stemmed from my imagination about how I might have behaved in such an unpleasant situation, or perhaps I was just living his anger too vividly.

Either way this episode remains one of the darkest in my City life to date. It characterised the dismemberment of a proud bank, whose people – in London at least – were treated in the shabbiest way imaginable. The cuts (metaphorical and actual) ran deep at the time and the scars remain; some faded, some visible.

But this moment stood out during a period of personal turmoil. The integrity and humility of such a genuine man fanned the flames of hope against the dog-eat-dog mentality in which we waded in the City from time to time.

I will return to the circumstances that forced together two of the world's largest banks at the time but for now let's just say that one of the casualties showed the world of finance how to behave, and believe me, it needed a lesson, and often still does.

I am a firm proponent of the 'what goes around comes around' philosophy. However much time passes, many of us will never forget the events of those few months, and interestingly the Warburg people haven't either. Call it sheepishness, or an apologetic shrug of the shoulders, perhaps. But they were aware deep inside of the corruption of the whole process, and the damage it would do to people's lives. What could they do? Us, or them? It was brutally simple, and it should be remembered that redundancy was always accompanied by a pay-off, so there were compensations. This was deceptive, however. The efforts required to take a brokerage firm to the top are generated by huge team effort. The bringing together of egos, excellence and eccentricity – qualities overflowing in the City of London – develop a powerful momentum which can be unstoppable if harnessed correctly. Talk to people who took James Capel to its pre-eminent position in broking during the '80s, who will also tell you that it was one of the nicest places to work to boot. When you lose that, it hurts.

Make no mistake, the former Head of Sales at UBS (me) who pitched up at SBC Warburg was full of vitriol and unhappiness. I genuinely resented what had happened. I hated the sycophancy and the half-truths that accompany financial services mergers in particular.

All the management-speak gets churned out, but no-one says what they really think. People pussy-foot around the difficult issues simply because they are scared to voice their thoughts for fear it will compromise their prospects. For one thing the SBC Warburg sales force was not a patch on the UBS team. And that is not just me talking, the client base was unanimous, but remember the rules of any merger – the firm taking over keeps the lion's share of the personnel. Paddy Fitzpatrick, the mild-mannered Head of UK Sales with SBC Warburg, was a reluctant executioner, but he had his orders, and I was duly given my list of victims for the axe.

James Tregear, Head of Pan-European Sales, was a wild-eyed and unconventional figure. Mind you, he wasn't the only one, and the rather more staid UBS figures soon found that a Warburg offsite contained rather more bonding than was normally expected. It was all part of the reality, which was that we at UBS were definitely outsiders.

Petty acts of humiliation were rife. I had an excellent assistant at UBS named Susie Pugson. She kept morale up during the difficult times and was a huge support to me personally. Yet when I attempted to bring her with me to SBC the idea was firmly blocked. "We have plenty of assistants here, and we cannot justify more," I was informed. Well, as good as Susie was, I couldn't fight that battle as well. Redundancy was a great financial option for her, but the decision itself was so unnecessary. Even more so when I found out that my new assistant was romantically involved with a member of the sales team, but on the quiet. The sound of stifled chuckling could be heard around every corner.

Unsurprisingly I fell into Goldman Sachs' offices for an interview with more enthusiasm than I should have had. My heart couldn't possibly be in it – I was well aware of the cultural differences between Goldmans and the rest of the market.

It was an environment which was aggressive, very corporate, individualistic and single-minded. Did it promise success? And how! But it was not for me – despite this I went through the process, and the exotically named Huit Pot, Head of Equities, had his claws into me. He sounds like some character out of the Vietnam War, but was in fact Dutch. He was a Goldman partner, was very convincing and keen to have me. His sidekick Robert Markwick conducted the charm offensive, very effectively too (for a Cambridge man); I was nearly there, a trip to New York and Goldman Headquarters being the only outstanding issue.

However, a long weekend ski-ing in the French resort of Courchevel interrupted the flow. My wife and I linked up with Mark and Sarah Rutherford for a couple of days on the slopes and some late nights on the town.

As my former Head of Sales at UBS, Mark was someone with whom I shared many business thoughts and ideas. In many ways he had given me my big break at UBS by making me a team leader, a first step to senior management. My next break came with his departure to Deutsche Bank along with John Smith, the UBS Head of Research. Despite a short-term hiatus, that event led to my appointment as Head of Sales.

But the way I found out about Mark's resignation was truly bizarre, and could only have happened in the City. I was sitting at my desk one morning and Suzanne called to speak to me. After some small talk she suddenly ventured: "So what about Mark's news, then?"

I frowned and asked: "What news?"

"Well he has resigned, hasn't he?"

I looked around and saw an empty chair, but his jacket was still draped over the back of it.

"Well I saw him this morning and his jacket's there. How do you know all this anyway?"

It transpired that Suzanne had bumped into Sarah Rutherford that morning, who had assumed that everyone at work would know about Mark's decision.

But I was unconvinced and Suzanne put the phone down, only to redial shortly afterwards: "Oh, there was another guy, called John, Head of Research or something …"

Oh my God, John Smith.

By now I was feeling physically sick. It surely wasn't possible. The two bosses of the business resigning simultaneously.

At that very moment, locked away in the bowels of UBS, John and Mark were indeed trying to persuade Hector Sants to accept their resignation – no easy job. Hector apparently spent seven hours trying to talk them out of it, before admitting defeat.

They had been bought by the Germans from the Swiss, and their departure plunged UBS into turmoil, well for a while anyway. 'The graveyard is full of indispensable men'; never a truer word.

For years after that we laughed at the fact that it had been my wife in a casual moment who had given me the news of the double departure. However, unbeknown to me, that weekend in Courchevel, the Head of Sales and Head of Research at Deutsche Bank were at it again, this time planning an exit to Donaldson, Lufkin and Jenrette (DLJ), the US investment bank, known primarily for its research.

As Mark quizzed me on my serial unhappiness at UBS, the Alpine beer was slipping easily down my throat, and my tongue was loosening.

"Would you ever leave?" he asked politely.

"Would I?" came the splutter. "I am nearly out, as it happens. "

He raised his eyebrows. "Where?" He almost choked on his own beer as the words 'Goldman Sachs' tumbled unbidden out of my mouth. I was mildly irritated that I had shown my hand so readily to him, a feeling that was somewhat alleviated when he revealed his own plans.

Hector Sants would lead the new DLJ International Equities divisions, and I could be one of the first joiners. A blue sky. A dream. A start-up. A risk. Perhaps it was wishful thinking on my part. It was all of these things. But, as beer turned to wine then spirits, Mark persuaded me to go to the United States and have a look.

I weighed up the arguments and concluded there was nothing to lose. Mark had described this caring, sharing, homely bank, where the Head of Equities looked like JR Ewing from *Dallas*, and the chairman had played rugby in South Africa, but had settled in the United States. DLJ was apparently called the House that Research Built. Rumour was that when you joined senior managers called your wife to congratulate her.

Time to wake up, Halliday, from this fairy tale, which hardly sounded like an investment bank on hard-nosed Wall Street. Still I caught the plane, with a limp excuse to Warburgs that I had 'flu'.

I was extremely nervous of being recognised en route, and sure enough at

JFK airport I was hailed by a familiar voice, which belonged to someone from Wimbledon. In no time my wife was hearing gossip at the school gates, something which should have been a closely guarded secret.

Amazingly DLJ was exactly as described: pure quality and full of great people. I was whizzed through all the departments in a hectic, non-stop day, punctuated only by a steak lunch with the Head of Sales. He and Mark were in full selling mode, at least until Mark spilled his glass of wine all over the table, an accident which somewhat interrupted the flow. I was relieved it hadn't been me.

Sometimes in life things are meant to be, and I knew that I was about to pitch myself into the unknown. But the feeling of enthusiasm in this place was tangible. After UBS and Goldmans, I was intoxicated with the atmosphere, the ambience and resolved to join.

That night we went for dinner, accompanied by another UBS colleague, Rob McCreery, who was based in New York, and who was also considering joining DLJ.

The wine flowed as we reflected on the day, and possible momentous decisions. Mark Rutherford has a prodigious ability to produce winning arguments, and that evening he was in his element. He weighed up pros and cons, knocked back the doubts, stopped to place special emphasis on a particular point –it was a veritable master class in persuasion, although nothing that hundreds of people in the City hadn't experienced themselves for so many years when dealing with him.

There was a pause, most probably caused by exhaustion. It had been a long day, and alcohol plus fatigue were taking their toll.

I looked at them both, took a deep breath and stuck my hand out: "I'm in," I said. Mark stood up with a beam on his face and wrung my hand. Nothing more needed to be said.

Rob McCreery looked incredulous. "You can't just do that. "

"I just did, " I retorted. We had not discussed money, or my role, or holidays, or anything. I just knew I wanted in.

Some months later Rob was also at DLJ. He confessed to me that he was very affected by that evening, by the fact that I had felt so able to commit unconditionally. To this day, I don't quite know why I felt so confident about that decision. But when I returned to England the easiest thing was to walk in and resign from SBC Warburg.

"You idiot," they said. "We are going to be the best. Why leave?"

But I was already looking straight through them. I checked out good and proper. Let the adventure begin. Let's see what we could build.

The following two years represented the most rapid build-out of an investment bank that the City has ever seen.

We started life above the Marks and Spencer food hall on Broadgate. Well at least lunch was on hand. And we were soon addicted to 'Percy Pig' sweets. It was the disaster recovery centre for DLJ's US business, but was adequate for our purposes.

We interviewed morning, noon and night, cajoling, coaxing, persuading, reassuring, eulogising… you name it, we did it. There was a motto we adopted throughout this period 'Don't hire arseholes'. Candidates, we decided, had to buy the dream, feel the pulse that we could feel. We were proud to say that people were at DLJ because they wanted to be, not because they had to, it was fundamental. Yes we would pay people well, but it was the purity of the offering and a break from the traditional model that we were selling.

When we were thirty-strong the chairman came over to meet us. He was called John Chalsty and had played rugby in his native South Africa for the University of Witwatersrand and Transvaal Under 19s. His pep talk was inspirational.

Slowly but surely we built up a team of people whose quality was undisputed. It was a huge tribute to the firm and its culture that it could attract such talent. And we had such a laugh along the way. I remember being so excited about our first proper piece of research that our drinks analyst had published. In the first six months we only had a Drinks and Transport team. For many weeks the sole topic of conversation ranged from Allied Domecq to British Airways. It was enough to drive anyone to drink.

So when I strode into the smart new offices in Broad Street to examine our virgin effort, I was more than disappointed to find an empty desk. No package of documents. Nothing. The analyst, Ian Shackleton, was fuming and somehow we felt cheated. The post room denied all knowledge of any delivery. There was no option but to telephone the printers. Oh yes, it was all done and prepared for transport to our offices (and our clients). The truck company was the next on my hit list. Oh yes sir, we took six boxes to our offices. Well where were they then? In security. Of course. We had forgotten to instruct anyone to collect research and get it distributed. The simplest of things and we had overlooked it. Well, humble beginnings for sure, but we never made that mistake again.

But these were little things – in reality we were building a great business. All areas were growing, clients were beginning to notice us and what we could achieve, the dream was turning into a reality.

DLJ was fifty per cent owned by AXA, the giant French insurance company, so there was constant speculation about this stake and AXA's ultimate and underlying intentions. Conventional wisdom suggested that because of our Chief Executive's presence on AXA's main board, we could control our own destiny. It was a question often asked during the interview process. However vehemently we put forward the argument for self-determination, it was a question that was left hanging in the air. It was as if we were crossing our fingers and hoping it was true.

Meanwhile the year was 2000 and the market was booming. DLJ was almost break-even in year two, a quite remarkable achievement. Somehow we were too busy to think about our own existence, or indeed our future. Our proposition to service the client base was working, all research teams were producing innovative analysis and our clients were paying. It was almost too good to be true.

The first time clouds appeared on the horizon was in the latter part of 2000. We were celebrating our second year when a major strategy seminar was called in London.

Despite our rapid expansion, we were still too small to play with the big boys in the market. Did DLJ have the stomach to lay down further investment? More importantly did AXA, our fifty per cent stakeholder, feel that it could support such an expansion?

When people joined the firm they always asked what could happen if AXA decided to sell its stake. We had fine-tuned our response to a tee: namely that AXA had promised DLJ that it would do nothing without mutual agreement. Thus, the argument went, we were safe because DLJ was ambitious and hungry to grow. Our destiny was in our own hands. This explanation would allay any worries, and in all honesty nobody gave it too much thought.

It was summer 2000 when the dream world was turned upside down. I had been on holiday and, rather unusually, Mark Rutherford had suggested a catch-up dinner the night before my return to work. After a few polite questions about my holiday, Mark came to the point. AXA had, after all, decided that it wanted

Sophie and Alexander in cheeky mode.

My two favourite people.

Happy times.

Mother and Father in festive spirit.
Always supportive, especially at away matches.

Unaware that a young Oxford Student was about to step into the big time from nowhere.

The offload – standard practice, though in today's game almost extinct.

Spot the cheeky face – Moor Park Prep school.

St Benets Hall 7 a side team – we got to the Oxford Colleges Final remarkably with only 60 students in the whole college!

A rather bolchy 22 year old, on the cusp of the England team.

Oxford Univ v Australia – plus 3 Ella Brothers, what an experience. We lost, just.

Grand Slam 1991 celebration – should have been a year earlier, but all the sweeter for that!

End of an Era, my last England game. This squad won back to back grand slams, never to be done again?

Three Marathons for CRY, a fused ankle no obstacle!

Ireland 1992, one for the i-spy book, a Halliday try!

I faced Malcolm Marshall and Joel Garner but Courtney Walsh was probably the best of the lot. Jonathan Webbs' cricket was precise, a little like his rugby.

Sophie and Alexander meeting Nelson Mandela – once in a lifetime opportunity.

Who could have imagined we would meet the great man two days after visiting his prison cell.

to sell out and had come to an agreement with the DLJ board. I was still relaxed because the conventional wisdom was clear: we could only do a deal which would suit us, perhaps a commercial bank with investment banking ambitions, of which there were plenty.

I could scarcely believe my ears when I learned the name of our buyer – Crédit Suisse First Boston, the Swiss-American giant. They had offered $12 billion in cash and the offer had been accepted. It was a done deal. There was no way out.

For a while I felt physically sick – this was no merger, we would be chewed up and most likely spat out, certainly in London. I just couldn't understand it, we had been sold down the river and I experienced a profound sense of anger. All the hard work of the last two years had been for nothing. All those promises to our employees, all the reassurance that our future was safe, were now just so many empty words.

Worse still, over the previous two years we had interviewed scores of Crédit Suisse people, but we hadn't liked their attitude, the culture by which they lived, or the way they did their business. They were not team players, they were out for themselves. It was a dog-eat-dog mentality. It was alien to our philosophy at DLJ, and now this was to be our future.

As I waited for the formal announcement my anger turned to despair. I was overwhelmed with a feeling that I had let people down. They had trusted us and we had failed to deliver. They were dark and painful days.

Wall Street went berserk when the announcement hit the wires. This was the largest cash takeover in the history of investment banking, and the DLJ stock price rocketed, making multi-millionaires of a number of DLJ executives. In the US there was a sense of disbelief. Joe Roby, the Chief Executive, was booed and pelted with paper as he walked across the trading floor. I would have reserved my best throw for this turncoat. In hindsight, of course, Mr Roby had pulled off a masterstroke. The third quarter of 2000 (Q3 2000) was probably the all-time peak of any Bull Market anytime in financial history. From the Swiss point of view (in hindsight) this was the most value-destructive deal done in the history of the financial services industry.

CHAPTER 16

Dismemberment (2000)

Day one of the deal set the tone in a depressing and inevitable fashion.

I took a call from one of my friendliest clients, Alex Popplewell at Mercury Asset Management. "I thought you may wish to know what was said to the sales team of CSFB at their morning meeting." I waited with grim expectation of the corporate spin they would employ.

Alex's words still shook me. I was shocked to hear how forthright Martin Newsome, the Head of Equities, had been. In essence he indicated that there was no intention to expand the current numbers – or put another way, all DLJ personnel were destined for the scrap-heap. We all knew that CSFB had done the deal for the US piece of the business, but to be so extreme seemed to be reckless and even unnecessarily ruthless.

Hector Sants called our first management meeting. He, of course, had known all of this, well in advance. He had prepared the script well, and he put out a very constructive message in which he stressed that the combined firm would represent the best of both sets of personnel.

I snorted openly with derision and Hector turned angry eyes on me. First impressions often dictated subsequent behaviour – he was keen to stamp on gratuitous dissidence. But when I recounted my story his eyes widened and attitudes in the room hardened visibly. Hector did his best to discount such comments, but suspicions had been aroused.

The situation went from bad to worse; essentially the firm put up a corporate two fingers to CSFB and everything represented by the company, when their senior management announced that they would arrive to conduct interviews there was zero cooperation. We were there because we wanted to be, not because we had to be. Offers were rolling in from competitor banks, who could see a real opportunity to hire people previously thought unapproachable.

It has to be remembered that the Bull Market was still alive and well. Banks were making record profits and there was consequently plenty of cash to spend. Expansion was the watchword.

As the growling continued between both sides it was decided that the big guns from the US would be sent over.

It is a fact universally acknowledged that senior management will only react after a crisis has erupted. Perhaps it is easier to see from a little further down the organisation, whatever the reasons, it has always amazed me that when a logical reaction to events is greeted with incredulity by those in control, had Crédit Suisse stopped to think, they would have realised that from day one they had to do a supreme selling job. Perhaps they didn't care, but how about this statistic? When CSFB acquired DLJ their stock price was 120 Swiss Francs; in the year following it plunged to twenty SFr, and some five years later was trading at forty SFr. At the height of the opprobrium following the takeover, the combined group traded in market capitalisation terms at less than the value of CSFB on its own before the bid. Quite clearly the market took a view of the whole thing.

Anyway, it was not until day twenty that we heard that a genuine big-hitter was flying in from New York.

Brady Dougan was the Global Head of Equities at CSFB and he was clearly destined for great things – witness his subsequent position as Chief Executive of the investment bank.

None of us had ever heard of him, but he was tasked with persuading senior DLJ staff that there was genuine merit in working at Crédit Suisse. It had obviously been made clear to him that, as things stood, the chances of this happening were zero.

My time came to see him, on a one-to-one basis. He seemed pleasant enough, but strangely lightweight. I had been expecting passion and persuasion, but got neither. His opening gambit was to ask me about rugby – fair enough, and a safe topic. Before I had got going, he then told me he knew nothing about the sport, but did I know that CSFB sponsored the Hong Kong Sevens? As it happened, I didn't know, but found this a strange direction for the conversation to take. He was on a busy schedule and we were surely wasting time.

Not that I had a bad opinion about the premier rugby sevens' tournament in the world. Some of the great sevens' games had taken place there over the years, usually between Fiji and the New Zealand All Blacks. In those days England had never competed, the only Anglo-Saxon representation generally coming from the odd invitation team, over there chiefly for a good time. The most notable statistic I ever heard was that the average beer consumption per person per day was fifteen pints. I think that paints the picture.

I soon found out why Brady Dougan continued to mention this meaningless sponsorship event. With an innocent face he posed his killer question: "Ever thought of working in Hong Kong?" Well I suppose I could see it from his point of view, a top executive making an obvious link and boxing off the problem, which was what they should do with me.

I wanted to throw him the most withering look imaginable, but did not quite have the courage. I patiently described that my wife was a Fulham GP and my children were ensconced in London schools. Besides, all my clients' relationships were in London.

His neat solution having been rebuffed, Brady seemed to lose interest. So did I. I was somewhat incredulous that he hadn't bothered to ask my bosses how he should approach me, nor how I might respond.

Yet, this was somehow so predictable of the arrogant Crédit Suisse attitude towards us. Meetings such as this continued to set the tone, and we were coming to the grim realisation that our new employers were the antithesis of the culture that had been built within the walls of Donaldson, Lufkin and Jenrette.

And we kept asking why we had been sold down the river to such a buyer. The despair and upset was hard to overstate. The momentum of our development had appeared to be unstoppable. The dream of changing the traditional make-up of an investment bank was now shattered. How were we to help safeguard the future of all these people? It wasn't that we hadn't made some mistakes in our hiring, but by and large we had constructed a group of people who all believed in each other. We were a genuine team, pulling together, interdependent and selfless.

To begin with we tried to keep everyone together. Perhaps we could all be transported as a huge team to a DLJ-like business. The inquiries we were fielding seemed promising at first – big commercial banks with no investment banking arm – perhaps they would be prepared to buy us lock, stock and barrel.

But we couldn't control such a situation. In the end cracks appeared in all these ideas – the pipedreams of all time.

It was over, and rather like a group of escaping prisoners, we were splitting in different directions. But of course that was the only solution. The next step was about self-presentation, a new job, securing the future. We all had to make individual decisions.

Mark Rutherford and I spent hours together, debating the options. We also spent many hours in Crédit Suisse, showering plaudits on our sales colleagues. It was vital that they received good offers from Crédit Suisse. Then they had a benchmark on which to judge competing offers from elsewhere. For those employees who would definitely not be taken on, our job was different. How to represent them to the broad market, push their case to head-hunters or competition banks and ensure that they had somewhere to move on to.

There were two extremes of this that spring to mind. We had a junior technology salesperson who had potential, but was very green. But in 2000 the tech world had gone crazy and all tech analysts/salespeople were in demand. I took a call from UBS, my old house, who were inquiring as to who was available. I waxed lyrical about our young recruit (not to be named to spare his blushes) at the same time warning that CSFB were going to offer the salesperson a large financial package. If UBS wanted to sign them up they had to hurry and pay up. Which is exactly what happened, and one member of the DLJ team slipped off to UBS on a ridiculous pay packet, some four times what he had been earning at DLJ. It was the least we could do.

At the other end of the spectrum, and during the latter stages of the process, we were handing out advice to Crédit Suisse Sales Management on certain potential hirings. A number of our top sales personnel had declined to go to CSFB, hardly surprising, and they were getting desperate. New York had mandated them to bring some DLJ people on board, or it would look extremely embarrassing. After all the essence of an investment bank is its intellectual assets, in other words, its staff. There is little point in paying out $12 billion if no one moves across.

One day we took a call asking for our final opinion on one individual. We advised against the person being hired, partly due to the fact that the individual in question had caused us a lot of trouble, but also partly because we just did not feel like sponsoring this particular person. However, the person's luck was in – there were so few DLJ people remaining who were available that Crédit Suisse simply had to hire a senior figure, so they took the person on, at an outrageous salary. We just shook our heads in disbelief.

As the days passed people's destiny became clearer. For some the DLJ decision had been a final one and there was no wish to consider careers elsewhere. James Graham was one such, a sales trader from Morgan Stanley who had real *nous* and was highly respected in the market. He had a history of heart problems, which also meant he had the whole situation in perspective. Mind you he took an extreme option and emigrated to New Zealand.

As for myself I was knee-deep in consultation with CSFB as well as with other houses, including Lehman Brothers, an alternative which was becoming ever more interesting.

By now CSFB had decided that they wished to hire me, although not in Pan-Europe. Despite the welcoming smiles, the incumbent sales management had no intention of letting me loose on their patch. Senior CSFB names such as Richard Mulder, James Flaherty and Ian Marsh in fact were actively resistant.

The globalisation of equity markets was in full flow at this time, and indeed one of our major calling cards had been the excellence of our US product, so we were all armed with this, as well as developing the European effort. So when CSFB proposed that I set up a global desk, it did not sound like the worst of ideas. In any case, it put off, for a few more days, the fateful day of decision, particularly when they suggested that I fly to New York.

Terrified that they might actually persuade me to take them up on their offer, I declined for some spurious reason, but agreed to a video-conference call with their Head of Equities Sales and Head of Research, Tony Engel and Al Jackson respectively. Thus the scene was set for the final act of the shambolic affair.

To begin with I sat in a darkened room at the top of Cabot Square, Crédit Suisse's main building, staring at a blank screen. Then I spotted someone whom I thought was the IT guy. He was a really scruffy individual, but when he peered into the screen and called my name I realised it wasn't. He didn't introduce himself, so I took a punt. "Is that Tony?" I ventured. He recoiled in near horror at the suggestion. OK, I thought, it's Al. He looked absolutely shattered, and for good reason – he had been interviewing most of DLJ Research, or should I say, trying to persuade them to join CSFB, our US research ability was way north of Crédit Suisse and would definitely add to the Crédit Suisse franchise. He started ranting at me, as if it were my fault that the DLJ people were refusing to sign. I was beginning to feel uncomfortable. Then in came Tony and the real conversation got going.

Al Jackson kicked off: "So why do you think a global role at CSFB will work?"

"Well I don't necessarily, " I responded with incredulity. And, biting my tongue, I continued: "I think I am here so that you can persuade me that there is such an opportunity. "

There was a momentary silence, which no-one seemed inclined to break. Then Tony Engel attempted to pick up the pieces, it was too late. My reluctance had turned to disdain. A few days later I informed Hector Sants of my decision to decline the CSFB option. My thoughts had turned to Lehman Brothers. The DLJ dream was over.

Many months, and even years, on, I am constantly asked about DLJ and its awesome reputation. "Was it really as great a place to work as people say it was?"

I can say with certainty that there has never been an investment bank like it, and in all probability never will be again. It was like a family, people were drawn to the culture, it had the lowest staff turnover on the street. DLJ staff were team players and immensely loyal, yet remained true professionals. After all, they were ranked No6 on Wall Street overall, when measured on a per capita basis probably top.

Despite finding great homes to go to, we all felt the pain of disappearing off the map after only two years. We had achieved a two per cent market share in that time and break-even status. Not bad for a bank that was constantly being confused with a worldwide courier company.

Just two years on hardly any of the DLJ personnel remained. They had either retired, refused to join, or had smiled their way into a massive redundancy package then headed for the exit at the first opportunity.

CHAPTER 17

Esher – A Surrey Idyll

In 1983, when I was about to hit the top with England rugby, I first encountered Esher – but not the rugby club. This well-to-do town, tucked between Hampton Court and Walton-on-Thames, was synonymous with discreet wealth and was classic commuter belt. There also happened to be a rather useful cricket club, stacked full with ex-public schoolboys. Two of my fellow lodgers in London, Andrew Bernard (also a Downside contemporary) and Tim Elliott were committed team members already. So it was logical that I should join up and that year we won the Surrey championship. I had particularly happy memories of that season, and many famous evenings were spent in the Albert Pub, and twenty years later, this is still a sporting ale-house, frequented by cricketers and many sports players alike.

But on the rugby field, Esher in the '80s suffered from the disease called 'divine right' – in other words, they thought that a proud history was enough to guarantee them a position as part of rugby's élite. But by the early '90s, the club was languishing in London League Two, a far cry from the days when clubs such as Harlequins and Bristol were on their fixture list.

Most of their players were used to training once a week after a long City lunch, then working off the week's excesses on Saturday afternoon. Fine, if you are playing Old Wimbledonians or KCS Old Boys but hopeless for anything more.

It was against this backdrop that in late 1992 I took a call from Ross Howard, club stalwart and future president. I had toured with him to California in 1983 with Lloyds Insurance, and we knew each other well. He politely inquired how I was going to fill my empty calendar, now that I had retired from first class rugby.

The thought had crossed my mind too: back-to-back Grand Slams, a World Cup final and fifteen years of first class rugby. Do you just walk away? How can you turn off a switch that has been permanently on for so long? While looking forward to spending more time with my family, and Suzanne was expecting our second child that October, could my Saturday afternoons just disappear into a haze of domestic and retail experiences?

Ross had decided to drag Esher into the new rugby world of achievement, commitment and success – words not associated with this club. I was intrigued, and saw little downside to deter me from accepting a role as the Esher coach. It had originally been mapped out for Peter Winterbottom, but he had decided not to retire – so they ended up with me!

It was then that I met the team manager, a character called John Inverdale – now of course a household name. I could see that he was incredibly motivated to take Esher to the next level and as I listened to him speak, I also realised that he had very special talents – so fluent and clear on what qualities the club needed to develop in order to succeed. He is still there twenty-one years on, engendering the same enthusiasm, despite being at the centre of much of BBC's sports broadcasting. The reason? He cared, and still cares, deeply for the club, he was frustrated that so much potential was being wasted.

I arrived at the club one dark, dank evening to be introduced to the players, only one of whom I knew at all. His name was Howard English, whom I had met socially a number of times. He also worked in the City – but then so did many of the squad. It was a frightening experience, and I felt like a new boy going away to school for the first time and meeting new classmates. I rustled up as stirring an opening speech as I could, promising a new era and urging commitment, loyalty and all those great qualities that I expected from rugby players. At the finish, I paused, uncertain what should happen next. Then a spontaneous round of applause broke out and I felt that perhaps we were already bonding.

The reality was starkly different. Ross Howard now describes the look on my face when I saw the first match against Charlton Park, a Kent Club neighbouring Blackheath. One pit next to another would be a good description! My new team gamely tried to show its new coach what was in the locker – it was a sobering afternoon all right. Silk purses and sows ears sprang to mind, but I resolved to give it my best shot regardless. I quickly identified that we were half a dozen players short if we were serious about promotion the next year. So when we finished mid-table, I went scouting.

The secret to the next few years' success lay in persuading one of the rugby's great entrepreneurs to sign up to the new Esher, a certain toothy Scot by the name of Hugh McHardy. It is only the game of rugby that can spawn such a character – he played for Harlequins and Scotland B in his prime, so was no mean player. I then toured California with him in 1983 – it was there that he taught me to do a 'swerve', as I certainly couldn't sidestep, in the unlikely surroundings of the vineyards of Napa Valley. Despite our intention to go wine tasting, I had taken my training kit – remember it was 1983, and I was taking things seriously. Well for half an hour anyway – take a kilted Jock into a California wine lake and you are likely to drown. Somehow we got back to San Francisco in one piece!

Hugh then became a very successful coach of Rosslyn Park in Division One, before I tempted him to play (into his forties) for this lazy giant of a Surrey club. He was inspirational, even if no one could underst and a word he said – Scottish is vaguely unintelligible anyway, more so when all your front teeth are missing.

Together with a number of other first-class rugby imports, we suddenly had a team. Gradually, I managed to persuade the majority of the club that twice-a-week training was an acceptable sacrifice for weekend success. Turning up on time for the away match bus was another triumph for the team. For home games, we would meet for lunch. On the pitch, I constructed two or three strike moves for our attack ball, and we had basic rules for kicking. No rocket science, but enough to craft a win. And win we did, achieving a club treble of the league, the Surrey Cup and the junior team of the year in 1994-5.

What a great time we all had, and people started to dream. Andy Cooke, the team captain, suggested that I should be England Coach – steady on! In truth, a lot of committed people had turned Esher into a side with which to be reckoned.

As anyone with a junior club will know, such achievements are terrifically exciting. And they usually manifest themselves in a significant amount more alcohol being consumed. Esher was no different, and numerous excuses were found for parties and general celebrations.

It was not just Hugh McHardy who was the catalyst for such a turnaround in the club's fortune. Julian Davis, the roly-poly London Welsh prop, added huge experience to the front row as well as much needed ballast. Pete Vaughan, ex-Blackheath No8, was a steadying influence, apart from being a Mel Gibson look-a-like (well, according to my wife!). At No10, the siege-gun boot of ex-Harlequin Ray Dudman was an invaluable weapon at this level. He could kick the ball comfortably from one end of the pitch to the other, without wind assistance. Ray was totally unflappable, accepting anything and everything that was thrown at him and dealing with them in the same unflappable way. His demeanour verged on the monastic, probably just as well given the nature of the rest of the team.

These senior figures lit the touch paper for Esher's eventual progress into the Second Division. Once the momentum starts to develop the circle becomes virtuous, and everyone connected at Esher is rightfully proud of its achievement.

As a vice president now, I always make it to the club annual dinner. Apart from Inverdale's capacity to attract formidable speakers year after year (Jeffrey Archer, Andy Irvine, Max Boyce, Martin Bayfield) – I had to do it twice (at late notice I may add), it is an opportunity to be among friends who have enjoyed great times together. To be at the heart and soul of an amateur club is to know the reality of rugby, and to recognise the traditional ethos of the game, and enjoy the fact that it has endured into the twenty-first century. Relationships with players and supporters alike can be even closer than those formed at the highest level. The respect and friendship is so unconditional, and there are no agendas. Of course, let people not think that junior clubs cannot produce stars. Wade Dooley and Preston Grasshoppers spring to mind (incidentally the England lock was discovered by Dick Greenwood).

I first saw Dominic Chapman, a winger, playing for Esher colts, mainly because he wanted to be with his mates, not because he wasn't good enough for the XV. He was the fastest thing I had ever seen on a rugby pitch, and that includes David Trick and Rory Underwood. He also had phenomenal balance as a runner and could sidestep off both feet. Quite a talent.

I kept him at Esher for a season but had already mentioned him to Harlequins as well as the England U19 selectors. Sure enough, in no time he was beating a fast track to national honours. He scored a hat trick on debut for the Harlequins away at Orrell, all from long range. What a debut! And I found to my amazement that Tom Hudson, my old fitness (fanatic) coach from Bath, was Director of Sports at Surrey University. He regaled me with promises that he would turn Dominic into an Olympic athlete, let alone an international rugby player. Tom always thought big, but then he always delivered. The season was 1995/6, and professionalism was upon us. Dominic was being paid piecemeal, match by match, and being a modest man this was sufficient, until I inadvertently stepped in. I was at a stag night attended by John Kingston, the Richmond coach. He declared that he was hunting for wingers, and I drunkenly told him that the Harlequin twenty-year old would play for England and was an obvious target. What then happened was mind-blowing: Kingston offered Chapman a contract, which he of course accepted. Who wouldn't, given his precarious financial position at Harlequins, but Dick Best did not see it that way. He promptly stripped his young protégé of all Harlequin kit, and demanded the club car back immediately, at the risk of police being informed that it had been stolen. No doubt the story has been embellished, but take it from me that Jeff Alexander, Harlequins, England B and émigré to Esher, had to exit the Stoop without any shoes on his feet.

However, the underlying strength of this fine club manifested itself most obviously from the way in which it reacted to its biggest challenge over its proud history. Put simply. Howard English, the Esher centre three-quarter, collapsed and died on Thursday 14th October 1994 on the training pitch, turning the club's world upside down.

It was a still autumn evening, and for once I had a full turn-out of the Esher squad. This was in no small way due to my anger at the pathetic attendance of the previous week. Of course, it had been raining, so very few people made the effort – not special to Esher I guess, but irritating nevertheless. We were trying to make an impression in the league and the cup which was hardly going to happen if we didn't train. I really laid into them utilising my finest invective. All known adjectives were employed as I explained to them that if I was out in the rain so would they be.

Eventually I had exhausted my vocabulary and suggested that we might train quite energetically that evening.

Howard was the one person I genuinely knew at the Esher club. He was a merchant banker at Morgan Grenfell, married to Stephanie and had three young children: Sebastian, Sabrina and Titus. The whole family was well known to me, mainly through my wife Suzanne. He loved his rugby and was a fine player. But it was strictly a pastime for him – had he taken it seriously, he could easily have played senior rugby. As a fellow centre, I could see his comfort on the ball, his confidence and his enthusiasm in taking on the opposition. All these things are critical in good centre play.

As ever, that night, he took up my challenge and delivered a great performance in the 'semi-contact' game I had constructed. Some time before the end, though, he approached me asking for a time out, claiming fatigue. I thought nothing more of it, and told him to go to the touch line for a rest, while I turned away to continue with the tactical piece of the training session; it was a few minutes later that our winger ran over, screaming at me to come and see to Howard.

He had collapsed and was unconscious on the ground, clearly in a bad way. One of our forwards was a traffic policeman, and placed him in the recovery position. But on taking his pulse, he became very concerned that it was so weak. He started to give mouth-to-mouth resuscitation, and the realisation dawned on the team that Howard was critically ill.

The ambulance had already been called, and as we waited I took the mobile phone and called home, in order to get the telephone number of his wife, Stephanie.

By the time I called her, the ambulance was on the pitch and the paramedics were grimly trying to resuscitate Howard. There was little that I could say other than to follow their instructions, in telling Stephanie to get to the hospital, and make sure that she was accompanied.

That the club then went into shock is an understatement. Events became a blur, and the atmosphere was surreal, with people wandering around aimlessly, in a daze. Only minutes before it had been just like any other Thursday, now someone had died during a rugby training session.

When I look back, there is always a sense of wondering if such a tragedy could have been averted, and I suppose that is a natural reaction.

The diagnosis was that Howard had suffered a massive heart attack. So the chances of him surviving this had been minimal, but it does not prevent you from questioning why this should happen to a man of thirty-one, apparently fit, and with a very young family. And, of course, there is no answer.

Esher reacted as only a rugby club can. We dedicated our season to Howard and his family, and set about organising a dinner to celebrate his life and raise money for his children's trust fund.

It was tough in the early days, as everyone felt the loss so keenly. This was nothing compared to the pain being felt by his family. But as the weeks went by, the club seemed to develop a real sense of purpose. We kept on winning, and plans for our dinner started to take shape.

Sure enough, the following April saw the realisation of a number of goals: Esher was on the crest of a league and cup double, and had been named Club of the Month. We had gone twenty-three games without defeat – what a tribute and an amazing response of the club to such adversity.

That month, also, the dinner took place at the Porter Tun Room, in the Chiswell Street Brewery in the City. Together with Ross Howard, the chairman, and John Inverdale, team manager, I had called in every favour I knew from the rugby world at large.

Among the 650 guests – a figure which far exceeded our expectations – were to be found most of the top internationals of the day. Apart from London-based players, a number of Bath and Northampton international players made the trip and Steve Smith, a former England captain and British Lion, travelled down from Manchester as one of the guest speakers. We were also lucky to have Cliff Morgan in attendance, one of the finest rugby players of his generation. That is saying something, given the era in which he played and that he was a Welsh fly-half!

As for the auction, an important part of the evening, we managed to obtain the services of the 'Colonel', aka Nick (NJW) Stewart, a larger-than life entrepreneur, whose boundless enthusiasm allowed us to raise a sum of money beyond our wildest dreams. We were also indebted to a maverick contribution by Mick 'The Munch' Skinner. He grabbed the microphone and offered to cook a prawn meal in the winner's back garden. He also threw in a pair of Victor Ubogu's braces for good measure (without reference to their owner of course). How could people resist? Anyway, Mick wasn't taking no for an answer.

Four pairs of hands went up, and Mick allocated a sliding scale, upwards! £250 went four times to £1000 – and the poor unfortunate soul in the corner found himself landed with it. He happened to be none other than Mike Parsley, a UBS Trader who was on Skinner's table. I absolved him of all liability to pay. But to his eternal credit, he insisted on providing a cheque for £1, 000 – I hope he has had his prawn dinner, because I never did follow it up.

Another great moment of the evening was provided by Will Carling and Rob Andrew, who walked around late in the evening signing their names in return for a fiver into the champagne bucket. God knows how many hundreds of pounds were added to the total!

I made rather a lengthy speech – mainly to thank all the attending celebrities. I possibly went on too long, but people did understand that this kind of evening made it appropriate. I read out a lovely note from Stephanie, Howard's wife, offering her own thanks for the evening and urging us to drink hard, as Howard would have done. We needed no second invitation! Finally, we had decided to award the 'Howard English Memorial Trophy' for that season. It was a wonderful looking cup and we sought out as the recipient a player whose qualities were admired by all, as a team man and loyal Esher player. His name was Steve Matthews, and he played in the second row. His hands were like plates, although he would be the first to accept that his handling in open play was a little variable. At 6ft 6in and with a well-weathered look to him, Steve was the guy you wanted on your side! But he was a gentle giant in a way, and for Esher to do the league and cup double that year, as well as be named the junior team of the year, was a huge record for a man who had contributed as much as he had.

He was a worthy winner of the inaugural 'Howard English Memorial Trophy', and there wasn't a dry eye to be seen among the Esher players as he collected the trophy. To his great relief we did not put him through an acceptance speech.

And so, the evening eventually closed, with a sense that we had all delivered the sort of dinner of which Howard would have approved. Rugby as a game had showed how much it cares about its own. Howard did not die because of a rugby injury, but he was on the rugby field at the time, and he was a member of Esher RFC as well as a good friend – that was enough.

For myself, the second year into my fledging coaching career had been an exceptional period in my life, when unprecedented success was accompanied by unimaginable distress and sadness, not just because of Howard's death, but because the family was known personally to me.

I did not really know many of his friends in the North of England and North Wales, but there were many. It has always been a slightly difficult situation, in that I was the last to see Howard alive. I have always been (and am still) ready to talk about that night, but everyone has the choice of asking, or not. For me, it remains a defining moment of my own life, in that so much of what I had achieved and had held dear appeared rather meaningless in the face of such a tragedy.

The fact that this chapter appears at all is down to the permission of Stephanie and Rupert, her now husband and proud father of her fourth and fifth child, as well as superb stepfather to Sebastian, Sabrina and Titus. I wished to write Howard a tribute, but one which fitted with their view of how it should be pitched.

Even more so because, unbelievably, Howard's son, Sebastian, collapsed and died of a similar heart attack some ten years later, aged fifteen, also on a rugby pitch. The manner of Sebastian's death still leaves me stunned, and brought back many harrowing memories.

All that I can say is that rugby, as a game, will pay tribute in its own humble way. Rugby was a passion for Sebastian, as his headmaster mentioned in the funeral address. It reflected his own qualities – modesty, sharing, consideration and tolerance for others. Teamwork; what greater tribute can there be, and for these characteristics to exist in one so young.

Howard and Sebastian are two people who will always be in my thoughts, but as much as mourning their passing, I prefer to remember their achievements in their all-too-short lives.

Out of such adversity, I was introduced to Cardiac Risk in the Young (CRY) by Rupert and Stephanie, a charity which researches into the reasons behind such sudden deaths. They also provide screening which can identify the symptoms, as well as engage in bereavement counselling. They have made such progress over the years that they have many success stories to tell about young people who have been saved by their actions and awareness raising. Regrettably though, twelve young people a week still die needlessly.

I am a patron of this amazing charity, and proud to be one, as we seek to reduce and eventually eliminate all such terrible occurrences.

CHAPTER 18

Harlequins – Up for Auction, Going, Going, Gone (1997)

When professionalism took hold in the mid '90s, you could see that this was going to be a particular challenge for the multi-coloured Harlequins rugby team.

By now, well retired, I was coaching the Quins backs after the three-year spell (1992-95) spent coaching Esher. But this was short-lived since a full time job and daytime training were hardly compatible. I stood down from the role with great reluctance, not surprisingly, given the emergence of a young Will Greenwood in the centre who was a joy to coach. I went on record as saying that pound for pound he was the most talented midfielder in the country, and that was in 1996.

Unfortunately he did not last very long, departing to Leicester shortly afterwards. It was the first sign that rugby clubs had to change their attitude towards their best players. Will was employed by HSBC in the City. Rather like myself, some years earlier, he was having to rely on the goodwill of his employers to train during the day. You can hardly blame the clubs for jumping at the opportunity to train in daylight after years and years of running around under floodlights, but it wasn't so easy for the players. Will went to Dick Best and explained the problem, seeking some flexibility, but Dick was having none of it, and insisted on full attendance. This just pushed Will into the willing arms of Leicester who needed midfield players and could see Will's potential.

The first I heard of anything was when Dick called me to try to persuade Will not to leave. I couldn't believe that we had allowed such a talented player to slip through our hands, and he became a major component of Leicester's success over the next few years. This was followed shortly afterwards by the club having to pay a significant amount of money to stop Jason Leonard going off to join Saracens. The stakes were rising sharply, and a period of exaggerated excess was just commencing. Quite simply, the clubs and the union did not see it coming, but situations like these were becoming more common.

Every club was embracing the new regime in different ways, while the Rugby Union was still resolutely in denial. Why else would they not have contracted the England players, allowing the clubs to take ownership of players' financial lives?

Quins made Dick Best director of rugby and invited the Beckwith Brothers, who were major names in the property world and responsible for the 'Riverside' chain of sports/leisure clubs, in as investors. At the same time a number of trustees were appointed to look after the 'golden share'. This was a way of protecting the membership from predatory behaviour, i.e a takeover of the club against the members' will, or any action which prevented rugby being played at the Stoop Memorial Ground.

So, shortly after my retirement as coach, I took a call from Colin Herridge, the secretary (and a member of the RFU). He proposed that Peter Winterbottom and I should become trustees, as well known ex-players and in honorary positions only. It seemed harmless enough, even if there were papers to sign and the odd meeting to attend. Little did I know that I was to become embroiled in two major scandals, one of which has never seen the light of day, until now.

Dick Best was at the centre of one of them. Somehow, professionalism had brought the worst out of him; I think that even he would admit that now. His relationship with the players, now as their employer, inevitably plummeted.

He would accuse certain people of not trying, threatening to impact their wages, with obvious consequences for key issues such as mortgage payments.

This maverick behaviour eventually impacted on the long-term health of the club. Life was a series of confrontations, upsets and generally amateurish behaviour. I was taking an increasing number of complaints from the players who were desperate for change, threatening to leave the club if nothing happened. Eventually matters were brought to a head, and at a team meeting the chairman Roger Lester surveyed a vote of no confidence. A show of hands, and Dick's career at Harlequins was effectively over. At the time, it was suggested that this was a personal issue between Dick Best and Will Carling, and that Will was pursuing a vendetta. Certainly, they had long since fallen out. But this move had nothing to do with Will; it was simply fashionable, and expedient, for the media and Will's detractors to suggest it.

I was hopelessly compromised, as a personal friend and colleague of the Harlequins' coach. Knowledge of the squad's intention was a difficult and invidious fact of life. But the events played out and in time Dick bowed out, settling his contract on the steps of the court. None of the players wanted to testify, despite their views. You can understand the choice between keeping your own counsel and refraining from public criticism of your coach, versus the club putting its hand in the pocket to make the problem go away.

Dick went on to be the successful coach of London Irish for a number of years. He is now an agent in rugby's professional game, and an occasional TV pundit. Dick Best may have outlived his usefulness at the Quins, and perhaps familiarity bred contempt, but his contribution to Harlequins, England and the game of rugby in general can hardly be overstated. He was a giant in every sense, and his team talks are still comfortably the best I have heard, bar none!

While all this was going on, a far more sinister development was overtaking the club. It was becoming clear that the overwhelming financial burden of early professionalism was taking its toll. The whole viability of the business model was based on the effective sale of debentures to finance the new east stand. Harlequins took a very amateurish approach to this critical piece of the jigsaw. The marketing initiative was under-funded and amateurish. My former playing colleague Jamie Salmon got involved for a while and was one of a number of people who was eventually shown the door. A similar situation was occurring down the road at Bath as most former players seemed to be finding some sort of employment. After a time the club faced a stark truth: it was running out of money.

The trustees had a series of grim-faced meetings, mainly around the fact that the Beckwith Brothers were unprepared to underwrite the club with the bankers. Instead they were ready to assume a majority holding in the event of the Harlequin club effectively going under. At this stage I started to panic. Apart from the fact that the trustees were mandated through the golden share to ensure that rugby was played at the Stoop Memorial Ground, we would be seen to be selling the club down the proverbial river. I was not ready to be associated with the demise of a household name in rugby circles. Visions of Beckwith leisure developments all over the famous old ground danced around in my head.

Finally it was crunch time. Our backs were up against the wall; we did not even have enough money to pay our caterers. The banks were sympathetic, but unyielding. The unpalatable was about to happen, and a weekend was set for a series of meetings with the Beckwiths to discuss a transfer of the golden share. We had no option.

On the Thursday night, I was at the UBS offices in the city and due to go out for the evening. A great friend and colleague was about to take up a post in South Africa, and we were giving him a good send-off in the bar under the building, the Brasserie Rocque. By mid-evening, I was ready to spill the beans. The unfortunate recipient of the story was a colleague on the corporate side, David Wilson. As I revealed, in somewhat garbled fashion, that the Harlequins was on the cusp of bankruptcy, he suddenly took an interest.

"So, how much money do you actually need?"

"Oh, probably £2m," I muttered dejectedly.

He mused, "I think I might know someone who would be interested. His name is Duncan Savile, a multi-millionaire from Australia. He is a rugby nut and he would jump at an opportunity like this." I gaped at him and laughed sceptically but David was insistent.

"Look," I said, "I am not fooling around here. We are going under in three days, and there is no time for speculation." We had moved all of a sudden into business mode.

"I might be able to contact him; he is in Australia, I'll be back." He returned swiftly to his office, while I staggered on through the emotional send-off for our colleague, Johnny Sutton, a Scot and a true rugby fan. We had often bantered over the years; not only was I half Scottish, but I had played the Scots a grand total of seven times in my career. As we became awash with alcohol, back came David Wilson; he had made contact and Duncan Savile was coming over on the next plane.

I sobered up pretty quickly at this piece of news and the next morning I called Edwin Glasgow, our senior trustee. He took some convincing that this was not a tall story. But finally, he gathered together Roger Looker, the chairman, and Colin Herridge, a fellow trustee and Harlequin. I do not profess to know all the details of the ensuing events, but Savile arrived at Heathrow, was taken to the ground, took one look and shook hands subject to the usual due diligence.

Put simply, the Beckwith Brothers realised the game was up, and sold out to Savile. I am of the opinion that they would have closed down the rugby club over time and turned the whole area into hotels a (leisure centre), corporate development, and no doubt the trustees would have been held liable by the club. As my employers at the time had no idea I was even involved, I knew I was breaching stock exchange rules over 'conflicts of interest' so I heaved a huge sigh of relief that not only a famous rugby club was snatched from the jaws of insolvency, but I was off a potential hook.

Duncan Savile and his right-hand man, Charles Jillings, even came to UBS to meet me in order to get a different perspective on the background to the whole situation. These days I often laugh about the whole episode with David Wilson; funny to think that the future of the Harlequins had hinged on one phone call to the other side of the world.

This spelled the end of my involvement with the Harlequins at all levels. Not because of any falling out, but because the fight for professional survival was well and truly under way. You cannot play around in the face of such a challenge, and I had neither the time, nor frankly, the inclination. As my first serious club, they will always have a place in my heart, especially as I feel at least partly responsible for their continued existence. But as most people will know, Bath rugby was and is in my blood, and that's the way it will stay.

CHAPTER 19

Toothless Lion
(2001)

It was the autumn of 2000 when I was asked to be a selector for the British Lions' Tour of Australia but rather more importantly the same time that my father fell ill. At first we simply heard that he was playing less golf than normal, then that he was short of breath and feeling tired. Well thats allowed at the age of seventy-six and we thought nothing of it. My mother and father came for Christmas that year and it was clear that it was more than that. A persistent cough and unusual tiredness even when surrounded by two grandchildren who would galvanise any grandfather.

Two weeks later, I took a call from my mother who had just accompanied my father to hospital to remove fluid from a lung. She was worried and so were we, as he was admitted for an exploratory operation. Being a Lions' selector didn't feel at all special and I used spare time to go down and visit. My mother had referred to his strong emotions all of a sudden and I couldn't work it out. As I walked through the wards, surrounded by sick people, I wanted there to be more hope and more optimism but I felt very uneasy.

My father was very wobbly, constantly asking about my mother as I tried to give him a pep talk about getting through his op. No one writes the script on how to talk to one's father when you are petrified that he may be terminally ill. He seemed slow to react and almost as if he had made his mind up that things were bad. The nurses were on hand to serve up a lunch to question the very word, and my nose wrinkled so I couldn't blame him for turning it down. But somehow I knew it wasn't that… I left the ward with a heavy heart, though blagued to my mother later that he had been in good spirits.

Moving on to Bath to view Lions' possibles in the Bath Munster match was a welcome distraction but my father was never far from my thoughts.

Three days later we assembled at the hospital to hear the outcome of the operation and my brother and I were crushed to hear that he indeed had cancer and it was terminal. Any treatment would be palliative and he had probably a year at most. We delivered a version of that to my mother and sister but no one was fooled by the language, and we had to face the grim reality.

But we had no inkling of his sudden and massive deterioration. He seemed to switch off, incapable of any adult conversation. My son Alexander, aged nine, kept asking: "Why does Grandpa keep talking about the trees and plants outside?" when all he had been used to was constructive banter and constant advice, often with an ironic smile. Both my children adored him to a fault, as all their grandparents, and they were stunned by the change.

First he wouldn't talk, then he wouldn't eat and refused to respond to questions of any sort. The doctors were baffled, and we fought desperately to get some clarity. They considered electric shock treatment, another operation even, and all the while my father went downhill at an alarming rate.

We all wish we could say goodbye to people we love, and that is probably the most painful part of his dying. My mother read him countless books and played his favourite music, but nothing got through. We all dealt with it in our own way, but with the outcome preordained.

It was 4 a.m in early March 2001 when my mother called to say he was finally gone, and even though we all knew it was coming, nothing can prepare you. I immediately got up and hit the road to Dorset from London.

We went to see him for the last time, and in all honesty his passing was a relief because watching him fade away had been very painful, especially as it was totally inexplicable. I reflected that he must have subconsciously rejected his illness from the start, and shut down totally when he realised it was serious.

The funeral was at his local Catholic Church in Wardour, deep into leafy Dorset, and my brother Christopher made a stirring tribute, hitting all the right themes and we often smiled at the memories it inspired. He was buried in a hillside cemetery overlooking the church, in a totally peaceful part of the countryside.

Derek Gordon Halliday was a proud, principled, yet humble man, who supported his family from an early age when his father and brother were killed in military action. He and my mother went through many hardships to bring up the family as best they could. Christopher, my dear sister Deborah and I have much to thank him for. When my mother handed over to me the scrapbooks he had constructed of my rugby career, I found many articles, pictures and comments I never knew existed. He had never told me about these, and I felt very emotional that he had cared so much to do that, all the while in the background. I still smile when I remember him proudly showing me the 'Grand Slam' tree which he planted in his back garden to celebrate the 1992 triumph in which I played.

Nonetheless it was with great sadness that I continued with my Lions' duties, and appreciated yet again that I had received another major perspective in my life, this time the loss of one of my cornerstones.

Playing for the British and Irish Lions is the pinnacle of every Home Union rugby player's career, and the Red Shirt has been worn by some of the greatest exponents of the game in the British Isles. The immortal party of 1971, which toured New Zealand, then turned into the great Barbarians team of 1973 – everyone remembers *that* try by Gareth Edwards – was for me the epitome of what every rugby player craved.

So to have missed the British and Irish Lions' Tour of Australia in 1989 through a desire to protect my fitness had to have been a really low point for me. I often reflect on that decision, particularly as it allowed Jeremy Guscott to make his mark in world rugby. He and Brendan Mullin replaced myself and Will Carling, who was suffering from shin splints. Having debuted for England with three tries, he then astounded everyone, including himself, by scoring a remarkable try to help the Lions win the crucial second test versus Australia.

My medical advisers however, had warned me that effectively playing all year round was likely to result in an earlier finish to my career than I wanted, so really I had no option. Roger Uttley, the Lions' coach, wrote to share his disappointment. But he expressed pleasure, with his English hat on, that the decision would extend my career with England – and two Grand Slams, a World Cup, plus two knockout cups proved his point.

But whatever the compensation, the lack of a Lions' tour still hurts. Think back to the 1971 team who conquered the All Blacks, or the dramatic win in South Africa for the Pride of 1974 and 1997. Tours such as these turn players into legends, whose contribution to the game will always be remembered but most importantly any Lions' tourist reflects upon an unforgettable rugby experience.

It was no secret amongst the players that I found touring difficult. My wife wasn't that keen on seeing me disappear overseas and stockmarkets tend not to shut down for weeks at a time. Always tricky.

I readily confess that when asked if I played for the Lions, I respond that I was selected, but did not tour; that may be a liberty, but I felt that it was my right.

Twelve years after missing out in 1989, and although it hardly made up for my previous absence as a tourist, I was thrilled to be involved as a selector. A number of the press were critical of the fact that I was not a full-time professional coach and therefore not qualified to make such important selections, particularly as it was clear that I would be instrumental in picking the three-quarters. I was of course highly indignant that I was deemed unsuitable to recognise midfield and wing talent when I saw it; it was I who pushed for Jason Robinson as well as Rob Henderson, who were both a revelation in that dramatic first test in Melbourne, so brilliantly won by the Lions. I also insisted that Scott Gibbs should not tour, because he had clearly stopped looking for space and instead was hunting physical contact. That may be fine at one level, and he was still a mighty player for Wales, but it wasn't good enough to enhance the skills of the likes of Brian O'Driscoll or Jonny Wilkinson. Scott is an all-time favourite centre of mine, but he was one season too far, and he probably knew it too, as one of rugby's honest men. His exploits in New Zealand in 1993 and South Africa in 1997 will rightly go down in Lions' folklore, and of course he is one of rugby's 'hard' men. I always used to think that his bespectacled features, suggesting a mild-mannered individual during interviews, were a contra-indication, belying the brutal reality of his physical potency and presence on a rugby field.

Scott's centre partner on those two tours was Jerry Guscott, and it was my withdrawal from the 1989 trip which allowed the selectors to take along the brightest young talent of the time. He had made his debut in England's match versus Romania, because of Will's injury. I too played in that match, which turned into a saunter in the Bucharest sun. Jerry scored three tries, although he was outdone by Chris Oti who touched down four times. That match was a real try-fest. Despite the modesty of the opposition, I had a dream of a game creatively and Jerry was the first to compliment me. I also received praise from Will, who was doing some television commentary. But Will's schoolboy human nature got the better of him during the match, when he made a disparaging remark about my recently acquired hairstyle. Of course, I did not find out that I had been made an object of fun on national television until I returned to England. Will was rather pleased with his role of style guru. Some weeks later, while England celebrated a fine end to the season, my own international career as a centre effectively came to a shattering end, when Jerry scored a simply wonderful try to help the Lions win the second test versus Australia, and in so doing marking himself out as the Golden Boy of British rugby. Of course, nobody dared to intimate that I would be left out of the England side, but they did not need to. As it happens, in the winter of '89, I forced my rugby to new heights although I knew it was in vain. But I was so used to adversity by now that it washed over me and I silently committed to keep going no matter what – and I did.

My own lucky break to become seriously involved with the British Lions was down to Andy Robinson, my former Bath and England colleague. He was a player for whom I had the utmost admiration and respect. At Bath, he had the tough task of filling the giant-sized boots of Roger Spurrell, one of Bath's best. But fill them he did, and more, as one of England's most creative back-row forwards ever. And I include Peter Winterbottom, Tony Neary and Neil Back in this assessment.

Andy's rugby brain was incomparable, and contributed hugely to Bath's dissection of many a midfield. He rarely died with the ball, always held it in two hands and could pass like a three-quarter. I loved his evil smile, probably inherited from Spurrell, and he lived on the edge of the offside line. Many less talented players appeared more times for their country. His appointment as England, and then Lions', coach was the first recognition of his ability to read the game from both a back's and a forward's point of view. His performances as Bath coach, e. g. winning the Heineken European Cup, put him in a prime position to further his coaching career.

The Lions' assistant coach position did however create some problems for him. He had a commitment to England, and lacked the time to view all the likely candidates, particularly the backs. It was because of this that he decided to call for some help, and I initially received the enquiry from Fran Cotton with whom he had been discussing the situation. He asked whether I would be available, with a special brief to look at the English three-quarters. I was thrilled, if a little shocked, to be asked, and of course I was keen.

But my problem was one of making the time I needed to commit myself for a few months of rugby-watching, in my capacity as a full-time investment banker. Unbeknown to us, fate was about to intervene at just the right time The year 2000 had seen a rampant stock market and my company, DLJ, was under offer from Crédit Suisse First Boston. My decision to reject CSFB and join Lehman Brothers meant that I was placed on three months' gardening leave. A great coincidence, but also extremely convenient for me, and a spot of Lions-hunting seemed just the ticket.

But the three months touring round five nations was a real eye-opener. For example, a rainy day in Cork (isn't it always, second only to Manchester?) saw me comparing the fading skills of Gregor Townsend of Castres with the flawed talents of Ronan O'Gara of Munster. Getting back to a Putney dinner party was a struggle, but also a blessed relief.

The Lions' coach was Graham Henry, now coach of the All Blacks. His selection as a 'non-Brit' had raised many eyebrows, particularly since Clive Woodward was in contention. I myself found him good enough company, and reasonably shrewd. But he was not an integrator, or passionate about the job in hand. He was simply a professional doing what he was paid to do; I don't think he quite ever got to grips with the Welsh *hwyl* of Derek Quinnell or the sardonic humour of John O'Driscoll, both former Lions and fellow selectors.

I think that it was surprising to find ten Welshmen in the tour party, and there were plenty of commentators who thought that half of the English 'A' XV should have been selected. Perhaps, but the Lions are not an England derivative, and, besides, the Welsh had played stunningly, overturning France on their own ground. We were seduced by that performance, as much as underwhelmed by the Scots and Irish teams who failed to perform, particularly up-front.

The selection meetings were fascinating. At the best of times, Graham Henry and Andy Robinson appeared inscrutable. The furrowed brows and eyes set deep in their faces made it impossible to know what they were really thinking. The intensity was frightening: "Lighten up, boys," I often murmured to myself. Perhaps I should have said it out loud; one off the major criticisms of the tour was the level of intensity both on and off the field. Maybe a little more 'recreation' would have created the freshness required at the end of a long season.

It was a staggering statistic that the Lions failed to score a single point in the last twenty minutes of the three test matches. Australia were there for the taking, no doubt about that, and we had the right players on the field. I would say that. But think back to the controversy of previous Lions' tours, when other commentators would have picked entirely different teams! None of that this time – simply fatigue, through too much training.

During my three-month tour of the rugby citadels of Europe, there was a great opportunity to get to know two of the games greats: Donal Lenihan and Derek Quinnell. One of my great international memories was the England v Ireland match of 1988, the 35-3 thrashing we administered to the Irish under Donal's captaincy. This was the birth of the now-famous England theme tune, 'Swing low, sweet chariot', derived from the crowd's delight at the try-scoring exploits of Chris Oti, the black England winger at the time.

Donal had to make the post-dinner speech at the Hilton hotel in front of 500 celebrating Englishmen: "I had the privilege of playing today in a six-try spectacular – unfortunately we scored none of the tries" and won over the audience with grace in defeat and a wry sense of humour. But make no mistake, he was hard as nails and the Irish pack were always a handful, particularly at Lansdowne Road. Fists often flew, with his partner in crime, Willie Anderson, not far behind. I always took care not to be pinned at the bottom of an Irish ruck; a white shirt was fair game for an Irish boot. Video replays and touch judges would have enjoyed hours of intervention and citing.

Donal was almost vitriolic over Clive Woodward, which was an interesting dynamic for myself and Andy Robinson. Clive obviously thought he should have had the job, and advertised this pretty aggressively. To be fair, he had a point. It seemed on the face of it a strange decision to appoint a Kiwi like Graham Henry when we had a qualified local choice. The only good thing was that he probably wanted to beat the Aussies more than we did, anyway. Andy and I rarely mentioned Clive's name as it generally caused Donal to bristle.

I would have loved to tour with Derek Quinnell – twinkling eyes, larger than life, genial, almost a modern day St Nicholas in demeanour. You could see why the Welsh dominated European and world rugby (through the Lions) in his era. He had passion and commitment; when he waxed lyrical about a player we all sat back and listened with a sense of amazement. How could he find so many adjectives to describe one player? Many a time I sat next to him and his delightful wife at some match, enjoying their running commentary. Either or both or their sons, Craig and Scott, would often be playing and if there are a prouder set of rugby parents I haven't seen them.

It is strange that one moment in time can often define an individual. Derek's immaculate pass which led to Gareth Edwards' famous Barbarians' try against the All Blacks will go down in memory. He must have pulled both hamstrings catching the previous offering from Tommy David – and claimed that throwing the ball at someone's ankles was a pre-planned move from Llanelli!

The first test match of the 2001 tour remains a stunning reminder of the popular support for the Lions. Much of the ground was swathed in red, and this clearly stunned the Australians who had to dig deep to stay in the series after their defeat in the first test. The Lions unfortunately had little in the tank after a tough season and too much training.

As a concept, of course, the British and Irish Lions are steeped in the amateur ethic. Many voices are calling for an end to this anachronism in what is now a professional sport. How wrong they are – for me it was the biggest miss of my rugby career. A Lions' tour represents the biggest personal challenge for a top British rugby player – how to integrate your ability with a peer group you normally try to knock the stuffing out of. There is less process, more commitment of body and soul to a noble cause – perhaps the antithesis of professional attitudes.

I admit to considerable anger when I read the comments of Iain Balshaw after the 2001 tour. Here was one of the most talented young players of the modern era. His form had dipped alarmingly, and he failed to make the test team. Instead of looking inward, he blamed everything else for his problems. More than a few England players wanted their own systems of doing things. Shame on them; they diminished both themselves and the Lions' history with their comments.

CHAPTER 20

The Rugby Fighting Union – A Battle for Control (1998-2003)

Playing for England was always my dream and I would have done anything to wear the red rose. Having had that dream dashed at the age of twenty-three because of an injury also made the second time round even sweeter.

In those days we all talked of the goodwill of our employers to give us time off. And whatever the glory or pain resulting from an international weekend, it was back to work on the Monday. Every match was an adventure, a few days filled with privilege, police escorts and free hotels. Running up big bills was the norm, and always led to conflict with the RFU council, which hated the thought of us getting out of control – ordering a hundred steak sandwiches at 3 a.m in the Hilton Hotel did not go down well, nor did the ritual emptying of the mini bars in our rooms, wherever we stayed. Fair enough in a way, we could do the maths – 70, 000 people paying £50 each was a lot of money, and we were doing this for free, so what was a few hundred quid among friends?

It is now accepted wisdom that England versus Australia 1988 – Will Carling's first game as captain – was a turning point for English rugby, after the mediocrity of the mid-80s which had culminated in the World Cup fiasco of 1987. And what a game it was against Australia at Twickenham in 1988, end-to-end stuff, and crammed with quality running. The outcome was undecided until the last minute, when I rather gracelessly secured the winning try – one of only two in my England career.

But it was also the occasion when I experienced at first-hand, and for the first time, the meanness of the RFU. In those days I drove a Ford Sierra. Now Ford just happened to be the main sponsor of the RFU. All the union officials drove around in leather-upholstered, luxuriously finished, top-of-the-range

Ford Scorpios, presumably free of charge. It was a great perk, one which, of course, did not extend to the players, who were all considered amateurs.

On my way to the Thursday training session prior to the match, a stone struck my radiator and the vehicle eventually ground to a halt. It was a major repair job. I appealed for help, but was told no way, even though Ford, I'm sure, would have sorted it out for me. I was given the equivalent of a first class return rail fare, leaving me approximately £500 out of pocket. I was distinctly unamused.

Worse was to come, something which would result in a five-year fall-out with the union.

As I have explained already I had agreed to play on in 1991/92 at Will Carling and the England management's request, because some young players had not emerged quickly enough to make the step up to international rugby. I had agreed to this knowing full well I was causing long-term damage to my ankle, which was becoming increasingly arthritic. Even though I was very fit, I was training only once a week, with extra sessions in the gym and swimming pool. The medical management guaranteed that any post-career operations would be carried out at the union's expense. This seemed fair, especially as we proceeded to win those back-to-back Grand Slams, as well as reach a World Cup final.

Two years after my retirement, I was picked to run a committee which would help identify the next group of international players. Paul Ackford, Chalky White (one of England's top coaches), Don Rutherford (tech director RFU) and Geoff Cooke (England team manager) were part of the committee. I was proud to have been asked, and we set about the task with enthusiasm. Soon I was given an early opportunity to develop the next pipeline to build on the success of the early '90s.

At the same time, my ankle was finally giving in, after two seasons of cricket in the Surrey Championship. I needed an operation to take out a number of boney fragments called oesteophytes which were causing me a lot of pain. So, in line with the agreement I had struck with the RFU doctors, I made contact to tell them my news. Doctor Ben Gilfeather, who was still in charge of the England team, agreed to arrange everything at the RFU's expense. That is, until I received a letter from Dudley Wood, the secretary of the RFU.

He informed me that they could not create a precedent by funding treatment for ex-players, and regretted that I would have to bear all the costs. I think I was more hurt than angry as I felt they had reneged on a clear commitment. Nevertheless, I immediately resigned in disgust from the committee I had just joined. What sort of payback was this, after all my years of commitment?

I did get over it of course – life is short. Four operations later, I had a fusion which fixed the ankle at ninety degrees, courtesy of two metal screws. I am in reasonable shape and even ran a marathon recently, but no thanks are due to the RFU.

In today's professional world, health and safety is paramount, not least because the non-appearance of top players costs everybody money. It is, after all, the day job and the growing world's demand. The presence of high profile names is important. Think of how many extra people turn up to see the likes of Jonny Wilkinson for example.

My immediate post-career experience was one step towards a recognition that 'amateur day' practices had to change. During the time of my fall-out with Twickenham I coached Harlequins and sat on the Barbarians' committee.

Then one day in 1998 I took a call from Fran Cotton, the former England and Lions' prop and a senior member of the Rugby Union Management Board. His call was to introduce me to ten years of something rather different.

Cotton, a veteran of three Lions' tours, and a front row forward who had performed with distinction for England both here and around the world, was also a highly successful businessman managing Cotton Traders franchise for sports leisurewear. I was intrigued by his proposition to join Club England, a standing committee of the RFU, to help administer the newly created professional game in England; to manage the appointment of England coaching personnel; as well as clear the way for the advancement of potential England players. It was an amazingly wide brief, and it didn't take me long to accept since Fran was highly persuasive and it sounded very exciting.

However, a few weeks after my acceptance, I started to receive official documents from the RFU council. Fran had omitted to tell me that council membership was part of the package. I made it clear that I had limited time for this and he reassured me that I only had to show my face from time to time. I was dubious, but the die was cast – I was in!

Will Carling had once famously described the committee as 'fifty-seven old farts'. Now, suddenly, I was one of them, although I begged to be called a 'young fart, since I was probably fifteen to twenty years younger then most of them. Will's point was that they were all out of touch with modern rugby thinking at the top level, and he was probably right, but there are some 300,000 active players in the country who also need looking after.

Nevertheless, I soon found out just how tortuous it was to get any decisions made. Broadly speaking, you had paid officials of the union for whom this was a day job; retired, well-meaning amateurs with all the time in the world; people like me with ideas but no time, who carried weight because of their ex-player status. Put these three groups together, and the result is generally chaos, and not just because of the crazy number of people involved.

Jeff Blackett, the disciplinary officer at the union, made an effort to resolve the overpopulated committee. He proposed, rightly, that it be cut in half and put forward a persuasive argument. Does any county need more than one representative, and do the British Army, Royal Navy and Royal Air Force each need a council member?

I remember laughing inwardly, as the council, like turkeys, took one look at the prospects for Christmas and the inevitable impact on their positions, and promptly set up a working party to consider the implications. The recommendation they handed over was for a three-year moratorium – of course. One senior member scoffed: "If it's not broken, why fix it?" which summed up exactly the predicament.

Nevertheless, this was a brave new world, and I had to pick my way carefully through the protocol, trying to understand what was expected of me. The bulk of my work was with Club England and there were two main topics on the agenda: getting the national team back on track after the disappointing 1999 World Cup, when there was huge pressure on Clive Woodward the new(ish) coach; and working out a sustainable agreement for the release of top players from national duty, with the premiership clubs, who naturally had their own agenda.

I knew Clive well, having played against him at the tail-end of his career, until I effectively replaced him in the England team. We shared many common views, and were firm allies in the fight to get our national game in shape. He was probably the only person who knew how to deal with the chief executive Francis Baron.

Having survived the inevitable inquest following England's quarter final exit, Clive and his team suffered a number of Grand Slam near misses, which whilst frustrating gave the squad vital experience and a resilience borne out of adversity. The losing feeling, for any top sportsman, is not one you want to go through too often.

His technique was very simple: he argued strongly for what he believed was necessary, mainly around facilities, extra personnel, and anything which he believed would give his squad competitive advantage – and if he couldn't get agreement, he would bring it to a head, even threatening resignation. Fran Cotton, as chairman of Club England, unfailingly lent his support. Talk about sleeping with the enemy, Baron and Woodward both wanted success, but for different reasons, and this unhealthy alliance paved the way for Clive's eventual departure.

Put simply, Clive could not understand how the 2003 World Cup victory had not resulted in a significant change of attitude regarding the availability of top players to the national side – in fact things had got worse, and the RFU negotiators led by Francis Baron and Graeme Cattermole, the chairman, had failed to get any significant preparation time for the 2004 Six Nations, or beyond. The clubs, having delivered improved player availability in the run-up to the 2003 RWC, now decided it was their turn to extract a pound of flesh, and refused to allow the requested release time for their players. The other frustrating aspect was that Baron and Cattermole simply did not understand how to negotiate this tricky situation, which irritated Clive even more.

Clive was bitterly upset: "We win the World Cup having been the best prepared side in the world. Now we are the worst prepared – what was it all for?" It was completely unacceptable. What it really reflected was a total breakdown in relations between clubs and the union, driven by a war of personalities between the RFU management and many club owners. There was a clear ambition: the RFU wanted control of the clubs and the players, but had no means to achieve it. The impasse eventually led to a five-year stand-off, immensely damaging to the game in England, and something that condemned the national team to years of underperformance.

Player release was another thorny issue, yet the lead-up to all this had actually been quite promising. My direct contact with the clubs was an initiative set up by Fran himself. I was to be part of a group identifying how much money the RFU should hand over for access to certain top players. It was clear to everyone that we simply had to get agreement, the clubs owned the players through their contracts, and we couldn't force them to release their best assets without compensating them.

The main drivers of the group were Rob Andrew, the director of rugby at Newcastle, not a difficult choice given his background, and myself. Also involved was the RFU performance director Chris Spice, as well as representatives from Wasps and Leeds. In addition, and on a separate note, Fran and I would get a buy-in from Leicester, Sale, Harlequins and Bath. We left

Northampton and Gloucester, whose owners were hell-bent on conflict with the union, especially Francis Baron. The others formed a useful majority.

The sum to be committed was £1 million with more to come. We were very hopeful of a good result, and painstakingly came up with a series of recommendations. Rob Andrew and I reported back to our various bodies, and seemingly we had a deal. I was delighted, especially as I had taken a couple of days off from the office to get this done.

Some days later, as the plan was to be unveiled, I took a call from the chairman of the clubs, Howard Thomas. He wanted to confirm the amount being allocated to each player for a term of release to the national squad, which I did. He then asked why they had been changed around, a fact which really shocked me, and it transpired that Francis Baron had altered them. I put the phone down and immediately challenged Baron, as we were both attending a council meeting later that day. It became clear that he had simply wanted the last word. I was gobsmacked, as well as confused by the motivation behind this show of control.

An agreement of sorts was reached, but a sense of mistrust was building.

The reappointment of Clive Woodward in 1999 after RWC q-final defeat by the Springboks was critical to our eventual success in 2003

CHAPTER 21

Good Night, Good Knight

In the days following the World Cup win of 2003, there were many celebrations, and the cup itself was taken up and down the country and displayed in front of all England's supporters. One match dinner was held in Bath, attended by the likes of Matt Tindall, Ian Balshaw and a host of famous old Bath names. Andy Robinson of course was also there, and I publicly paid tribute to him as a key part of the triumph; in my view he had never received enough accolade for his role in the long journey from 1999 quarter finalists to eventual winners.

Clive Woodward's knighthood was well deserved, but Andy's contribution was often understated; he was that kind of guy, very much in the background, yet still doing great work.

His time was soon to come, however, as the squad started to unravel through a combination of retirements, injuries and loss of form. It seemed as if the players had been holding on for the World Cup, and once it was over had given in to all the stresses and strains they had ignored until then, not to mention the adulation they enjoyed everywhere they went, which must have been a continual distraction.

A poor Six Nations' campaign and a sound thrashing on the following tour Down Under, led to questions about Clive Woodward's succession planning. So when the clubs started to flex their muscles for the next World Cup, which was still four years away, Clive threw in the towel, frustrated by the perpetual lack of player availability and a perceived lack of support from his employers. You could hardly blame him given what he had achieved. I sat across the table from him as he hammered home point after point. The whole of the England Club committee sat there helplessly, unable to offer a solution. His very public departure laced with acrimony towards the RFU management, was wholly understandable.

Clive's legacy is, in my view, permanent. Some people decided that he was simply blessed with good players, but rather like Geoff Cooke in the '90s, Clive took training methods, selection and a no excuses mentality to a different level. He had to force through so many new initiatives, which did make him unpopular. He cost the union a lot of money. Put bluntly, he built a culture of success, winning consistently against the southern hemisphere, and nearly always at Twickenham. We became the best in the world, and not just for a week or two!

However, once gone, he was history, and the ready made replacement, Andy Robinson, was an obvious call... wasn't he?

Surely it was time for a rethink, to spread the load, since Clive was unique. A one-off. He just could not be replaced. There needed to be a team manager, a head coach and a more dynamic performance director. Chris Spice, the incumbent, had been sidelined by Clive, and was simply a process man. It was time to replace him. I told Andy as much, and urged him to include this in his presentation. He asked if I would consider being team manager, which at first took me by surprise, then got me thinking. Perhaps this was a role I could fulfil, meaning of course a departure from my job as investment banker. I soon realised also that my role as one of the selectors had been compromised. So, in accepting that my name could be put forward, I called John Spencer (now the Club England chairman), and withdrew from the process. At the same time, I wished Andy luck with his interview and waited.

There was really no other alternative to Andy, and his credentials were impeccable. Shortly thereafter, he was appointed England's head coach. The rugby world was delighted, the legacy was intact and he was an obvious choice, but in my view only if he was going to be surrounded by appropriate support.

Francis Baron was having none of it; he appeared to have lost control in the Woodward era and gave the impression that he was not prepared to let it happen again. So he point blank refused to appoint an England manager or another performance director, despite the fact that this was the direct recommendation of the selection panel. I was stunned, and told Andy he ought to resign immediately; he simply wouldn't succeed without effective support around him. Unsurprisingly Andy backed himself to succeed anyway; he was that sort of guy. And anyway the greatest prize in English rugby was available to him. Baron had promised to review the situation, but he warned Robinson that he had to work with Chris Spice, even though the two had already fallen out. It was a recipe for disaster.

I urged John Spencer to make Baron rethink, but there was little anyone could do. We were simply unpaid advisors versus full-time personnel, who were ultimately accountable.

So the post-Woodward era lurched forward, ill-conceived and with little chance of success. There were painful scenes as Andy Robinson suffered every set-back that could possibly be experienced by an England team, which was then in transition. Selection decisions were questioned (e. g. Mathew Tait), and every loss was keenly felt, given that we were the reigning World Champions. Previously untouchable players took out their frustration on the new coach, and the rugby public was beginning to wonder where it had all gone wrong. The shock of the Argentina match, when England were soundly defeated, had everyone wondering whether the team was wearing the shirt with the pride we all expected. The inevitable, and belated, replacement of the ineffectual Chris Spice by the acclaimed Rob Andrew simply added to the pressure. Rob's support of Andy was lukewarm at best, and the resignation of a proud man seemed inevitable.

When it happened, the media – hardly surprisingly – focused on the individual. Andy's anguished face was splashed across all the newspapers, and contractually he had little right to comment on the chain of events. The bottom line was that he was set up to fail, and his biggest mistake was to accept the unrealistic conditions surrounding his appointment instead of digging his heels in. He may have had shortcomings, as do we all, but with the right level of support he, and England, could have been successful, instead of which he became a major casualty of the Woodward backlash, a victim even of the leadership hiatus in the RFU.

I have never quite got to the bottom of the Graeme Cattermole resignation in 2004. He was the chairman of the Rugby Football Union's management board and was continually at odds with Francis Baron, throughout his tenure. While there may have been good reasons for the constant battling, still it made for a very fractious environment which was frankly unsustainable.

This led eventually to an attempt to unseat Baron through a coordinated move led by Cattermole. He had clearly failed to gather enough support and paid the ultimate price and had to resign. He made an emotional speech to the council and then walked out whilst the council looked on in embarrassed silence.

Whatever the details behind this, there was a vacancy left for the chairman's position. This was an important decision. As amongst other responsibilities the chairman reviews the position of the chief executive.

There were plenty of ideas flying around either from inside or outside the council. One name was reverberating on everyone's lips, that of Jack Rowell, director of rugby at Bath, ex head coach of England, my old Bath coach, a former executive of Dalgety (a food company). And non-exec of four quoted companies, possibly over qualified!

In the light of my past association with Jack, I was asked to contact him to see if he was interested. Jack did not mince his words, handing down a resounding yes. He was clearly the outstanding candidate with his level of background and experience. But he had to win the vote of three significant bodies: the nominations panel; the council; the game, through the AGM vote.

He won the first vote by a street, given the criteria employed by the nominations panel. Then he made a capable, if nervous, presentation to the fifty-four-strong council, and there were enough supporters to give him the two thirds majority he needed. It seemed as if he had made it through and was destined to be chairman. I felt good that someone of such standing in the game would be able to lend his considerable intellect to solving many of our on-going issues, mainly centred on unifying the clubs, Union and players. However he still had to win the backing of England's clubs, which was almost like a trade union block vote. For example, the biggest contributor was Yorkshire, for historical reasons, with some ninety votes. This reflected the fact that they used to be the hotbed of England's rugby. No longer, of course, but they still had plenty of power, as did the likes of Cornwall, Gloucestershire and the armed forces.

While a small group of Rowell supporters thought up some tentative marketing plans it became clear we had totally underestimated the process and what it would take.

One of the other contenders was Martyn Thomas, a long-standing council member and an extremely vocal critic on a number of issues. However, he was conclusively defeated, in a council and nomination panel vote. So I naively thought that was the end of the story. How wrong I was. He knew the rules much better than I did – in fact the only vote that mattered was at the AGM. I will leave it to others to judge on the logic – the massed ranks of England's club appointing the chairman of the RFU, who would oversee the most important executive position within world rugby. If Thomas succeeded then the clubs would be overturning the decision of their own elected committee.

It was soon apparent that the Thomas camp was conducting an effective campaign across the country and through the media. Jack and I were depicted as representing elitist rugby, and that his appointment would signal a hijacking of the union by the professional game. They were very simple scare tactics and highly effective – however, if anyone had stopped to think, it would be remembered that Jack spent more than thirty years in amateur club rugby.

The game was split down the middle and words were increasingly acrimonious. My frustrations were boiling over as I could see the momentum going away from us. Eventually I took a call from Jeff Blackett, the disciplinary officer and an influential voice. He was concerned about the split that was developing, and wanted to find a solution. He had spoken to Martyn Thomas and had a proposal to put to me. Martyn would step down in favour of Jack, on condition that he would himself be deputy chairman and sit on the management board. It would involve a rule change by the RFU but Jeff thought that this was achievable.

I was perfectly happy with this. It seemed an ideal compromise, and everyone was in agreement. We all decided to meet in a West End hotel in London. Those involved were Jack Rowell, Martyn Thomas, Jeff Blackett, John Spencer (chairman of Club England) and myself. The atmosphere was tense, to say the least. Jeff made a proposal and we all shook hands. The meeting was over in twenty minutes. I allowed myself a moment or two of congratulation and was back at my office desk within the hour. But it was all too good to be true. I was on my way to a meeting when the phone rang. It was Martyn Thomas and he was brief. His campaign team had told him he was likely to win the AGM vote and therefore he had reconsidered his position. I said this was not about winning but making the right decision. But I could not change his mind. I was obviously furious, as was Jack, and Jeff was totally bewildered. The bottom line was we had to resume the battle and Thomas was indeed right. In the end Jack lost comfortably and Thomas was to preside over the council for seven long and difficult years.

When you look back at those times of infighting and chronic underperformance of a national team at all levels, I find it hard to forgive Francis Baron and Martyn Thomas. Whilst there were plenty of other circumstances at work, I hold them responsible for creating those conditions, wilfully and often with little regard for the games interests. They seemed to thrive on division and conflict. This is not to ignore Baron's many achievements off field, improving the RFU balance sheet and overseeing the construction of the magnificent new stadium. Nor do I underrate the many hours spent by Thomas on RFU business – but I formed the view that over the years he simply was out of his depth and his departure in 2011 was long overdue.

Perhaps Rowell would have failed, but we would have then held him accountable. Perhaps we would have forced him to delegate more to people who were better placed to make decisions. In general, sport administrators love to have control and it's so unhealthy.

I remember many years ago being sent constantly to the headmaster when at school as I was always badly behaved – nothing too serious, but always just enough to warrant me being disciplined in one way or another. However, I never thought that I would also be called in to the Rugby Union offices like a naughty schoolboy, but I was. It summed up the immense insecurity of the whole set-up. On this occasion I had been publicly critical of the management board, and they weren't letting me get away with it.

'The Way Ahead' was a project which laid down a blueprint of the future of the game in England and how it should be structured. A consultancy group had been brought in to take views from all sections of the game and had come up with a proposal.

When Francis Baron presented this it was met with a mixed reaction. For example, how much would it cost – rumours put it at £1 million – and did this company have the relevant experience to ask the right questions?

Despite misgivings we went ahead with it, the RFU council was divided up into groups and we all put forward our views. Many constructive thoughts were put on the table, input which we were told would form part of a presentation to the wider game. I had one major reservation. The senior professional clubs seemed not to be part of the process, a fact confirmed by the CEO of the clubs, Marc McCafferty. How could we determine a way forward for the top of the game without consulting the main participants? They would have to be at the core of any workable plan.

Despite all the good intentions the concept was fatally flawed. It was like constructing a pyramid and leaving the top section unfinished. Moreover, by the time the consultants came to ask my views as a national member and part of Club England, the report was nearly written. Any observation I had could not have been incorporated in it and the people I met appeared to have little understanding of the key issues.

Chairman of the RFU for seven long years, not to mention a few other positions collected along the way.

As the media took more and more interest, I made these views known which did not go down well in the corridors of power. So I was called in to Twickenham to account for myself to the Chief Executive, Francis Baron and the chairman of Club England John Spencer. To be fair John was very supportive and fought my corner.

Nevertheless I was given a severe warning and told that the management board took a dim view of my criticism and that they had taken it personally. I maintained that the current structure of the management board was hardly suited to key decision-making in the professional area. I was sceptical that they had all the relevant information, especially when neither the CEO of either Premier Rugby or the Players Association was represented. We agreed to disagree and I made an apology for any personal upset. For the record the outcome of the whole review was predictable – nothing happened, although it would not surprise me to learn that they probably did spend a million pounds. Today you would struggle to find anyone who would admit that the review had ever taken place.

For this period the clubs and the RFU had fought a running battle for control of the players – effectively the game. In this professional era players were contracted to the clubs, so the RFU had to negotiate for their release for international duty. If only the union had contracted the players at the start of professionalism, then, arguably, there would never have been a problem.

As all sides continued to talk a good game but deliver nothing, John Spencer asked me to set up an 'Elite Players Group'. The mandate was to bring together the clubs, union and players in an informal working party to attempt to hammer out a deal. It seemed as if the members of this group had a good chance of success: myself, Rob Andrew (performance director), Jason Leonard (National Member), Mark McCafferty (CEO, Premier Rugby Ltd), Phil Winstanley (secretary PRL), Damien Hopley (CEO, Professional Rugby Players Association).

We duly met on half a dozen occasions, working on all practical aspects such as elite player availability, welfare management, compensation and prioritisation of fixtures. The key ingredient here was cooperation. We all wanted the same thing – a practical and workable solution which would allow for a successful club structure, a top three national team and a development plan which would allow young players to come through the system successfully and rise to the top of the game.

Rob argued hard for what he needed, but was sensible enough to indulge in some give and take. At last we all agreed and frankly a lot of the key decision-making was driven by common sense. It remained for Rob to present his conclusions to the management board. This was the last stumbling block.

Happily, Rob's recommendation was unanimously approved and a multi-year deal between the RFU and the PRL was finally unveiled. A new dawn awaited English rugby or at least many of the excuses put forward for a poor performance had now been removed.

As for me my job was effectively done. The arrival of Martin Johnson signalled a new phase and Club England was replaced by the Professional Game Board (PGB). For various reasons that did not include me. Broadly speaking, neither Martyn Thomas nor Francis Baron were prepared to have me involved, rather they preferred to sit on the PGB themselves, despite their minimal knowledge of top level rugby. My outspokenness counted against me just when I had an opportunity to operate without politics dogging me every step of the way. I guess that sometimes you have to accept that you are part of a particular moment in time. When it passes, you must move on. Which I did.

Clive Woodward, I admired him as a player as well as a Coach/Manager. He had passion and spoke his mind. In my book the best qualities you can have.

CHAPTER 22

South African Interludes (2005)

Johann Rupert, other than being chairman of the multi-billion pound conglomerate, Richemont (Cartier, Dunhill, Montblanc, Van Kleef), has been for many years a senior figure in South African rugby, owner of the Blue Bulls, and an influential character behind the scenes at a national level. For him to have become caught up in RFU politics was an unlikely situation, but he was another businessman who found out how difficult it was to negotiate a path through the administrative minefield of UK rugby.

I first met Johann in a business capacity. He had a corporate relationship with Lehman Brothers through his holding company, and I was keen for him to come and talk to investors. Eventually we met courtesy of Allan Lamb, ex-England test cricketer with whom he and Ernie Els (the golfer) had been drinking the night before – Johann, as can be ascertained from this, is a very knowledgeable sports fan. He also has a very strong personality, and was soon telling me the rights and wrongs of world rugby, as well as the numerous shortcomings and failings which underlie, and indeed were the probable cause of many of the problems in English rugby. As a result of that meeting, besides a commitment from him to visit the office, I got an invitation to the Dunhill Links Championships, both as guest and later as player. What an experience that was!

It was some months later that I took a different call from him; this time he was talking to me in confidence, in my capacity as an RFU council member. It was 2004 and he had a plan to buy Rotherham, a near-bankrupt club in the North of England, refinance it as an amateur club and assume Rotherham's current professional position. His plan was then to relocate it in London, where the new club's playing headquarters would be centred. He would include a number of South African players, but did say he would adhere to the then limits on foreign players. An academy would be set up in line with RFU policy and he had ideas for global TV coverage, no surprise given his media connections. With the number of South Africans living in London, he anticipated enough crowd support, and claimed that there was already interest to sell out the ground.

It was intoxicating stuff, but it was also dynamite. Getting the RFU to buy into this radical idea looked like being a Herculean, if not impossible, task.

Johann, having revealed to me his plans, stressed the confidentiality of the situation, given the sensitive nature of the project. His agent had briefed *The Times* newspaper, which was extremely keen to run the story, and so I made a call to David Hands, their rugby correspondent and Mark Souster, his deputy. They agreed to keep everything under wraps until the right moment presented itself, although, like all good journalists their appetites were whetted.

My next step was to inform the RFU's chief executive Francis Baron. It is fair to say that his reaction was tepid at best. There was a process to go through, and a formal application to be made, which would then be ratified by management board discussion. To take over a bankrupt club, and relocate it to London under a new name was ground-breaking and complicated. Meanwhile, it was critical that the news should be contained, which was becoming increasingly challenging.

Johann and I went to work on the proposal with the important backing of Fran Cotton. The chain of events which then unfolded was breathtaking and scarcely believable.

There was a European Cup match taking place in Toulouse to mark the opening round of the Heineken Cup. All the rugby media were in attendance, and gathered in a cafe on the morning of the match. Imagine their surprise and immediate interest when Terry Burwell (an RFU employee) walked in and told the whole story of this South African billionaire, who was trying to take over an English club. Souster, who was there, went off the deep end, and called me immediately in a state of rage. His story was blown, and sure enough the *Sunday Times* featured a full-page spread about Johann Rupert's attempt to gatecrash the premiership the very next day. It also carried a picture of Johann's wife, Gaynor, and a more general piece about his business connections. For a deeply private individual, this was an outrage, and I had to hold the phone away from my ear as he let rip when he saw the article. He made it clear that the proposed deal was off, regardless of the RFU decision. From a personal and a business perspective, I was mortified. Terry Burwell's actions were unacceptable. Why had he felt entitled to do what he did? I was determined to get to the bottom of the leak.

With Johann's words ringing in my ears, I called Fran Cotton (the chairman of Club England) and Graeme Cattermole (then chairman of the management board). Cattermole in particular was furious, and went directly to Francis Baron to demand the removal of Terry Burwell. There had apparently been a series of incidents under investigation, but this was the first breach of confidentiality that could be linked directly to the head office of the Rugby Football Union.

Shortly thereafter I was contacted by Francis Baron himself. Nobody could have known that *The Times* had prior knowledge of Rupert's intentions, and that I was also in the loop. Thus, the RFU had been well and truly caught out. But what was the motivation? Could it simply not accept the emergence of another powerful owner of a premiership club; was this regarded as a threat to their dreams of overall control? This is pure speculation, but what other explanation could there be?

Baron was in a tight spot, but he was not going to put his hand up to me. I suggested that he interviewed Burwell and take the appropriate action when he admitted the truth – realistically this was not going to happen. For where could Terry Burwell have found this information, and who could have authorised him to leak it? Francis Baron was no mug; he insisted that Mark and I produce sworn affidavits testifying to the events described. Neither of us was prepared to do it, which gave Baron a way out and in the end he merely gave Burwell a verbal warning.

What a farce! The RFU had been caught red-handed distributing sensitive information to the media, while not having the guts to admit that it had done so.

The contrast between this unhappy episode and what happened to my family and me the following year could not have been more stark.

When you look back the ultimate sporting heroes appear in the most unlikely guises and define themselves, not just through their achievements, but also in the way they are viewed by a particular sport and the world in general. If you are a rugby supporter, from whichever country, there can have been fewer more influential moments than the Rugby World Cup Final, when Nelson Mandela appeared before the team, the crowd and the sporting world with a Springbok shirt on his back. Given the fact that Afrikaaner supremacy was symbolised by their rugby, an almost exclusively white sport, this was some kind of statement that they were all in this together. The rugby match became a test of a new, integrated South Africa, a true Rainbow Nation. Their subsequent victory over the hot favourites, the New Zealand All Blacks, confirmed this as some kind of sporting folklore, even if the reality of a post Apartheid society is still a work in progress some twenty-five years later. There was no doubt in the mind of most rugby people that Nelson Mandela had pocketed a major piece of sporting history by his actions. He became a total icon, if he wasn't already, and the thought of meeting such a man has topped many peoples' wish lists.

Imagine that turning into a reality for me and my family.

We were visiting South Africa for the very first time with some good friends and their children, combining a safari trip with a few days down in the Cape. Glorious weather greeted us on arrival in Johannesburg and we piled into a rather pokey minibus for the four-hour trip to Madikwe, situated on the South African-Botswana border. We soon appreciated the massive difference between the haves and have-nots in this unique country. The plush town houses with forbidding walls and intimidating barbed wire fences left an indelible impression on us all, reminding us at every turn of both the stunning wealth and the crime problem so often referenced in Africa. In no time we were gawping at the corrugated iron shacks that lined the roads as we made our way deep into the countryside. It seemed impossible that in a country of such opportunity poverty is a way of life for the majority of the population. It was a sobering sight, and I could see that the children were very subdued as they took it all in.

The bouncy roads soon morphed into dusty tracks, as we approached safari land and almost inevitably one of the tyres suddenly blew. No AA or RAC in this part of the world, although a dozen or so passing vehicles stopped in the shimmering heat to offer their assistance. Rust-bound tyre nuts proved to be resistant to all human effort, but we kept our sense of humour in the thirty degree heat. On the eventual arrival of a replacement vehicle, we managed to get to our destination as the African sun set with worrying speed.

Jaci's Tree Lodge was our first real experience of the African bush right on the edge of the game reserve, with rooms built into the trees and connected by wooden walkways. Everything was suspended above the bush floor, so the threat of snakes, scorpions or other undesirable creatures was mercifully nullified.

The Madikwe Game reserve is a burnt looking wasteland, unlike the amazing scenes of the Serengeti. But there was abundant wild life, and we had our fill of the Big Five – well four anyway, as there wasn't a leopard in sight. The traditional South African cuisine, especially Kudu, was amazingly tasty and we were well looked after – but three days was enough, and we sped off to Cape Town with great excitement.

Whatever the pictures of Table Mountain may reveal, they are nothing compared with the real thing seen with the naked eye. As we came round the corner from the airport I could appreciate why people rave about it, and once into the city the backdrop dominates at every turn. We never tired of gazing up to the mountain, especially when the clouds enfold the tabletop with an eerie smothering forward march, only to evaporate when falling down the mountain.

As any tourist will tell you, there's a regular three day circuit to take in the sights – Table Mountain, Camps Bay, Cape Point, Robben Island and of course the winelands – all of which we did in glorious weather. It was ironic that the visit to Nelson Mandela's Robben Island prison would prove to have such an impact on us.

On our last day I made contact with Johann Rupert, who is now of course a major investor in the Saracens rugby club. He invited us all to lunch in Franschoek, where his wine farms are based, and it seemed an ideal way to finish the trip. We loaded our bags into a hired minibus, all ready for the return flight from Cape Town to London Heathrow. Our cooperative bus driver was very cool that we would roll into the bus a few hours later after a long and liquid lunch.

Johann and his wife Gaynor were in fine form. He is such a character, and both families were fascinated and enthralled by his many stories of South African life over a number of decades. So we thoroughly enjoyed our last lunch washed down with some Franschoek vintages – South African wine is undoubtedly among the best in the world, and when you combine it with the local crayfish or a dish of Kudu, the combination is very difficult to beat.

Johann then sprang his surprise on us – "Hallers, why don't you all stay on for a couple of days longer?" I was nonplussed, and declined politely – after all, flights were booked, bags packed, a return to school scheduled for the children, and not least there was also a return to work beckoning me. He seemed irritated by my response and turned his attention on the children, who of course were all too scared to say no. We were all thinking this was just a piece of Rupert humour, until he revealed why he had asked. His daughter was due to interview Nelson Mandela in Johannesburg two days later, and he would introduce us as well. There was a stunned silence as we took in the prospect. Johann had it all planned, he would call his assistant, rebook our flights from Johannesburg, put us up in his estate accommodation overnight, and fly us up from Cape Town tomorrow. The whole conversation seemed surreal, but he was deadly serious and we soon realised this was a total one-off opportunity, especially for the children. How many young Western kids had Nelson Mandela met over the years? Probably a mere handful.

Nervously, we allowed ourselves to accept this incredible invitation, and the next two days were to pass in a blur. Firstly, we spent the night just up the road in his late father's house, which was now used for entertaining guests and friends. Digging out clean clothes, calling the UK, delaying home plans, all those practical details were put in place, and some very excited English travellers clambered aboard Johann's private plane the next day for the two-hour trip to Johannesburg, the children rather impressed that they didn't have to show their passports as we took our rather exclusive seats. Once there, we relocated to Johann's house, and went downtown for a traditional steak and red wine meal, quite a staple diet in South Africa. We were again struck by the levels of security which were significantly higher than Cape Town: barbed wire everywhere and high, forbidding walls guarding many residences and even our dinner venue was within a very safely protected area.

The next day dawned hot and bright as we nervously awaited our guests' arrival at lunchtime, and there was a small welcome party also in place, with some musicians invited to sing for the former President of South Africa. It was midday when the Mandela entourage arrived, and he was taken on a buggy around the beautiful gardens before coming over to greet us. He was very frail and barely walking, but his eyes shone brightly, and he was clearly looking forward to his afternoon. Having visited his prison cell where he had spent twenty-seven years only two days previously, I could scarcely take all this in. We were all mesmerised by the sight of him, and waited in the background to seize our opportunity to say hello.

When the moment arrived, we all lined up, and Johann brought us to his side. "Madiba," [Madiba is his Xhosa clan name and the name by which most South Africans address him], "I want to introduce you to some English friends of mine."

It has to be said, he was mildly disinterested in us four adults, we received a cursory handshake and a smile – fair enough, he probably has to undergo countless such introductions – but when he met the children he was very animated and spoke to them for several minutes each, asking about school and wanting them to say 'Hi' to their friends and schoolmates in England. It is well known that Mandela said the thing he missed the most in his time in prison was the sound of a baby crying and children talking – he hardly saw his own children during his imprisonment. So it was simply a breathtaking moment never to be forgotten. I told Sophie and Alexander that they should always treasure the experience, and remember it for the rest of their lives.

After some more music, it was clear that Mandela was very tired and his 'team' who had accompanied him were adamant that it was time to go. He departed in the same understated way that he had arrived, and I was struck by his humility as well as by his sheer presence, which had affected us all. Johann gave us some fascinating insights into the months leading up to Mandela's release and the difficult times following.

After all, the traditional Afrikaaner rule was about to be diminished forever. It seemed to me though that there was a realisation that the situation could not continue, as the country by the mid-80s was in total isolation from the rest of the world on many fronts. I, myself, for example, had never had the opportunity to play rugby in South Africa since my whole career spanned their time out of international sport. The change that Mandela wrought after his release from prison in 1991 is already reflected in the history books, but it was still incredible that he should use the platform of a Rugby World Cup Final to make his point by donning the Springbok jersey.

I felt so privileged, as a rugby player, to have spent albeit the briefest time in his presence. And for a man such as Nelson Mandela to recognise how rugby could bring people together speaks volumes for the game's unique characteristics.

CHAPTER 23

Lehman Brothers
(2008)

The final word on Lehman Brothers' battle for survival echoed down to the trading floor at about 8. 15am on September 15th, 2008. The Head of Banking had called a meeting and opened with, "It's over. I am sorry. Go home. And good luck." Simple as that – game over. 25, 000 people out of a job and the firm in bankruptcy.

On the fifth floor, where the heart of Lehman Brothers in Europe had pulsed so strongly for so many years, we were in shock. The US and European equities business had become best in its class and it was inconceivable that we were looking into an abyss. To be clear, we were engaged in the conventional advisory business; doing company research, and providing advice to institutions that looked after people's pensions and private wealth.

Not for us the perilous geared investments in the US housing market, the complexity of fatally-flawed fixed income products, or the fashionable practice of securitisation packages. However, we had all been moored to a collapsing pyramid, and we were now paying the price.

The atmosphere on the fifth floor turned toxic very quickly. It rapidly became common knowledge that the United States office had cut us off, and in the process had pocketed a chunk of money – seven billion dollars to be precise. We simply could not get through to them by telephone or other electronic means, and it was clear that they had left us to fend for ourselves. While we all understood that, in dire times, people have to look after Number One, this was unbelievable. It was cowardly and unworthy. We saw the true colours of our US colleagues.

Anger, astonishment, disbelief, incredulity, we ran a veritable thesaurus of emotions, but, in the face of the Lehman collapse, all that quickly turned to fear, then to thoughts of survival. For some there was no alternative but to pick up possessions and leave as it sank in that 25, 000 people around the world were suddenly unemployed, and that no-one was going to come to the rescue. It was every person for him or her-self. A rumour started that the police were arriving in case of a confrontation and soon journalists and photographers were clustered around the bank's entrance. Security men apparently weren't allowing people back into the buildings, computers were being disabled and mobile phones turned off. And all of this before lunchtime.

We were told there would be no salary the following week, that our pensions had been frozen, and that healthcare policies no longer applied. In other words, in a period of two hours, everybody's lives had been totally dismantled, emotionally and financially. The feeling of helplessness was overwhelming.

I raced down to the ground floor reception and eyeballed a security man I knew well who was overseeing the chaos. He reassured me that we still had access in and out of the building and shook his head when I told him about the rumours flying around. I returned to the fifth floor and bumped into John Phizackerley, one of the architects of the Lehman equity business and now CEO of Europe. I confronted him with the fact that I had been blocked by Vodafone from transferring my mobile telephone number to a personal account and that our phones may be turned off. This mattered to me because I didn't possess a landline. If my phone was cut off, I would be rendered *incommunicado*. To make matters worse, I was organising a charity rugby match of some magnitude that week, the Help for Heroes game at Twickenham, and we were expecting 50,000 people. I couldn't afford to be uncontactable. 'Phiz' reckoned things wouldn't get that bad, and gave me a name to call for reassurance, which I did. Vodafone were, indeed, in talks with our administrators and had frozen all accounts but thus far had not cut us off. Well, that was something, I suppose. In the meantime, the texts and calls were raining in from concerned friends and relatives. What could I say? We were gone.

Newswires started humming as the enormity of the financial disaster dawned on people. CNBC showed live footage of Lehman US employees rushing around in New York, emptying their offices of possessions. Tears were shed and, in some cases, hysteria set the tone for a sudden exodus from Bank Street, Lehman's European headquarters. What an ending!

Lehman Brothers had built a top-class research franchise and employed some of the best people in the City, if not the world, through the first part of the new millennium. On a *per capita* basis, we were without peer, a statistic backed up by clients and surveys alike. But the terminal shock of Lehman's bankruptcy turned the division into a disorganised rabble – you'd have thought an incoming category five hurricane had given us an hour to leave the building. Hundreds of people headed for the exit, much to the delight of the waiting news cameras and crews. The plight of a broken business and its human consequences was broadcast live around the world. It was almost like a public execution. Suddenly, and fortuitously, my phone rang; I picked-up the incoming call. It was Ronnie Lamb, chairman of the Oxford Rugby Trustees. He delivered a prepared speech, as if to a condemned man.

"This must be a very difficult day for you all." – Come again?

"And I don't wish to be insensitive." – What on earth was coming next?

"But," he paused, "where will this leave the Varsity Match sponsorship?"

He ended weakly, probably regretting that he had made the call.

The background is that I had been instrumental in persuading Lehman Brothers to take on the annual Oxford versus Cambridge rugby match sponsorship at Twickenham, which would have linked us to the two premier universities in the world and give the Lehman brand a big boost in the UK – but it was hardly the time to bring this up. It was about 500th on my list of priorities that morning. I almost told Ronnie where to go, instead I bit back the words and gave him the only answer I could. "Look, Ronnie, we'll find someone else, I promise you, but it's all over for us – and if anyone credible calls you to replace our sponsorship, go for it!"

I thought of the many business/charity relationships which were ending; the Lehman foundation donated tens of millions of pounds every year to worthy causes. These would be further casualties of the hubris and insane behaviour of some of our senior management, perhaps tiny in relation to the implosion of the firm as a whole but nevertheless highly damaging to the beneficiaries.

As many former Lehman employees are now in the fortunate position of having been re-employed by the Japanese bank Nomura, I often reflect on how we had ignored all the warning signals. Sometimes, as in all walks of life, the seeds of disaster are lying around and can be seen years before the fateful moment. For example, England rugby experienced a horrible five-year run of underachievement since winning the World Cup in 2003. The systems put in place post the departure of Clive Woodward were so hopelessly inadequate, one didn't need to be a rocket scientist to see that the impact would eventually be felt.

In Lehman's case, the signs were much more subtle. However I do remember watching a video conference of Lehman's full-year presentation hosted by the CEO Dick Fuld, back in 2000. It was the first time I had ever seen him 'live', having joined the firm only three weeks previously. It wasn't so much a presentation as a testosterone-fuelled rant. Lehman had almost been taken over by Deutsche Bank in 1998 but the company's record-breaking set of results seemed to have cemented the idea that Lehman could survive on its own, and anyway it certainly didn't need the 'help' of Deutsche Bank. Fuld was maniacal. He ranted: "Deutsche Bank. Where are you now? I can't see you. Come on, where are you?" He repeated this a few times as if he had single-handedly rescued his firm from their clutches. In truth, he was the heartbeat of Lehman Brothers and this sense of proprietorial behaviour was a hallmark of his style. He was gloating.

I became a managing director two years after joining Lehman Brothers and saw more and more evidence of his autocratic decisions. Very few people dared to question him. On one occasion, he announced to the London business during a 'major presentation' that he had reversed the firm's dress-down code as though everyone was looking scruffy. "You need a suit of armour when you go to war," he declared. Our eyeballs rolled. What *was* he on!

Yes, the profits stacked up and great people joined the firm. We were on a journey and Fuld's entrepreneurial attitude empowered people. There was plenty of business around and we made sure we were part of the never-ending bull surge in the market. How else could we proudly forecast a figure of $20 billion revenues by the end of 2007? What a pinnacle from which to fall.

But had we bet the bank? We were all encouraged to take more risks in every possible live product and, sure enough, it was paying off. In 2005, I attended a managing directors' presentation at Bank Street. Fuld started talking about the $150 Club, meaning he thought the stock was worth double the current level. We all made a quick mental calculation – as owners of stock ourselves as a lot of our bonuses were awarded in stock. This was a meaningful comment but more so for him as he was already a 'share billionaire'.

Then he paused. "But what really concerns me," he went on, "is arrogance. If we are arrogant about ourselves, we will never get there." He was right of course. The best operators have loads of humility; the world's best team sportsmen spend most of their time attributing their success to the support around them, either on or off-field. Because it's true.

Ironic, then, that these words of warning would be ignored by the very man who uttered them. All of us at Lehman, in London anyway, were blown away by Dick Fuld's breathtaking arrogance as things went from bad to worse. He actually said that if he found a 'short seller' of his stock, he would tear open his chest, and eat his heart in front of him to teach him a lesson. What sort of human being is that?

In 2006 my boss Rob Shafir left the firm. He was our inspirational Head of Global Equities. He was a leader, looked you in the eye, asked your opinion, made decisions, stood by them, joked and laughed, paid compliments and offered constructive criticism. He was Lehman Brothers through and through and had seen us through 9-11 when Lehman Brothers' employees watched the bombers fly past their windows from the top of the World Financial Centre. He co-ordinated a 3,000-person mobile phone conference call to inspire the firm to fight back, since all our employees had lost their offices and were operating out of a Manhattan hotel.

I knew Rob well and he was a rugby fan, having spent a number of years in the UK, so he caught the bug. We hit it off from the start and in no time we were sharing the vision of where Lehman Equities could go. After all, in 2000 we were outside the top fifteen brokers in the market. I had been appointed Head of European Sales in London and he wanted me to know how hard he was driving the firm towards a pre-eminent position in equities. Ultimately it was his inspired leadership, together with Roger Nagioff his co-head in London, which took us to top five in Europe as well as number one in the United States.

He also gave me the mandate to knit together the Lehman global equities research and sales franchise, which contained many political challenges. He would make a habit of calling me from the States most days on the way to his office in order to ask for updates. I got to know him extremely well and our thoughts were very much aligned. He used the 'f' word a lot, but it seemed to add weight to his words rather than offend people; another Gordon Ramsay, perhaps.

Yet despite all this, Rob left the company for no apparent good reason. And when he walked out of the building for the last time, the number one equities house in the US rose as one to applaud him. I was told the standing ovation went on long after he had closed the door behind him and I can believe it. I understand that he left because Fuld imposed a budget on him which he knew was unattainable. Rob is an honest guy – we all trusted him totally – and when he decided to achieve a target, it rarely eluded him. But Dick Fuld attempted to drive the returns of the business way beyond attainable levels and if anyone stood in his way, they were out. We should have spotted it.

In came Bart McDade, now notorious for his role in Lehmans' demise. He emerged from fixed income, once the engine of growth, but later perceived as the catalyst for the impending disaster. In his tenure as Global Head of Equities I never swapped a single word with him and if he ever visited Europe, it was fleeting. He possessed a look and character which were dull in the extreme. He inspired nothing and nobody; unfit, in my opinion, to wear the mantle of his predecessor. It was McDade who was with Fuld until the bitter end and eventually helped sell the Lehman US business to Barclays. He left the rest of the company to fend for itself and then, once he had done his deal, had the audacity to send us an encouraging e-mail suggesting that everything would work out OK. Finally, he left the newly-formed Barclays Equities business after being paid an obscene amount of money. What a legacy!

In 2008, the year after McDade became Head of Equities, I achieved what I considered was my greatest business honour – the chairman's award. It was for 'extraordinary client service' and only fifty people receive the accolade every year. I was certainly flattered to be honoured in such a way. I had mixed emotions, though, since I had separated from my wife some six months earlier, and my personal life was now very different. I flew to New York for the celebratory dinner in the prestigious New York library. There, at the ridiculously early time of 6. 30 p.m, we assembled to receive the plaudits from Dick Fuld. It was strangely impersonal and I never actually shook his hand. It almost seemed as if we were there for his personal gratification. Coincidently, I sat next to one of the most powerful men in Lehman Brothers by the name of Mike Gelband. He was head of global fixed income, the powerhouse of the Lehman Brothers' machine. To be clear, this was a multi-billion dollar revenue business and Dick Fuld's 'baby', in that we had been the global number one player for many years. He was forever applauding the resilience of all the products and their growth capabilities but despite the excellence of our equities business, we always felt like junior partners.

The Americans have a habit of finishing work by 8 p.m, then going home. A 6.30 a.m start means exactly that, and they hardly drink or eat anything, which is pretty amazing given that apparently twenty-five per cent of the US population is officially obese. Well, not the Wall Street jocks; up early and into the gym, skimmed milk on the cereal, lunch-time salads, etc. Doughnuts and Ben and Jerry's cheesecake ice cream were definitely off the list. So, for them, a business dinner was something to get through as simply as possible.

I wasn't too impressed that there was so little conversation on the biggest night of my business career. My evening stuttered along and Mike Gelband was so withdrawn it was almost embarrassing. It was the second quarter of 2007; the multi-product fixed income business and the multi-layered mortgage business were about to explode, or should I say implode. Mike resigned a short while later, for months protesting against the risks we were running. As with anyone questioning the Fuld strategy for any length of time, they were shown the exit.

The firm tolerated no post-departure criticism, as evidenced by the amount of share options which were accumulated over the years and could be removed at a moment's notice. It was a very clever system; load the employees with so much stock that they would have a vested interest for many years, whether with the company or not. So it was very laudable to throw a load of poisoned darts as you walked out of the door but very costly. At the time, the high percentage of employee ownership made Lehman Brothers a very loyal place to work in but it also stopped any objective or constructive criticism. That was a terminally bad thing.

So with two of the 'best operators' leaving so soon after each other, it should have told us all something was not right and that trouble was on the way. Mike was then parachuted back in to try to sort out the mess – way, way too late, of course. And Rob Shafir had become one of the key players in the Crédit Suisse Group – hardly surprising for a man of his capabilities and inspiration.

Finally, my own personal alarm bells were ringing at the end of 2007. Two years earlier, I was asked to manage the financial sector industry group in London. This was a new initiative which coordinated the functions of sales, trading, research, derivatives, corporate access and fixed income/ banking where relevant. The aim was to increase revenues from all the cross-trading opportunities which existed in such a large organisation.

This concept was the brainchild of Mark Rutherford, my boss. He was also my most enduring business partner in the city, as well as a close personal friend. We worked together at UBS before he set off for a management position at Deutsche Bank. He then persuaded me to help and set up the international equities department at a US bank called DLJ. Finally we had orchestrated a mass move to Lehman Brothers in 2000 after our acquisition by Crédit Suisse. So we had plenty of history. When he proposed the concept of the industry group leader role I was immediately enthusiastic. It was entirely logical as the role would by definition break down the barriers that often exist in investment banking, which could be very revenue generative.

This structure would force people to work together for the good of the team – the challenge was to persuade everyone, but they would get paid for their collective effort.

There were five industry groups created, and I took on financials. The profitability of banks around the world was exploding, a function of cheap credit and high margin products such as derivatives. Unfortunately, as things turned out, it was precisely these types of products which were to bring the world's financial system to the brink of disaster.

Over a two-year period my group more than doubled revenues and by the end of 2007 had generated 200 million dollars. The model worked like a dream – we used all available information within the bank to leverage our opportunities, especially in trading flows and in achieving corporate mandates.

The crowning example was ABN-AMRO, whom we defended against the Royal Bank of Scotland (RBS) in the most ill-advised deal of the time. The Royal Bank shareholders and the British tax payers are still paying the price for that crazy decision.

Before anything had happened we had detected unusual trading activity and excessive volatility in the shares and we informed the management of ABN-AMRO that this was signalling that they were a possible takeover target. We ourselves were conducting a lot of business in the shares. They were sceptical at first but we continued to prove that we knew what we were talking about.

On the day that the hostile approach by RBS was announced, Lehman was rewarded by being appointed by ABN as defence adviser. Our strategy had worked and by the end of the deal our bank had generated at least 100 million dollars of revenue from this single situation. This outcome was clearly as a result of the way in which we had approached the whole topic.

Trading management saw it a different way. We had taken very large trading positions in the stock throughout the period of the takeover and therefore there was significant risk for the bank. They were disappointed that I was not able to provide more help to them and they realised that my skills did not necessarily lie in the execution of big trading strategies.

I made this clear in the end of year review with the Global Head of Trading. While 200 million dollars was a great effort he wanted to turn it in 300 million and I advised him it was impossible. Partly because I thought the market had peaked but also because I wasn't capable of delivering that result. This was not the message he wanted to hear, because he was under pressure to deliver more growth as were all of the Lehman divisions. This was clearly coming from the top.

I eventually moved on to a more dedicated role in client relationship management and two of my colleagues, who were more trading orientated, took over. Within weeks the whole sector went into a meltdown as the financial crisis started to take hold at the beginning of 2008. Not their fault of course but it didn't seem as if the supernormal profits could go on for ever – unwittingly I had rung the bell.

Therefore in my own part of the business I was seeing the aggressive targets that were obviously being set throughout the rest of the bank and were paving the way for the eventual disaster that was to hit the bank later in the year.

And so, as we all watched a slow motion disaster take place before our eyes, through the whole of 2008, we shouldn't have been in denial, but we were. Already resigned to losing all our stock, we kept thinking someone would save the bank which had accrued $20 billion revenues the year before. Whether it was Warren Buffett, the Korean Development Bank, Barclays or even the US Treasury, surely nobody would allow Lehman to collapse?

Lest anyone think I am playing Pontius Pilate, I am not. We all went down together and felt every moment. And yet, many thousands of us believed the protestations of our executive committee and others just below them that we would get through it. There were a few people who knew what they had done, were out of control, had passed 'GO' a number of times and one hopes they can look themselves in the mirror every day. They know who they are and they will not be forgotten.

There are many who think that Mr Fuld will go to jail. Well, no tears from where I sit. But when I look back to that fateful week of September 15th, the collapse of my bank plus much of what I had worked for over a period of eight years, I also remember it as the most fulfilling week of my life in the form of the Help For Heroes charity rugby match.

CHAPTER 24

Help For Heroes

It was a blustery day in March 2008 when I took a call from Mark Souster, then the deputy rugby reporter on *The Times*, now that paper's correspondent. He was in a very emotional state, having read yet another article about the poor treatment of badly injured soldiers who had returned from Iraq and, in particular, Afghanistan. "Hallers, we have to do something about it." And, after a bit more chat, he came up with his big idea, "Why don't we put on a fund-raising rugby match at Twickenham?" I almost dropped my mobile phone in shock – was he serious?

Of course, like the rest of the country, I was totally disgusted at the current state of affairs, by way of background I had spent time at what was then RAF Headley Court in 1984 while recovering from my ankle injury and so it was easy to identify with the modern day rehabilitation centre which was looking after the injured soldiers when they returned to the UK. Headley Court seemed to be in the news constantly for other reasons, however – the poor facilities primarily, which had not seen much improvement from my day. For example, soldiers with life-changing injuries were having to use the public swimming baths in Leatherhead for hydrotherapy treatment because the Headley pool was inadequate. This in turn led to complaints by parents whose children were traumatised by some of the sights of the mutilated servicemen that greeted them whilst they were swimming.

No-one in the UK could fail to be touched by their plight, and the media was laying into the government for lack of funding and support. There was even a rumour that Headley Court would be shut down and all military personnel relocated to Selly Oak, the main hospital, which is situated near Birmingham. By contrast, Headley Court nestles quietly in the Surrey countryside and provides a comfortable setting for rehabilitation, both mental and physical. To close it down seemed unthinkable.

Into the scene stepped Bryn Parry, a former soldier, and his wife Emma. Their motivation was simple – raise money to provide better facilities. So the Help for Heroes charity was born. The public response was immediate, people relishing the opportunity to show that they cared. Millions had already been raised by the time we came along, but it was only the start and they were obviously enthusiastic when we mentioned the prospect of a charity match, though mindful that they were a very small charity so had limited resources themselves with which to help us.

Mark and I kicked around a number of possibilities: northern hemisphere versus southern hemisphere; a combined England/Ireland team versus a combined Scotland/Wales side; a services match, and many others. In the end, we thought that two invitation teams was probably the answer. Mark had already called Twickenham who were agreeable in principle to the concept, but made us aware of the costs of hiring the stadium, as well as the fact that the season was very busy and there were very few available dates.

We put out some initial feelers to the premiership (PRL) which controlled all the top players. They were very supportive – how could they not be? – but, mindful of fixture congestion and the possibility of players being injured while being contracted to their clubs. How would we deal with insurance cover etc? Everyone we spoke to thought it a great idea, but there were drawbacks across the board. We realised we were dancing around the whole thing – we had to make a decision regardless of the obstacles.

Were we prepared to have a go at this? Mark was on the car phone, I was on the mobile outside the Lehman Canary Wharf offices, watching the financial world spin past me, a rather grotesque contrast to what we were discussing. We had even looked at a servicemen's match only, and reckoned we could cover our costs – so where was the downside. "Let's do it," I said finally.

"What was that?" came the response.

"Let's do it," I said again. Mark was in agreement, and ultimately euphoric. The ball was rolling and the next twenty minutes were full of the possibilities. Game on. It was March and the match was set for September so there was no time to lose.

Early pieces fell into place. Firstly we brought in one more partner to make it a 'gang of three'. His name was Adam Cocks, 'Cocksy', twenty-seven years old, who had been on active service in Afghanistan. He had been blown up by a roadside bomb twice in one day, losing his best mate who was alongside him at the time. Cocksy had suffered shrapnel wounds and a broken leg, and was in rehab at Headley. I knew him well as he was in a relationship with Helen Fenwick, who was a great friend of Charlotte, my now girlfriend. We had all been deeply shocked to hear the news of his injury, and his involvement in the match seemed a great way for him to focus on something useful and positive while he recovered, since he was unable to work or be returned to army duties. Mark and I both realised that having Cocksy involved made this venture massively real – he was, after all, a representative of all the people we were trying to help. He was an inspiration to us all, especially when, unbelievably, he had another accident when back in the UK. He was on the way to recovery from his war injuries, when he was wiped out in a road accident, re-broke the leg (a lot worse) and also an arm. A few weeks later he rejoined the effort fully plastered. We had already taken him to our hearts – he never once complained and went on to play a full part in the arrangements despite the severity of his injuries… not much else to say.

We started to apportion responsibilities. Cocksy was assigned to negotiate with the H4H charity so that we could combine our efforts – after all they only had six full-time employees. He organised for us to meet their marketing team down in Headley Court and they showed us a promotional DVD – Mark and I were close to tears as we saw footage of the suffering endured by these brave men and the good humour they displayed through such hardship. Our resolve was immeasurably stiffened.

Mark signed off the agreement with Twickenham for the use of the ground (I had agreed to underwrite the cost) and Paul Vaughan, the RFU's commercial director, promised the full support of the marketing department – now things were rolling.

I just had to get the two teams – easy really!

The next step was to form a committee, and we soon found the ideal chairman. His Honour Jeff Blackett RN, RFU disciplinary officer, Navy Representative on the RFU Council and a senior Judge based in Lincoln's Inn, agreed to take on the job. Safe to say that without his supreme organisational skills we would never have got there. He brought together all the key elements for a successful outcome – the RFU, the armed services, the charity, the marketing etc etc, and importantly the accountability. After every meeting there were action points, which were realistic – after all most of us had day jobs. He also defined our objective: to put 50,000 people into Twickenham and raise £1million. Wow, it made us stop and think what we were now a part of.

There were two other vital appointments who were to make a telling difference. We desperately needed a full time 'point person' who could be the central figure for all the administration, marketing, sponsorship, media etc. After some discussion we agreed that this should be a paid position, so I approached an old friend, Jolyon Armstrong (all 6ft 7ins of him), who had such a background. He was the prime organiser of the Stella Artois tennis tournament, and had been heavily involved in Heineken European Cup and Six Nations rugby. He was ideal and, what's more, he had some time available.

The other person we persuaded onto the committee was Janice Ashby, who had immense experience in marketing and ticket sales. She had almost singlehandedly managed to increase the army/navy match attendance from 15,000 to more than 50,000 over a period of years.

I soon realised that this was a high-powered and opinionated group of people. A lot of emotion came out in the early meetings – at one point I had to remind everyone why we were there, and to stop the side-swiping. There was no rulebook for organising such a one-off occasion. In fact it was unique and we were all finding our way.

Jeff decided that we should meet once a month to review progress and as the weeks passed the committee grew in size to twenty or so. The services of course wanted their equal say, the MOD and even the Joint Chiefs seemed to have to be consulted at every turn. At the end of every meeting, the last point on the agenda was always the team, at which point all eyes turned to me. A crowd of 50,000 and £1m target was a pipedream without two teams which would excite the paying public. I was well aware of this and often glared back at them in exasperation – it was not easy! Jeff always took the pressure off by saying that this was well in hand, whether it was or wasn't.

What of the teams we had to select? Firstly the composition was decided: two from each of the services, a number of Under 21 players, who were unlikely to be governed by the strict premiership rules, and then whatever stars, past or present, we could persuade with agreement from their clubs. We also needed two captains, two team managers and some coaches. These turned out to be the most important appointments of all.

Mark had already approached Lawrence Dallaglio through his agent Richard Railton, to be a non-playing captain. I called Ieuan Evans, the great former Wales captain and winger, to be a manager. He was sunning himself on a beach at the time, drinking chilled Rosé – but he promised to give it serious thought. A call went out to Phil De Glanville, former England captain, to be the other manager.

Imagine our delight when all three agreed, and then, even better, Ieuan called to say that he had persuaded Scott Gibbs (Wales and British Lions' centre) to be the other captain. We had our four in place, and I felt sure that they would be very influential in building two quality sides.

Another early coup was obtaining the services of Mark 'Ronnie' Regan – England and British Lions' hooker. He was in the twilight of his career, and not currently being picked for Bristol. I asked the Bristol coach Richard Hill (a former Bath colleague) if I could approach 'Ronnie' and he agreed. Mark was an immediate 'yes' and, given his high profile in the game, I knew it was a coup for us.

Meantime I emailed all the premiership directors of rugby, notifying them of the fixture and asking for their support in principle, while understanding their own pressures. All responses were positive, especially from Ian McGeechan, who promised at least a couple of his best young players from Wasps. Phil Winstanley, secretary to the PRL (professional clubs) had mentioned it at the PRL board meeting, so all the club owners were now aware of the game, and of course they were all supportive, although getting current internationals to turn out, I knew would be well nigh impossible.

Because of the sensitivities of potential fixture clashes in the UK, we also reached out into Scotland, Ireland and the southern hemisphere. At one point Dan Carter of New Zealand expressed an interest, but sadly it wasn't to be.

On the coaching side, our new management team enrolled Jon Callard (England International and now kicking coach) and Nigel Redman (England and now National U20 coach) for the H4H team, and Phil Davies (Wales) and Eddie O'Sullivan (Ireland) to run what we were now calling the International team.

All we had to do now was select the two sides – I made it clear to everybody that getting forty players was the priority. Then we could work out who they were going to play for! I had, however, overlooked the fact that both captains were going to be focused on the quality of their respective sides, so the eventual selections all fell into line quite naturally.

It was at the Twickenham press conference that we got our biggest break. As we all lined up to face the press and announce formally the date of the charity match, Lawrence dropped his bombshell. He had decided to play! There was a stunned silence around the room – the profile of the match had just doubled. Imagine the look on Scott Gibbs' face – proud Welshman that he is. He fixed Lawrence with a long stare, took a deep breath and retorted: "Well if he's playing, then so am I!"

It was a defining moment – not for the first time the emotion was palpable. And alongside us, Cocksy was there in full military uniform, stick in hand as we had become used to seeing him, as the tempo of the conference sky rocketed. There were photoshoots for the three of them, any number of interviews – the media had suddenly realised something special was unfolding.

Over the following days, we managed to gain the services of a number of England and Wales Under 21 players – this meant that we had almost ten a side already. On reporting this back to the committee, I still saw some glum faces. Where were the internationals who would help fill the stadium? Two old legends, some young thrusters, and a dozen servicemen weren't going to do it. Point taken – it was proving too difficult to get the top names to take the risk, even though they were all for it in principle.

Our biggest moment was just round the corner, we suddenly heard that Lawrence had persuaded Martin Johnson to put on his boots for one last appearance. I punched the air in triumph and relief! It was an incredible development. I received an email from Damian Hopley, ex-England player and chief executive of the players' association. He wrote one line: 'The profile of your game has just gone through the roof.'

The media went wild salivating at the thought of two of England's 'greats' back on the pitch for one last time. The momentum became unstoppable – suddenly the England and Saracens' flanker Richard Hill and centre Will Greenwood were also prepared to give it one more go – so now we had five of England's 2003 World Cup winning team in place. It almost became too much when the incomparable Jason Robinson actually made contact with one week to go, complaining that he hadn't been invited and could he play? Dan Luger (England) and Martin Offiah (England RL star and ex Union Player) also signed up and suddenly the H4H team looked the real deal.

Meantime, the International XV Managers had also been busy. Ieuan and Scott had been flown to Basra to visit the troops and received huge publicity. Players flocked to be available. Gareth Llewellyn, the great Welsh second row, Colin Charvis (Wales, back row), Kenny Logan and David Hilton (Scotland), Justin Bishop (Ireland), Zak Feaunati (Samoa), Dai Evans and Dai Jones

(Wales), and then, the icing on the cake: through Mark Souster, Jonah Lomu, the iconic New Zealand legend, announced that he would fly over.

At the next committee meeting, there was a sense of disbelief that we now had two teams of superstars lined up – admittedly from yesteryear, but the mix was perfect – and not a single premiership club up in arms as had been the fear. Janice Ashby, in charge of marketing and ticket sales, was confidently predicting a crowd of 50,000. Could this really happen? Could we get to our target of £1m? It seemed possible.

Mark, Cocksy and I were in awe of what was taking place, from such unpromising, humble beginnings only six months previously, we now had something far beyond our wildest imaginings.

Added to all this, Jolyon Armstrong was convinced that we now had enough sponsors to cover all our costs (£350,000). Plans were put in place for a plane and a tank to be positioned in the West Car Park at Twickenham. It was even suggested that the match ball could be dropped onto the pitch via a Chinook helicopter. That idea was dismissed after a test run in front of military top brass went horribly wrong. As the Chinook descended slowly towards the pitch, the force of the downdraft blew the advertising boards fifteen rows up into the stadium – not a great way to start the match we thought, and those plans were aborted.

Publicity for the big day mushroomed – Sky Sports, led by Will Greenwood and Stuart Barnes did regular features, and even BBC Radio 1 DJ Johnny Vaughan urged Londoners to come along and support. Advance ticket sales were at 30,000 and Janice wore an ever more confident smile.

Meanwhile the whole RFU machine was whirring away in the background, driven principally by Richard Prescott (Comms) and Tracy Fox-Young. They were key figures for all the logistics and practical issues. I lost count of the many hours they put in for the cause, and no praise is too high for what they achieved.

With a couple of weeks to go, we were given the ultimate endorsement. The two squads were invited to 10 Downing Street to meet the then Prime Minister Gordon Brown – the issue of whether the government was diverting enough funds or not was forgotten – for all of us, it was a great moment of acknowledgement for what everyone had achieved.

It seemed as if nothing could go wrong, until it did – well for me anyway, and in a big way.

For a number of months the financial markets had been showing signs of real stress and my company Lehman Bros was right at the forefront, for reasons already explained. On the weekend before the match, the US Treasury held emergency talks with the CEOs of all the big US Banks in order to save Lehmans – an unbelievable prospect only twelve months previously. On Sunday evening I heard they had failed to reach an agreement, and that my firm would seek Chapter 11 on the Monday morning, i.e was going bankrupt. All hell let loose in the US, Far East and Europe as Lehman employees tried to come to terms with this disaster. And share prices plunged worldwide. Was the financial system itself on the edge of collapse?

I was completely traumatised. It was a personal nightmare. Concerned calls came flooding in.

It was then that I made a decision – I could not influence anything on that day or on following days. So why bother to try? I decided to ignore everything and concentrate on the forthcoming Saturday, I could deal with the future when the day was all over.

If I hadn't previously understood the meaning of the word perspective, I certainly did now. Which is not to say that I didn't care that I had lost everything over a weekend, but that there was something positive out there that I could achieve, in that grimmest of weeks.

On the Wednesday morning, the squads gathered at Twickenham – there was tension in the air, people didn't quite know how to behave. The army second-rower for the H4H team met Martin Johnson for the first time – "The biggest sporting moment of my life," he said afterwards.

After the medicals, there was a presentation by the head of the charity, Bryn Parry. He put on a short DVD detailing the work of the charity and showing distressing scenes of suffering, and during the showing you could have heard a pin drop. If the players hadn't realised what they were into, they did now. The meeting broke, and seemingly the intensity of the occasion had gone up a few notches.

Here I was at the home of rugby, where I had enjoyed so many experiences and such success. I was witnessing unique events coming together, and it seemed right that this was taking centre stage over anything else.

That afternoon we arrived at 10 Downing Street for a 3 p.m audience with the Prime Minister. He was a good hour late, reasons for which I found out the following day. He had been negotiating the Lloyds/HBOS deal in another room with Sir Victor Blank, the Lloyds Chairman. Given that Lehmans was broker to Lloyds and financials were my sector, this was a little too close to home! With a number of other Wall Street Banks on the verge of collapse it was understandable that this deal get done. I joked over following months that I was at No 10 for two reasons, on behalf of Help for Heroes and to get the Lloyds deal done. I am not so vociferous now, as the deal was a total disaster from a shareholder and a taxpayer's point of view.

Nevertheless, the audience went well and Gordon Brown was complimentary enough about the occasion while not missing an opportunity to stress how much the government was committing to the rehabilitation of injured soldiers. An unnecessary comment on such a day. Having been snapped outside No 10, Cocksy and I went across the road and got drunk – not before time, it had been a day of high drama and emotion.

By the Thursday, as event organisers, our work was nearly done. The two teams were safely in their hotels, training grounds had been established, and pre-match routines were in place. Word from both camps was that they were taking the game very seriously, especially the International team. Remember, Scott Gibbs had never won a match at Twickenham. This was definitely his last chance.

Disappointingly, Jonah Lomu had pulled up in training and would miss the game. It was our only injury problem, but the very fact he had turned up was a massive boost for the game. Tactically, we didn't tell the press till the morning of the game.

We were almost there, I spent the Friday evening in the bar with the coaches – we were all nervous but at the same time excited.

A crowd of 50,000 was expected, there was to be live Sky coverage, Prince Charles would be in attendance and there was a promise of clear skies. Bring it on.

The day dawned, cloudless as promised and by mid-morning I had set off from my little rented Mews house in West London.

As I approached the ground, I felt grateful to be fresh and ready – there was a lot to get right. When I walked through the gates, Twickenham was a hive of activity and looked a picture, bathed in sunshine. At this ground, I had won six cup finals, two Grand Slams, and had played in three Varsity Matches as well as a World Cup Final. Yet this was different and in many ways so much more meaningful.

Jolyon Armstrong was there waiting, and took me off to the sponsors' boxes, offering our thanks. Their contributions had ensured that the money raised through gate receipts would go directly to the charity, a great achievement.

The military were there in force, of all ranks, and were quick to proffer handshakes and best wishes for the day. My father, who passed away in 2001, had been in the Fleet Air Arm for thirty-five years and I knew he would have loved to have been there. I also recalled that my grandfather had been shot down over Basra some seventy years earlier, and is in fact buried there. All this, plus the help I had myself received from Headley Court all those years ago, it all seemed so appropriate.

The biggest challenge was yet to come. It had been decided that I would make a brief speech before kick off to acknowledge the efforts of so many people. There was no doubt in my mind that this was crucial moment when we had the crowd in our pockets, and they could appreciate fully the nature of the occasion.

In addition, there was a DVD provided by the charity which featured Mark Ormrod, who had lost both legs and an arm in Afghanistan. We planned to show it on the big Twickenham screen just before kick off. We also had the task of ensuring that Prince Charles and Camilla, Duchess of Cornwall, were safely in their seats so that they would see all the pre-match events.

Come 2 p.m, the ground was already filling up, as if the crowd realised that the pre-match atmosphere was to be found inside the stadium, not outside.

First the Help for Heroes flag was carried aloft around the ground by a number of soldiers, and everyone erupted into spontaneous applause as they made their way.

Then out came the two teams, one heading to the right, the other to the left, as planned, to acknowledge the crowd. Pictures of Martin Johnson, Lawrence Dallaglio and others flashed up on the screen as they ran out. The noise and applause grew to levels that I hadn't experienced even before an international. It was heartfelt and very moving. The lump in my throat grew, although I knew I had to hold myself together for the speech.

Eventually the two teams came to face the royal box, and it was announced that I would say some words on behalf of the charity – Sky cameras zoomed in and I was off. Mark Souster, whose original idea this was, and Cocksy, the symbol of our efforts, stood alongside me, and they were the first people I mentioned.

There was a long list of thank-yous and luckily I had rehearsed well, so didn't miss any important names, before asking the crowd to watch the DVD. There was total silence as Mark Ormrod told his story of how he was coping with no legs and only one arm. His was a story of optimism and hope against the background of such adversity – I defy anyone in the stadium to have had a dry eye, and the players were visibly moved. To a great cheer, I was able to announce that we had hit our target of £1m, and in fact exceeded it, apparently it was a match fit for the occasion, I have to admit much of it passed me by. We had got there, and had realised the dream. That's what mattered, and the charity Help for Heroes was known to many thousands more – which would result in better treatment for wounded soldiers.

I am still in awe of the whole adventure, and it represents the most meaningful experience of my life. It bonded me with an incredible group of people, who combined to make it happen. Rugby, when asked, stood up to be counted and acknowledged in its special way a massive vote of thanks to our soldiers, and showed it cared. The momentum this gave the charity is inestimable, and it all came about because on a blustery day in March one man bothered to make a call to another – if we improved just one person's life as a result, it was worth it.

CHAPTER 25

Pulling the Plug on Bath

The call from Andrew Brownsword came very much out of the blue. He had been chairman and owner of Bath rugby for more than a decade since the game had gone professional. It was no secret that since winning the European cup under Andy Robinson in 2008, the club had under-performed hugely in the professional era, despite a succession of high profile names being recruited, on and off the field. Many famous former Bath players had tried their hand as manager of the club, chief executive officer, head of rugby and just about every other executive title you can think of. In the first decade of professional rugby the most sensible structure was a decision made on the hoof, depending on what day of the week it was – or at least that's how it seemed more often than not.

Andrew wished to talk to me about a role with Bath, and I readily agreed to see him. My passion for the club was undiminished, and what is more the RFU was on the verge of completing a deal with the leading twelve clubs which would secure a longer-term financial outcome, in return for the England set-up having more access to international players. My involvement in this deal had been significant as described, but I had crossed swords so much with the 'powers-that-be' among the Twickenham hierarchy, that I was unlikely to be continuing on any sort of capacity in the game.

We met in a coffee bar down in Canary Wharf, where I was based with Lehman Brothers – the year being 2007 – financial markets were in a frenzy at that time and I was super busy, but there was always time in my life for rugby, and I could see that some involvement with Bath could be fun. In addition, my personal life had by now become pretty volatile since I had separated from my wife Suzanne and was living in rented accommodation in Westminster. Apart from the inevitable pressures which that situation brought, I was far more flexible in how I spent my free moments, and to have the opportunity to spend time in Bath was certainly an attractive one.

Andrew offered me a position as a non-executive director, explaining to me that having a businessman ex-rugby player was a role that was desperately needed down at Bath. In his view the off-field structure lacked credibility and he wanted to bring in some experience. My status as an ex-club player would also send a message to the Bath faithful.

I was intrigued. I had heard all the criticism of Andrew over the years, his lack of investment in the club, his bull-headedness and his reputation as a very tough businessman. I had no fears and indeed that was the challenge. It was also clear that he would likely become a seller of the club over time, and that had set my mind working on a possible plan.

So, on a number of fronts there seemed to be opportunity aplenty – and if I failed to make an impact I would just be another in a long line of ex-players who had given it a go. Where was the downside? I accepted Andrew's offer and he stressed that once I had introduced myself to everyone I should conduct a thorough review of the club on and off the field, but mostly the latter. My next act was to resign from the RFU Council and I quietly consulted one or two friendly faces on how I should best do this. I didn't want to appear hasty or be seen to be making a knee-jerk response, but at the same time I was being quietly marginalised, so I felt that it would be best if I were to disappear as quickly and as discreetly as possible.

I still shake my head sadly at some of the political goings on at the union. I was ostensibly the right person from the RFU to chair the newly formed Professional Game Board, which was set up to administer the professional game in England, once the deal with the clubs was signed. My experience at Club England had been doing precisely that for the RFU, and of course there had been my involvement with Harlequins. What's more, I had great relationships with the Players' Association and Premiership Rugby.

However, I already knew that as far as Francis Baron and Martyn Thomas were concerned my appointment was a non-starter. To my mind they were each of them control freaks in their own way, and so the promise that I was interested only in a rugby agenda may well have been irrelevant to them. They felt that I would be too close to the other stakeholders and not represent the RFU strongly enough. They also wouldn't forgive me for my oft outspokenness, when I felt they were ill-informed or self-interested. So they persuaded John Spencer, the then chairman of Club England, who had already made it known he thought I was the ideal candidate, to reverse that decision, join the board himself and support the appointment of both Baron and Thomas (as chairman) of the PGB. What a joke! Neither Baron nor Thomas seemed to have very much idea what they were doing, given their lack of experience of rugby at the highest levels; indeed the clubs had a deep mistrust of both of them.

But as Mark McCafferty, with his characteristic grasp of reality, said to me, what was the point of fighting these battles. The clubs had the deal they wanted (more or less), and frankly they didn't care who was on the PGB, because the big decisions had all been made. A fair enough point, and one which I had already worked out for myself. So fundamentally there was nothing left for me at the RFU. What is more, John Spencer had now been drawn into the web of intrigue and I felt he struggled to be up front with me on the facts. I couldn't really be too angry with all that since he was placed in an impossible position. Had he refused to cooperate he would have found himself out in the cold. But given all our years of working together with Club England throughout the glory years of the 2003 World Cup victory, and then the struggles since the departure of Clive Woodward in 2004, I was saddened that he couldn't look me in the eye and tell it to me straight.

So I wrote my letter of resignation, and sent a friendly email to the council taking my leave. It was all very constructive, although I felt emotional at the time since I had given nearly ten years of pro bono effort during a roller coaster time. I got some nice replies from a number of council members, who had become good friends over time. But there was not a single comment from the executives, not even an invitation to put my head in a dark place. How petty, I thought. Whatever opinion they had of me, my commitment to English rugby could not be disputed. My efforts over the years had been with one aim, the long-term improvement of English rugby's administration leading to success for our players. Whatever mistakes I had made along the way, and there were many, and however unpopular I was among certain members of the management board, a simple response to my resignation surely was not too much to ask.

I didn't dwell on it; there was no time to do so as I reminded myself when travelling down the M4 motorway to the greatest of Georgian cities, Bath, to enter a final chapter in my love affair with one of the loveliest of English cities and one of the proudest Rugby clubs in the world.

Of course, I had no idea what to expect from either the players, the administration or indeed the supporters and various old friends who were still connected to the club – after all I had lived there for ten years, so I knew people from all walks of life, be it business, social or sporting.

My first impression was that nothing had changed from my time at the club nearly twenty years earlier; there was a temporary stand or two, there had been one or two licks of paint over the intervening years, but the changing rooms were in the same place, the only difference from my playing days being that the plunge baths had been removed. Just as well, they are a particular invention of rugby which made sure you learned never to drop the soap!

The truth was that no investment had been made in the club for a number of years and it showed. I had some sympathy for Brownsword, because the on-going feud between the RFU and the clubs meant that the owners were always struggling to make ends meet, in fact most clubs lost money. Also the constant speculation about building a new stadium on The Rec meant that there seemed little point in injecting any money on a short-term basis.

But that was the bigger picture. More important was the operational side of the club, on and off the field, on which I had been brought in to advise and effect change. Brownsword had effectively given me *carte blanche* to make any recommendations that I saw fit. So I proceeded to get around the players and administrators and find out how everyone felt about the club.

Broadly, everyone was in a state of paralysis, no one was sure about the future of the ground; people were unhappy with the lack of current investment, and disturbed by the lack of off-field support.

It was difficult to know where to start, but I opted to listen to anyone who had a view. Some were old friends of mine, people such as David Jenkins, a former player, touch judge and commercial director. He was passionate about rugby and always had a view – in this case he was highly critical of Brownsword and his unwillingness to listen to any advice. This became a common theme, hardly surprising given the fact that Andrew was a highly successful businessman, self-made. No doubt he hadn't got there by listening to other people all the time.

It was also a sad fact that the early generation of club owners such as Andrew had received little or no help from the RFU as to how to manage their clubs. In truth, professionalism was an unwelcome outcome for the union, since Twickenham had lost control of the players. Without exception they had all signed up to the clubs, which were offering them financial contracts. This was in sharp contrast to the RFU, then run by Dudley Wood, who refused to accept that we were moving into an era of professionalism. Meantime, on the other side of the world, some of the top All Blacks' retired stars were visiting current players to sign them up to the NZ RFU before anyone else picked them off. What on earth had possessed the RFU to ignore the trend that was right under their noses?

So I did have some sympathy with Andrew. I liked the man himself – he was a hard-nosed operator, owning businesses in greeting cards, property, hotels and leisure to name a few. His involvement with Bath had been largely philanthropic and, after all, he had purchased the most successful club in English rugby history in one of the most picturesque cities in the world. Surely this was a low risk trade. But how wrong could you be? No one could make any money out of club rugby in the UK: low crowds, poor TV revenues and overpaid players made sure of that. The numbers simply didn't add up and so anyone who had got involved was locked in for the foreseeable future unless they were prepared to cut their losses.

It seemed churlish then to criticise Andrew, when he had been prepared to put his hand in his admittedly deep pocket. However, he had seemingly failed to apply his business acumen to the rugby club. There was no individual anywhere to be seen who had an understanding of the twin pressures at work. Andrew had simply brought in people who worked for or advised him, and they all seemed petrified of him. He was a little scary it has to be said, but he is the sort of man you have to stand up to, or he will trample you underfoot.

There were no board meetings, unless I was prepared to come down to Bath from London, and so very few decisions were ever made, except by Andrew, when he felt in the mood to make them.

With this backdrop it was very clear that there was deep-seated unhappiness and I set about trying to fix it. But where was I to start?

My first thought was to find out the player situation, establish which contracts were about to expire, and which players might be thinking of leaving. Although Bath paid well they adhered strictly to the salary cap, the limit placed on squad expenditure for a season. The intention here was to create a level playing field for the premiership competition. In reality a small number of clubs were far more ambitious than that and found ways around it, much to the disgust of Bath and others who kept to the rules. For example Leicester, Bath's arch rivals for many years, somehow managed to maintain a squad containing twenty-seven internationals, and Gloucester had twenty-five, and

I was well aware of the going rate for such quality players from what we were having to pay our own.

My first concern was Steve Borthwick, the England captain. He was out of contract at the end of season, as was Matt Stevens, one of the most talented forwards in the country. Lastly, our mercurial, gifted, but temperamental inside centre Olly Barkley was known to be fretful. The club certainly didn't need to lose any of these guys, as the approaching season had Bath as favourites to be in the top four by the finish. In addition they were the heartbeat of the side in different ways. Steve didn't appear very inspirational, but tall, broody and with eyes set deep into his face. But the players loved and respected him. I felt that he let his captaincy be impacted by the position he played in (unlike say Martin Johnson) rather than creative captaincy. Nonetheless he was a key figure. And I was forever hearing stories about his legendary focus on line-out calls.

Matt Stevens was the new model front row forward, jinking into the midfield with gay abandon, and selling dummies with his equally gifted hooker Lee Mears. I have to admit when I saw them at their best, I imagined that I might I have just let them occupy some of the midfield space when I played. Normally I wouldn't let a forward come near us unless it was to clear up some mess we had left. Midfield was the domain of centre-threequarters, and I am sure the likes of Jerry Guscott, John Palmer, Phil De Glanville – all Bath legends – would agree. Anyway, the last thing we needed was for Matt to leave Bath, I thought of him at the time as a probable future Bath captain.

Olly had somehow never fulfilled his obvious talent, but now with Butch James, the Springbok No10 alongside him, there seemed no reason for him to consider other clubs.

On inquiry I was assured by Nigel Laughton, our operations director, that the negotiations were going well and there was no cause for concern. My mild sense of unease that none of the trio had signed yet was assuaged by the fact that apparently it always took this long – but then why wasn't the agent returning our calls? However, I took him at his word and continued to spread messages of support through the club and give the impression I was making some early difference.

How wrong I was.

One morning in mid-November, and not long after a great win by Bath over our local rivals Gloucester which had placed us at the top of the premiership, I received a call from Steve Meehan, the Bath coach. Steve was an

Aussie with a wry sense of humour, but not that optimistic a person at times – justifiably so it has to be said. He had worked at Stade Francais with Nick Mallett and that was good enough for me, and without doubt Steve had a lot of talent. In the two seasons that I spent at the club we were the most attractive side in the country when at their best scoring great tries at will. Steve had plenty to do with that, but there was a *je ne sais quoi* quality to him, which didn't really endear him to players, so there was always an undercurrent there, of something that was not quite right.

His phone call on that late, autumn morning did not convey a great piece of news – Steve Borthwick had decided to leave Bath to join Saracens at the end of the season. I was speechless, not because of the fact that Borthwick was leaving, these things happen and in my line of work much more often than they should, the graveyards are full of indispensable people, as the saying goes. No, I was shocked because I had been told there were no worries and absolutely no chance of him leaving. I quickly identified that there was in fact no chance of him staying for a number of reasons and mentally I felt we should look ahead. Who should captain the side? How would we replace him? Would there be any collateral damage to contain? Then there was the little matter of the Barkley and Stevens' contracts.

Unfortunately Nigel Laughton had misread the situation and he evidently had no effective rapport with the agents and certainly not the players. However, it wasn't really his fault because ultimately he wasn't responsible. I kicked myself for not having stepped in much earlier to check that the simmering unhappiness at the club wasn't going to translate into mass departures. Being a top side made us targets for that for sure and there were still plenty of wealthy rugby-mad owners who would be prepared to spend the money.

It turned out that Olly Barkley was indeed thinking of leaving, and I went into overdrive explaining how foolhardy that would be – didn't he want to make a long-term England career for himself after all the disappointments? Butch James at 10 could only help matters, but Olly seemed to have an intent about him, which made me feel that he had already mentally checked out. I took money off the table as an issue, and frankly the interested club, Gloucester, hadn't offered much more than he was currently getting. It was the change he was after. He felt stale, and he thought that he just had to experience something different. After exhausting the conversation there was nothing left to say. However I made him promise to call me first when he had made his decision.

Honesty is important in the small world of rugby, and if you leave these things to agents then the story comes out all wrong, if at all.

I was walking up Regent Street when Olly called to say he had finally decided to leave. I was respectful and promised that we would have nothing but good words to say about him, and that if he ever wanted to come back (which he did eventually) then the door would remain open. I squashed all negative commentary inside the club and spoke positively to the media. Privately I thought he had made a rubbish decision and that he had been influenced by commission-hungry agents. I can't remember this particular agent's name, and I won't give him the credit of bothering to find out, but when I saw him at the Rugby Writers' dinner the following year I let him have both barrels. He was crowing about how well Olly was doing, and I almost hit him. That, though, is just not my style, so instead I informed him bleakly, in front of an audience, that he had ruined Olly's career, that he would fail at Gloucester and that I hoped the agent would choke on the commission he had earned on the transfer. It wasn't pretty stuff, but I was seething, and it was late on so my fury had been fuelled by a few beers.

It was a different story with Matt Stevens. He was chilled. He loved Bath and was planning to open a coffee shop with Lee Mears. He also had a very serious and credible agent in Richard Thompson, who ran Merlin Entertainment. Matt was a brand. He was an X-Factor finalist, a new model prop with charisma, and was a very likeable guy. I took a day off to negotiate his new contract – Bath were panicking after the double departure and didn't need a third. We at Bath all knew the meaning of the word leverage, and by the end of the meeting there was a very healthy financial outcome for Matt.

Having spent many years listening to egotistical brokers telling me how much they were worth, it was mildly amusing listening to Richard extract a major number for Matt. But he did it professionally

So, despite losing two high profile players we had at least managed to hang on to Matt Stevens and that really mattered to the club. Of course, Borthwick and Barkley were staying till the end of the season, so it was a delayed effect. Meantime Meehan and I discussed a replacement captain to see Bath through to the end of the season, although disappointingly not many names were forthcoming. I thought back to my Bath playing days when almost every player would have captained the team if given half a chance, and in fact there were sometimes a few self-appointed captains on the field of play who needed to be told to shut up. Remarkably the senior players came back to Steve and said that they wanted Borthwick to carry on since no one else wanted to do the job. I was amazed at their loyalty, but felt it was misguided. Well, I suppose I was wrong because Steve led the team to the European Challenge Trophy that year, which was Bath's first trophy for a decade. Of course it wasn't the premier trophy, the Heineken Cup, but the players deserved their triumph for their fine play throughout the season.

As I got more and more involved down at the club some facts started to emerge and they demanded action. Firstly we needed an executive off the field, someone who could take rugby-based decisions – it couldn't be me obviously, nor Steve Meehan. The incumbent CEO Bob Calleja had been pushed into the job by Andrew Brownsword and had no rugby background, nor did his legion of financial advisors.

I thought long and hard about the requirements for a role appropriate to Bath and their needs. When you looked back at professional rugby's brief history it was littered with ill-advised appointments, partly because nobody had a blueprint for a successful management structure. This had happened at Bath in particular, mainly because various former players had been shoehorned into action without the proper experience. So when the name of Phil De Glanville popped up. I was naturally cautious, but here was someone who for a number of years had been working in sports administration with Sport England, as well as being a former England captain and Bath player. Being highly respected inside and outside the game was a bonus.

We met up for a preliminary chat; a subsequent meeting with Steve Meehan confirmed to me that we had our man. It was simply a question of the terms and conditions and working out the process of extracting him. But there was another situation brewing which was to have a major impact on the eventual outcome.

The central issue at Bath was that Andrew Brownsword didn't seem really committed to rugby at Bath. As already stated his involvement was more philanthropic than anything else and he certainly wasn't prepared to invest any money, so the club was in a real quandary. In addition there seemed to be no way forward in developing the ground and building a new stadium.

To say this was an ongoing saga is an understatement. It had been discussed for years, the stumbling block being the charity commission whose articles of association meant that commercial activities shouldn't be taking place on the site of the rugby ground in the first place. Many people had almost given up the will to live as the years passed without a resolution. It really was the elephant in the room as far as the club was concerned and it was getting to the players as well. Poor facilities get you down – I don't think the showers had changed since my day and the training ground at Lambridge was always suffering from flooding, hardly factors that were conducive to quality performance.

As with all these things negotiation is the only way and Brownsword struggled with this approach. I couldn't blame him for his frustration, but to just give up on it didn't seem right either. All sorts of brinkmanship were employed – leaving The Rec for another site, relocating to Bristol, even merging with these West Country neighbours. As I found myself drawn deeper into the story I could see it was fiendishly difficult to seek a way forward.

The status ran something like this: a reluctant owner, poor facilities, an off-field structure which left a lot to be desired, a deeply unsuccessful team on the pitch – no trophies since 1998 – a pretty much broken franchise and hardly any voice at the premiership table; against such a backdrop it seemed at odds for me to consider buying the club. Well, that was exactly what I was thinking, with the help of one of my oldest friends, Mark Jackson, who was also the main sponsor of the club. There were four others who will remain nameless, but were all wealthy rugby-mad businessmen who were enthused at the prospect of being a part-owner of such a prestigious franchise. We had gathered together nearly £1. 5million which would just about give us the chance to get various balls rolling.

Brownsword was only too happy to talk to us – Mark and I were Bath men and had the right intentions in his book. This was an elegant exit for him. I had sought advice from Lord Ian MacLaurin, who was living near Bath and often came to matches as a sponsor. He was very supportive, and I knew that if the takeover came about then we would have a strong advocate.

Progress was slow, but eventually we came to be in Brownsword's Bath office with his advisers, Jeremy Hancock and Ed Goodall. We weren't entirely sure of their motives and they were very tight with information, probably because Andrew was in control and they didn't want to step out of line. Draft contracts were even in the offing, before he dropped his bombshell. "Of course, I want what I paid for the club." A little matter of £5 million.

I could scarcely believe it. We hadn't really discussed price, but there were no assets other than P shares, courtesy of membership of the premiership, he didn't own the ground, he had underinvested and the goodwill value had certainly been damaged over the years. Yes there was the matter of the Trustees of Bath Rugby, who had a share of the training ground at Lambridge and they had to be bought out, but he couldn't just demand what he had paid some thirteen years ago.

Our surprise brought out immediate irritation in him, as is the case with every entrepreneur who can't get his own way. The meeting ended in an *impasse* as we clearly couldn't just agree the price like that. We suggested that we would consult with our partners and revert, but we were shocked at the arbitrary turn of events.

There were other consequences. I had just about signed up Phil De Glanville to take on a senior role at the club, and he was preparing to talk to his current employers although clearly nothing was agreed yet. It required the sign-off from Brownsword before any further progress could be made. Except that he suddenly went *incommunicado* and wouldn't return calls. I was furious. I felt this was messing with people's lives and unacceptable. Meehan was bemused and suddenly all my confidence in being able to effect change was diminished in a big way. I had been warned by many that I would go the way that many others had before me, but I felt sure that this time it would be different.

When I eventually made contact Andrew told me he wouldn't confirm the offer. I could see everything unravelling before my eyes. Even an offer to go back and discuss the £5m club deal was disdainfully refused. Many months on it transpired he was in talks with a number of people to sell the club and Bruce Craig, the owner at the time of writing, had money to burn. As we have seen he has put his money where his mouth is, and it was much more than we had that's for sure. It is to be hoped all the money yields the return we all want from this famous old club.

With both initiatives dead in the water there was effectively nowhere else to go. But before I could step out of the picture a serious scandal erupted which was to set the seal on an already out of control premiership club. The suspension of Matt Stevens for failing a drugs' test had put the club in the limelight for all the wrong reasons. However, there was widespread sympathy for the man, and rightly so. Matt is a quality person who has become a close friend.

Following his suspension, he was treated quite disgracefully by Bath and the RFU. He was in reality suffering from an illness and the game simply threw out a ban and dropped him like a hot potato. I saw a lot of him during the second year of his ban and came to recognise the integrity of the man. His re-emergence as an England squad member is an inspirational story of someone dealing with adversity, living the dream and refusing to be beaten. A big hand to you Matt and may our game in England be ashamed of the way it dealt with the affair.

So it was with the five players banned on suspicion of cocaine abuse. They were treated like common criminals and, as with the governing body, it was all based on the ignorance of the club on how to deal with the situation. It is all very well to have a zero tolerance toward drugs, but Bath had no process in place to which they could refer, all of which left individuals to make decisions on the hoof.

In desperation I called Brownsword as I saw things spiralling out of control. The players' lawyer, the RFU, the players' union, the players themselves, not to mention their families, were all pleading for some common sense. Brownsword was noncommittal. He suggested that people who break the law should be punished and that was what he intended to see happen. No acceptance that a club with no moral compass had allowed poor behaviour patterns to emerge. None of these players were bad people they simply had a good chunk of money, were stuck in the goldfish bowl of Bath and were bored – none of this is an excuse, but the consequence of all those factors coming together was there for all to see and yet, frankly, it needn't have happened. The lack of interest and understanding shown by the club towards the players off the field was definitely a contributing factor. Now the club was paying the price.

Having said all this there was absolutely no excuse for the players' behaviour. When you consider all the money that is washing around in the pockets of young players who have little to do in their leisure time, then an accusation of serial drug taking has to be an indicator of a broader issue that needs to be addressed. There is nowhere near enough care taken over player welfare, lifestyle and career planning. When the academies were set up at the turn of the century the clubs effectively used them as a preparatory school for their senior players. There was very little effort to give them any kind of education or send them out to local businesses for example. You could say that the generally accepted criticism of players lacking leadership and character is a direct consequence of a poor vision by the game's authorities as regards the intellectual capabilities of its membership.

The eventual banning of the five players was inconclusive on the evidence actually received, but it heralded the departure of all of them, as well as the move to Saracens by Matt Stevens. The way in which Bath ignored the England international was, as I said, nothing short of disgraceful, mind you the RFU wasn't much better. Part of the issue is that the game had no prescribed way of dealing with drug abuse and so it buried its head in the sand when all human instinct and emotion cried out for a sympathetic approach.

I remembered many years earlier after my last game for England having my name drawn from the bag for a drugs test and I didn't care too much, because we had just won our second Grand Slam. When I had rehydrated after a few pints and could actually give a urine sample, I then became picky over the whole thing and refused to cooperate, thinking it a waste of time as I was retiring anyway. When the officials told me I would be found guilty if I refused, I yielded and handed over some alcohol-fuelled samples, but of course nothing else. How times have changed.

My eventual resignation from Bath was accompanied by a letter to Brownsword detailing all the promises which I felt he had failed to deliver on, and asking him in reality how much longer he could continue. Well, perhaps he already knew that since Bruce Craig was waiting in the wings.

My commitment to my old club remains as strong as ever, and while money is the name of the game now, so is heart and passion and emotion. When they can add those qualities to the processes at work in the pro game – not to mention a new stadium, fingers crossed – then Bath can assume its rightful place at the top of the game in Europe. The appointment of my old mate, the maverick David Trick, as club president, was a step in the right direction.

CHAPTER 26

Another Life Changer

When I look back the two years spanning 2007-2009 were life changing for me from a personal and business point of view, there is no other way to put it. We can all look back at the past and wonder about what would have changed if… big decisions you make… events which take place out of your control. It is also easy to reflect and regret, but in all honesty that isn't right, and I don't.

If my attempts to describe this time comes across as hectic, well it was, but it set the basis for a real change in perspective on my rugby, business and private life, not to mention the arrival of a new charity I decided to support.

In summary, during that period my marriage sadly ended after twenty years, Lehman Brothers in its attempts to be a global market leader went bankrupt, an event which almost broke the world's financial system and I became involved in the Help for Heroes Charity raising £1.5 million from a Twickenham rugby match. I also finally decided my fused ankle was ready for a marathon, a massive decision in itself, which I would run on behalf of CRY. Amidst all this I met Charlotte which changed my personal life forever.

In 2007 the financial markets were enjoying unprecedented activity, property prices were rocketing and there were many corporate deals going on. However the storm clouds were building over my company Lehman Bros, while optically achieving record results, and enjoying a market value of $40 billion plus. We were the next Goldman Sachs, apparently unstoppable, and that year my financials division was a $200 million revenue business. But the level of risk being taken was out of control. It's just that no one put their hand up to stop it all. I knew that it was getting scary. I was more and more embedded in Lehman's senior management and was seeing decisions at first hand which could not be justified, and which ultimately led to me standing down as Head of the Financials Group which I managed.

In the middle of all this, Suzanne and I separated, a tough thing for any family and I didn't underestimate the impact it would have. I did my best to ensure that Sophie and Alexander's lives continued in as least adisrupted way as possible, despite the obvious changes for us all. Their successful exams followed by university entrance reflected hugely on them, and I didn't underestimate Suzanne's role in keeping them focussed during a difficult time.

I initially went to live in Westminster, renting on my own at the top of Whitehall Court on Horseguards Avenue. I couldn't have gone to a more lofty position in the middle of London unless I had lodged in the London Eye. Every morning I woke up I had Lord Nelson looking at me. I reckoned he was 200 metres away from me on my eye line. We had more than a few conversations (one way of course!) over those months, as I digested that my life had changed forever. Many times I walked through a deserted Trafalgar Square at the crack of dawn to collect my car, and the end of day was a raft of essential admin, but it was the path I had chosen. Holding down a senior job with Lehman Brothers at the same time, which involved looking after other peoples' lives, was a challenge, let's just say that.

This was particularly so as I was now in another relationship. I had first met Charlotte in 2006, a perfectly innocent encounter which involved discussing job opportunities as she had just arrived in London. Little did I or she know that we would eventually fall in love with each other.

In my first months together with Charlotte, life was a whirl of hectic activity, business and social, not much time to reflect. My hours in our offices at Canary Wharf were incredibly full on, seemingly nonstop from 6.30 a.m through the day with no let up.

Out of the office, I soon got to know Charlotte's closest friends and acquaintances, not to mention her family. It's a fact of life that people make judgements, but they took at face value our feelings for one another and I was welcomed into her family. In addition, many of Charlotte's circle of friends are good mates of mine now, and I hugely value those friendships.

At weekends we often went out of London, sometimes up north and occasionally down to Bath, as I needed to watch some rugby given my position as a director of the club. Happily, Bath was operating at the top end of the premiership, I had reintroduced some old players back into the club, and people seemed content with the way things were. My great friends, the Jacksons, often put us up, and they took to Charlotte immediately – well why wouldn't they?

As the months passed, it became clear to me that the problems at Bath rugby weren't going to be cleared up with the owner Andrew Brownsword at the helm, and I started to wonder how long I could put up with it all. Then in September 2008 Lehman Bros finally went under, in a blaze of publicity. Somehow the collapse of a bank where I had given so much over an eight-year period didn't seem so cataclysmic when put in the context of the Help for Heroes' rugby match which I helped organise – I hadn't had my legs or arms blown off by an IED, or had another kind of life-changing injury. What's more, the advent of Nomura who bought the Lehman Asian and European business from the administrators seemed to indicate business as usual and yet another reincarnation, so I was back in action: same desk, different owners and very much poorer. I had now experienced three of the largest and most traumatic corporate unravellings in the financial markets (UBS, DLJ and Lehman). Thousands of people losing jobs, many of them good friends, and even if they ended up somewhere else it wasn't the same.

I completely accept the hostility to the banking sector. However, the large majority of people worked very long hours, had little or no holiday and if not at work were travelling to and from. People could lose their jobs on a whim, with no recourse and all the costs associated of living in such an environment. Once you were caught up in it, it was very difficult to step away unless there were powerful reasons. I was just about to find one…

Christmas 2008 passed quietly, and Charlotte and I went abroad for New Year; winter sunshine was essential, especially after a traumatic few months dealing with Lehmans' collapse. There was nothing more we liked to do than go away on our own. Back at home, a stroll round London at a weekend, or a night out at the cinema, it didn't matter much. However we were ignoring some gathering pressures – most people were aware of and embraced our relationship, but it wasn't all straightforward.

I undoubtedly wanted Charlotte to be part of the rest of my life, and we had been through so much to establish that our relationship was genuine. But there were plenty of pressures. For example, we wanted a relationship to exist between us and Sophie and Alexander, my teenage children, but that wasn't going to be easy in the early days, and nor did we expect them to just accept us.

Even now I wonder why we decided we needed a time out, but some two years after meeting each other we parted. We hadn't fallen out, quite the contrary, there was simply a feeling that we should have a break. I guess sometimes when there is pressure around you make rubbish decisions. I felt pretty desolate and days ceased to have any real meaning or purpose and all the time I was asking myself what on earth we were doing. Charlotte and I continued to stay in contact and we trusted each other and that this would all turn out OK, but in reality we both suffered. We had fought every pressure imaginable to be together, we still loved each other, so why were we throwing it away?

Meantime at the workplace, Nomura was draining me of all my energy. The post Lehman environment was as tough as you like, and absolutely no fun. Hardly a good mix when you are working fifty-five hours plus a week. In addition I was put in charge of the Emerging Markets business: fifty or so people from both Nomura and Lehman. It was one of the few businesses that had a crossover following the acquisition. The only problem was, that there was no business and Nomura's new management (ex-Lehman) didn't really believe in it. It was the first time in my career that I had to be disingenuous with my team. I couldn't tell them that I felt there was no future because I didn't have the right. So I simply tried to support them and encourage them to make the best of a terrible market environment. But it was so demotivating, most of all because I felt we should be investing in the markets, and produced much supporting evidence. But the Nomura agenda was to get the European business flowing – how short-sighted – and I have since been proved very right as Emerging Markets recovered very strongly.

I was of course still massively involved in European Markets, being one of Lehman's most senior managing directors for that business. I was regarded along with others as a key part of the new business, but here I was finding myself at odds with my colleagues, and however hard I fought I got nowhere. Psychologically I found it difficult to keep arguing, because the bottom line was that we felt pretty lucky to still be employed!

I think the worst impact of all this was that they lost me as a person. I live my business life with passion and conviction at the forefront, and above all I need to feel the support. I could feel myself emotionally checking out.

Getting to know everyone from Nomura Emerging Markets was tough, however good a people person I felt myself to be. Russians, Turks, Egyptians, Americans, Japanese, Eastern Europeans were just some of the nationalities – I felt like a member of the Diplomatic Corps doing rather a bad job of telling some of them they weren't going to be paid at all well, in fact many of them were going to be laid off. How do you make that judgement when you don't even know them to make the call. Worse still, I liked most, if not all, of them and I felt wretched.

The upshot of all this was that my working day was a constant struggle and, worse than that, the evenings and weekends now I was on my own were a matter of forcing contact with friends, or dealing with an increasingly difficult situation at Bath rugby. The obvious reluctance of Brownsword to stay engaged, and the drugs scandal at the end of the 2009 season not long after the banning of Matt Stevens, made me realise that there was little point in staying involved in such an environment.

Something had to give. Charlotte was still the only person with whom I could share everything. I had a welcome break in South Africa following the Lions, and as the summer approached life on my own in London was feeling like a real struggle. We both knew that we had to give ourselves a proper break and see it through whatever that meant, even though I had decided in my heart that it was the last thing I wanted.

It was during the summer of 2009 that I felt I had to bring everything to a head. I resolved to resign from my Bath rugby directorship, hand my notice in to Nomura and even more dramatically to leave London and go overseas. Like most people, we all have friends in distant climes who extend an open-ended invitation to come and visit. We rarely take them up on it, well I decided it was a good moment.

The Nomura decision was a big move but I realised that I simply had nothing more to give, and importantly it didn't seem to matter anymore. Mark Rutherford, still my boss after all these years, and one of my closest friends, was entirely sympathetic and promised to help me exit from the business in the best way possible. He also knew that from an emotional standpoint I was bleeding badly inside and couldn't keep going. I was contracted through to the following April and for the sake of morale at Nomura, my departure had to be pitched correctly, a lifestyle change rather than any discontent at the firm itself which would have been damaging to all of us. This resulted in a period of secret negotiations where absolutely no one could be in the loop other than the Nomura executive.

Despite Rutherford's best efforts to describe my situation and the reasons behind wanting to leave, they first tried to persuade me to stay and take on another role, thinking that I had simply become demotivated by the Emerging

Markets job. Well they were right but I wasn't trying to game them for more responsibility or more money. I was called in to see the boss, Rachid Bouzouba. He didn't know me that well being from a derivatives trading background, and he wanted to hear for himself my determination to leave. It was an emotional meeting, and I struggled to keep myself together as I went through a short summary of my business and personal circumstances. He soon realised that I wouldn't be persuaded, and the meeting changed its tone. He congratulated me for all my efforts and wished me well. In fact he offered his personal assistance if ever I needed it, which I massively appreciated.

I think we both knew that after twenty years in London at major investment banks and twenty-seven years all told, the adventure was finally over.

Again, I was having to keep a smiley face for the outside world, as there was a date set for the announcement following which I would spend as much time as needed to ensure a stable transition from a client and internal perspective. It was an immensely lonely time, but at least I had a plan on which to concentrate. In addition I felt huge loyalty not just to the team but to the firm. I knew and cared about hundreds of individuals with whom we had built a great business until the misguided ambitions of Dick Fuld took over. All the way through this, Charlotte was an unbelievable rock of support. She offered advice where she could, and was a sounding board always. It seemed irrelevant that we weren't currently together – we both knew that I couldn't go through all this without her. In addition, nobody knew me as well, so she appreciated the part she could play to help me. The biggest issue was that it was all a secret and had to remain that way. Charlotte loyally adhered to this through the weeks, and honestly I couldn't have got through it on my own.

Eventually Nomura set a date for September, and I resolved to go to New York to say goodbye to friends out there, and also take some holiday in France in the wonderful Cathar Region, rich in history and a favourite part of France for me. Places like Carcassonne and Mirepoix were an oasis of calm amidst all the changes afoot.

By now, I had made my final decision to leave the UK and travel abroad. I had no reason to stay in London, and every reason to leave. The plan was to go east to Hong Kong and beyond, and then to New Zealand for a while, ending up in South Africa. I had no timing agenda, but plenty of places and people to visit. Was I running away? Well yes, but I was convinced that whatever happened and however it panned out, I would be better for it. Sometimes you have to follow your gut feeling and there was an element of catharsis.

One of my last acts at Nomura was to check myself in for a medical, as I was allowed, and surprisingly found myself to be very fit, always good news. I was starting to train for the London Marathon the following April, which I had agreed to run for CRY – if of course I was back in the country which was by no means guaranteed.

However, when the doctor asked me to fill in the 'lifestyle' section, she was less impressed. Recently divorced, leaving job, no settled place to live, a broken relationship and leaving the country… my score was off the chart. She wanted to check I was OK, and with a deep breath I assured her I was dealing with it all, I wasn't drinking myself into the ground, or driving myself crazy. In a funny sort of way I had never felt as sure about anything in my life… being in the middle of a perfect storm was how I rationalised it to myself, and I was ready for whatever came next.

Soon the time was right and together with the Head of HR, an incredibly helpful guy called Geoff Goodman to whom I will always be thankful, we wrote the defining email. When it was released, I was there to tell everyone that I simply needed a break, that there was nothing personal with Nomura, and I stayed around for six weeks to prove it, talking to clients, handing over to colleagues and generally providing reassurance. It all worked well, the firm was happy and I had at least three leaving parties, each one more drunken than the last and I allowed myself to drift into melancholy as my departure date loomed.

There is something surreal about leaving a place which was, for eight years, an adventure of unbelievable proportions, going from a small time boutique to a global powerhouse. To live through the collapse of Lehman and come out the other side, then to leave your mates with unfinished business, it didn't fit the way I had lived my life – I was always so passionate about everything I did. But when you know you can no longer commit, you know that you will simply let people down and that for me was even worse. I had lost the reasons to get up in the morning and give it my all, so I had to go.

We set a time one day when I would leave the trading floor, and I slowly cleared the last remnants of my desk until there was nothing except a bulging briefcase perched on my chair. The senior managing directors had gathered to say goodbye and it was tough to say very much, the emotion was beginning to build in me. Even more so when the entire trading floor got to their feet and applauded as I made my way across the room, past the sales and trading teams with whom I had worked for so long. Tears filled my eyes, and I wanted to stop to take it all in. But I kept steadfastly on until I was by the lifts, and it was done. I was out, free as a bird and with a world ahead of me which held any amount of uncertainty, but I wanted to embrace it with all my heart.

I managed to get a few miles down the road before the enormity of what I had done overwhelmed me and I had to pull over as I was in no state to drive. I had arranged a round of golf with Adam Cocks, who had fast become one of my closest friends and was joining me in New Zealand halfway through my tour. What felt like a good idea turned into a few hours of club swinging, which would have been better suited to a total hacker. Meantime Charlotte and I spoke and she wished me all the luck in the world and asked me to send her a postcard; it was a rubbish effort at good humour but she knew what a pit of despair I was in and was trying to drag some laughter out of me.

The next day I woke with a hangover of a different kind but focussed on the future. I was scheduled to leave for Hong Kong on the first leg of my trip a number of days later to stay with an old cricketing friend, Jonathan Orders, who lived there with his wife and three children. Then on to Vietnam and Singapore for a few days before moving on to the land of the Long White Cloud, New Zealand. It was an exciting prospect in anyone's book.

I spent time with Sophie and Alexander, who were, I think, a little bemused but broadly understood what I was up to – they weren't the only ones who were a little unsure as to what I was doing and why – but then no one could put themselves in my shoes. I promised the children that we would meet up for the New Year in South Africa for a holiday. In the meantime of course Sophie was at university and Alexander at school so they wouldn't really be missing me for that time which extended almost to Christmas. In today's world, being in contact was going to be very easy.

Charlotte and I met for the last time before my departure, which was close to unbearable. It was as if we knew the greatest test of our relationship was underway, even though we weren't even together. As we tried to talk things through, we were both overwhelmed by what we had experienced in getting me to this point. I handed her my car for safekeeping, and a series of telephone numbers of key people if anything should happen to me. After all I was off round the world, and at this point I really felt that I may never come back. She eventually went home and I was left with my final preparations.

It was 2 p.m on a beautiful Sunday afternoon in October when the taxi came to my door at Harcourt Terrace. I had checked my things over and over, I was truly ready. I wheeled my recently purchased North Face bag to the taxi and the two smaller ones followed. Then I looked round, the street was empty, almost eerily so. I remember an imperceptible shake of the head and a deep breath before I swung into the back seat, feeling vaguely sick. Was I really doing this? As we sped towards Heathrow, the sun was bright in my eyes but fading in its strength as the autumnal days were coming to an end.

We reached the terminal in good time, and I decided to get some Hong Kong dollars. A rather pretty girl at the counter smiled sweetly and tried to make conversation – "Well sir, is this a holiday you are going on?" I said nothing, venturing a weak smile.

Once checked in and in the departure lounge, I purchased a travel bag, ditching the Lehman one in a nearby bin. It seemed symbolic and another show of moving on. Although I knew there was something and someone I could never move on from.

The flight was called, and as I boarded I finally knew this was real.

CHAPTER 27

An End and a Beginning

It was in New Zealand when I received a text from my friend Jeff Blackett, the disciplinary officer of the Rugby Football Union, telling me of Francis Baron's resignation.

I was three months into what I had termed my 'gap' year, but what was in reality an effort to make some sense out of everything that was going on in my life – it is fashionable to talk about a mid-life crisis or such-like, but I prefer to say that a whole series of events had taken place all in one go, and I needed some time to take them all in – preferably 12, 000 miles away on the other side of the world.

I had arrived in the land of the Long White Cloud to play some golf and taste some wine – a somewhat different experience from being taken to pieces on a rugby field in New Zealand. I was accompanied by my good mate Adam Cocks, or 'Cocksy' as he was known. Cocksy was in the army and a veteran of the war in Afghanistan.

While I had come on from Hong Kong, Vietnam and Singapore, he had flown to Auckland direct from London. This was the first time he had been on holiday since being blown up twice in one day in Helmand Province, losing one of his best friends in the process. He had returned with a fractured leg, shrapnel wounds and concussive damage from a roadside bomb (IED) – only to be even more badly injured in a motorbike accident, which resulted in him re-breaking the same leg, as well as fracturing an arm. What a two years he had experienced. So this was a welcome break, so to speak, for him.

Cocksy was more than twenty years younger than me, but we had grown to be close mates. Our respective girlfriends were best friends, and we had spent many good times together, both before and after Afghanistan. He was one of the cornerstone inspirations behind the Help for Heroes' rugby match in 2008, an event which created a great sense of comradeship among all involved, and very much cemented our friendship.

When I was planning my trip abroad, he immediately expressed a wish to join me. I was also pleased because, although I was prepared to travel alone, having the company of a close friend would be a lot more fun. It was a great tour and we made a number of good friends – people were intrigued to meet two Englishmen cruising around with no agenda, and Cocksy was permanently fighting off the girls. We were taking in the sunshine of the South Island when I was contacted by Jeff.

There was no actual detail in his message, except for the fact that Baron was leaving after almost thirteen years in the post as chief executive of the most powerful and richest rugby union in the world. I had mixed emotions at the news. I was dispassionate enough to admire his achievements as a businessman: he had returned the union to financial stability and more in the new professional era, he had also sealed a number of profitable commercial partnerships, had overseen the construction and funding of a 250-room hotel in the South Stand, as well as the expansion of Twickenham stadium itself.

So I had no issues on many of his achievements. But he simply had no empathy with the game of rugby, especially the senior clubs, and sought to exert control at al times. It was crystal clear that he would never win that battle, and he never did, simply because there wasn't a battle to win. The professional game was ten years old, and the players were owned by the clubs so they had a very strong hand when it came to releasing players for internationals, and what that would cost. He had to understand the needs of the premiership, and to acknowledge the leadership there; he had to accept that there had to be a negotiated settlement, access to players and goodwill in return for money. Very simple.

Moreover, ever since Woodward had left in anger, Baron had presided over the structure of the England coaching management, with our ever knowing what he was doing. He had undermined Andy Robinson, and promoted Brian Ashton from within because it was convenient. Not that Brian wasn't one of the best, in fact he was a visionary, but there needed to be some clear thinking around the right structure, and so he failed as Robinson had and was consequently hung out to dry. But, as an employee of the RFU as well as being a man of great integrity, he said very little when he was removed from his position after the 2007 Rugby World Cup.

By this time of course, Baron had allowed the appointment of Martin Johnson in 2008 as England – England what? Manager? Coach? Director of rugby? Supremo? Head of performance? No one had the remotest idea what his role was, but apparently it didn't matter. He was the man whose personal credentials were unquestionable. To be fair to Baron, it wasn't his idea, but by now he seemed to have been emasculated by the very 'executive' chairman, Martyn Thomas.

Ever since Thomas's coronation as Chairman of the Union in 2005, he had been practising his own power-play. I watched him attempt to diminish Baron's authority, and he was the natural magnet for all those disaffected RFU Council members, who wanted to see the back of Baron – and there were plenty of them.

As they fought each other bitterly, at huge cost to English rugby (something for which they should never be forgiven), there was one moment of conflict which defined their relationship and signalled the beginning of the end. Back in 2005, the then performance director Chris Spice was at last removed. I liked Chris as an individual, he had a lot of good sense, but he didn't get rugby – hardly surprising given his hockey background, and his skills weren't transferable. Unfortunately Baron ignored both John Spencer's and my recommendation, claiming that Spice was liked by his department. So what?

As people considered the new vacancy, there was a clamour for the return of Clive Woodward, which became deafening and was most certainly supported by Thomas who was quite justified in having his view. Not that I disagreed, for me Clive was a shoe-in. However, could he build bridges with Baron, after the vitriolic nature of his departure, when he had slung various poisoned darts in Baron's direction? Thomas urged Baron to bury the hatchet and sanction Clive's return. In conversation with John Spencer, one of the selection panel and chairman of Club England, I was content enough. Woodward and Baron had lunch, and discussed a way of working together again. It seemed as if it would happen.

Until that is, Baron took a call from the chairman of the premiership, Dave Thompson, who was also chairman of Newcastle. He had decided that Rob Andrew was surplus to requirements and offered him to Baron on an effective free transfer, claiming that the premiership would find it hard to work with Clive. It was a perfect get-out clause for Baron. It denied Thomas and frustrated Clive in his return, all in the name of more harmony with the clubs – talk about killing a flock of birds with one stone. As a result, the interview with Clive turned into a very spiky meeting, and nothing like the *rapprochement* which

Clive Woodward, Andy Robinson, Brian Ashton. The brains behind England's RWC win in 2003. And all coached Bath!

Thomas was expecting. It became obvious that Baron was not prepared to work with Woodward, thus the appointment of Rob Andrew became a formality.

In Thomas's eyes, that was a treacherous *volte face*, and so the game was up for Baron; Thomas worked ceaselessly to engineer the chief executive's exit and managed to achieve it. While it was reprehensible that the two of them felt that their own agenda outweighed the national sporting interest, the fact was that, on Baron's departure, the void had to be filled, and people in the game hoped, understandably, for a new beginning.

While I felt very qualified to take on the CEO role at Twickenham given my business and sporting background, my strongest suit was the prospect of unifying the sport, which was riven from top to bottom. I had spent time on and off the field at both ends of the game, and I knew personally many of the key people in rugby. This was especially so with the premiership clubs, where many of the problems lay. Of course there was the small matter of running a business with a £200 million turnover – coincidentally almost exactly the same size as Lehman Brothers' Financial Equities business. In all honesty, the line management responsibilities at the RFU were nothing compared to the complications of dealing with the RFU Council.

I was also free and available, although the desolate beauty of the New Zealand coastline seemed light years away from Twickenham. Did I really want all the hassle which would come my way? The answer was very clear – of course I did. I had been touted as a possible successor to Baron for a number of years, but the questions were all theoretical because I was firmly entrenched in the City. This was real now, and my head was spinning with all the possibilities.

The time scale was likely to be in the spring, and that also suited me. My plan was to go to Australia, then South Africa and I guessed sometime when my head was in a better place, I would venture back to the UK. But I had to clear up one major obstacle, which was Martyn Thomas. My history with him was acrimonious, and since my departure from the RFU we hadn't exactly been meeting for dinner once a month. There seemed no way that Thomas would ever countenance my candidacy, however suited I was.

Jeff reassured me that he had spoken to Thomas about this, and was adamant that they had to choose the right person whoever it was – no personality issues could get in the way.

I took this at face value and when I returned to the UK to host my daughter's twenty-first birthday in January 2010, I called Martyn. We discussed at length the current situation and it was clear that the relationship with Baron was non-existent. That was a strange thing to hear, when it was their unholy alliance which had led to his appointment as chairman over Rowell all those years ago. However, he would not be the first person who had ever exploited such an opportunity. He promised me that whatever our history he would have no hesitation in endorsing me if I proved to be the strongest candidate.

So I made the decision to apply, set about updating my CV and laying out my plan to take the union and the game forward over the next five years. I sent it on to Thomas, who promised to forward it to the soon to be appointed head-hunters. Of course, absolutely no one knew about this except Jeff Blackett, in spite of the mounting speculation in the media on the various candidates.

Nor did I hang around in London, returning to South Africa shortly after Sophie's twenty-first. While I loved catching up with my family, having been away at Christmas time, my reunion with Charlotte had been traumatic. We saw each other pretty soon after I got back, and realised that we were still in love with each other, but unsure how to deal with it. This wasn't supposed to happen, surely after six months abroad I would be thinking differently.

After another six weeks in South Africa and a fortnight in Hong Kong, I was back again and entirely focused on the interview process for the CEO role. They were down to the last five, and I was one of them, although the head-hunters hadn't really been very clear on how it had all been narrowed down, and they more or less told me I was an afterthought. Again, Jeff assured me that I wasn't just some stalking horse so they could say I was part of the process before dropping me from a great height. Still after all my experiences in the City, something was niggling me, and it didn't feel right.

The three 'wise men' were all taken from the RFU Council. It seemed scarcely believable to me that there was no outside figure to provide some dispassionate opinion and add some objectivity to the process of selection. The out-going RFU President John Owen was talkative and friendly – we discussed England prospects and the failure to bring through younger players – what was my view on Johnson and Andrew? And how easily did community and professional rugby sit together? These were all reasonable questions, and John Douglas, the Surrey rep with a business background, invited my thoughts on transferable skills from financial services to sport – I had managed complex teams of bright people for many years, this was good territory for me. But Thomas was silent more or less throughout – I had written a ten-point plan on how I would deliver specifically, so there was plenty to talk about and test me on, but he said nothing. By the end of the one hour meeting, they crowed that there had been 100-plus applications, and were overwhelmed by the quality of the candidates – good decisions would be made.

Well, I am used to high pressure interviews, and this one was decidedly low key and amateurish, but the prize was a big one. As I left the head-hunters' office building, I wasn't impressed to bump into one of the RFU secretaries – this was supposed to be a private gathering. But the leaks at the RFU are legendary – within a day or two I was hearing that the five names of the final candidates were being freely bandied about. I was content to wait, and two weeks later the head-hunters called to say that they couldn't make their mind up.

Eventually I got the call, I wasn't being considered further, they thought they had their man. Fair enough, I had entered the contest with my eyes wide open, I knew the panel and I knew the history – if I hadn't been prepared to deal with it, don't get involved.

It emerged that the new CEO was to be John Steele, head of Sport England, ex-director of rugby at Northampton, ex-army and Scotland B rugby player. I didnt really know him, but assumed that he was as keen to take command as Thomas was to control him.

We didn't have to wait long for the appointment to unravel – after the usual comments of how ideally qualified John Steele was for the post, he started to clash with Thomas and others who were trying to dictate the agenda. I had played against John Steele some years earlier, and I had plenty of respect for him. I made contact and offered him a meeting to give him some insider thoughts on what he was up against – he declined saying he was too busy – that was a shame, because he completely underestimated Thomas. Thomas wanted to control everything, he was already chairman or executive of a number of boards within the RFU. There was only one eventual outcome.

The crux of the issue that led to Steele's departure was in his lack of communication with the management board. He seemed not to appreciate that he needed them on his side, and when the issues of the performance department and Rob Andrew were raised, Steele's unwillingness to consider all options counted tellingly against him. There was still a very strong desire to bring back Sir Clive Woodward, and regardless of the merits of this he couldn't just brush it under the carpet. But he was giving out mixed messages, and the frustrations were obvious. I can empathise with this – we all wanted clarity of direction and an end to the perpetual underperformance of the national game on and off the field. As the weeks went by, it was obvious that Steele was becoming extremely isolated, and Thomas's conviction that the new CEO would listen to him more and more misplaced.

The eventual removal of Steele was conducted with breathtaking ease, but it was soon clear to the wider public that the manner of his removal was totally unacceptable, if not illegal. There was rumour and counter rumour, briefings to the press and a sense that Thomas may have finally overstepped the mark. John Steele may have failed to understand how much the council and management board could still influence proceedings, but he was a decent man and had been treated appallingly. It crossed my mind more than once that this could have been me in this position, but at least I would have known that to proceed without the support of senior board figures was corporate suicide. However, what was even clearer to me was that Thomas didn't want a CEO, but rather somebody who would fit in with his own agenda.

As the discontent grew, the disciplinary officer Judge Jeff Blackett was asked to conduct a review of the removal of Steele and the conduct of the management board. Meanwhile, Thomas had become the acting CEO to add to the other roles he had at the RFU. In summary, he was in charge personally of just about every aspect of the Rugby Football Union, and I have to say I admired his *bravado* in thinking that this was sustainable.

Away from the politics, England meanwhile were talking a huge game at the Rugby World Cup 2011, when in reality all the chickens were coming home to roost. I certainly don't wish to go over old ground here. History has judged that Martin Johnson wasn't equipped to be the head coach and manager of the England rugby team, at least not without someone of similar stature and more experience alongside him. Too many old stagers went along for the ride – Johnny Wilkinson for one, which may sound like heresy, but it was clear he was well past his best and could no longer operate as an orchestrator of a back line. I watched him in a warm up game v Wales, when the England centre Ricky Flutey was trying to make a late bid to make the squad. It was seventy-five minutes before he touched the ball, I think if I had been playing I would have hit the ageing stand-off. Unbelievably Jonny Wilkinson got the Man of the Match award because he kicked some penalties and a drop goal. The adjudicators must have been watching another game. Other veterans such as Steve Thompson and Mike Tindall went along to New Zealand and were quite clearly not good enough.

Their lack of relationship with the media made them easy meat for a press corps, which was also unimpressed with England's boring style of play. England's exit at the quarter-final stage against France was dismal, and I watched the match in one of the great rugby pubs, The Sun Inn at Richmond, one of Jason Leonard's favourite haunts. The feeling of unhappiness was tangible, not just that we had lost, but how we had lost. It resembled the shambles of a game in the 1987 World Cup quarter final when we lost 16-6 to Wales and were never in the game. Ironically Johnson's men had a decent record over the last twelve matches, but never looked likely to progress. Add to that mix the various off-field scandals, some no doubt blown out of proportion, and the knives were out among the media and the grandees of the RFU.

This very public post-mortem of the woes of English rugby was played out alongside the mass condemnation of the management board, coupled with a recommendation that they be removed from office together with Martyn

Thomas. How on earth any constructive outcome could emerge from the shambles was further exacerbated by the leak of a players' feedback report on their own views of the RWC and their coaching team.

This was supposed to be an anonymous exercise so that players would speak frankly. They of course hadn't covered themselves in glory, but they had some caustic words for their management. Instead of being analysed and discussed behind closed doors, the report found its way into the *Times* newspaper. Apparently only twelve individuals saw the report which was highly confidential. How could it have been leaked? In today's world you can send emails which cannot be printed out and nor can they be forwarded to other people if you so decree it, but naively this restriction had been left off.

The outrage of Damian Hopley, the chief executive of the Rugby Players' Association (RPA), was understandable, and the ensuing inquiry to identify the mole of course led nowhere, despite the employment of a sophisticated private agency. Of course they could have found out if they had really tried, but instead Mark Souster, the *Times'* rugby correspondent, received the Sports Journalist of the Year award. To be fair, Mark handled the disclosures well, but this was hardly a scoop, just a cowardly leak of some sensitive material – we can all speculate on who would have done this, and who could have benefited from such an action. But all it really did was highlight even further the rotten core of the union. In fact people even started to suggest that the leak was a good thing as it supposedly got everything into the open. I concede that it might have been regarded as being cathartic.

Finally, the board decided to turn its vitriol onto Jeff Blackett who was leading this inquiry into the behaviour of the management board executives. It had obviously become personal between Thomas and Blackett; indeed it was Blackett whom Thomas blamed exclusively for the recommendation that he be removed from all his posts. He had been accused primarily of breaching confidentiality by leaking material to the press – something he firmly denied.

Ultimately, the whole tawdry scenario from top to bottom was a mess. It seemed to me that our game could stoop no lower, to apportion blame to Jeff Blackett, one of the few men with the universal respect of the game for his honesty and integrity.

Finally, and belatedly, the management board realised that it had lost all credibility by allowing the *status quo* to remain, and they informed Thomas he could no longer continue. After a tenure of some seven years, his reign was over. History will judge him more effectively than I can, but one of his final acts was to reduce Mike Tyndall's fine for being drunk and behaving in appropriately at the Rugby World Cup. The reason – he was too drunk to know what he was doing so this was a mitigating circumstance. Enough said.

What is certain is that he spent a huge amount of time on RFU business, and had an unquenchable appetite to take on multiple responsibilities. This was never sustainable, and simply left him looking autocratic in the extreme.

Also, people lost confidence in him when it came to negotiations within and without the RFU. This was a key failing – you can't get things done if there is a degree of mistrust.

Fundamentally he and Baron appeared ill-equipped to manage the complex issues at the top of the game. They lacked leadership and vision, and could not unify a fractured structure. Worse, they wouldn't delegate or listen to alternative opinions. They were highly political and seemed not to have the best interests of the game at heart.

We are still paying the price.

CHAPTER 28

Marathon Man

I had very little time to dwell on my failure to secure the CEO position, as I was still involved with Esher rugby club, which was battling against relegation from the championship, which is the division below the premiership and theoretically therefore the waiting room for elite rugby. So this was pretty much full-time in terms of trying to help a club which was batting well above its natural place in the order.

In reality no one had much of an idea, least of all the RFU, as to how this group of twelve championship clubs should be managed and helped in its ambitions.

The simple fact is that there is no vision as to how rugby clubs outside the premiership can progress, or even if they should at all, given their location, facilities, assets and such like. Clearly professional rugby cannot be sustained by more than an elite few. Yet how do you incentivise and encourage some clubs, yet make others aware of their practical limitations? Well the first thing you do is go and share your thoughts with that club, hear about their aspirations, offer advice, perhaps finance, certainly register interest. At the very least you lay out your own thoughts and vision. None of that has ever happened.

Secondly, if you expect certain standards to be maintained, you have to pay for them. This group of clubs were expected to survive on £320,000 per annum when the true costs were nearer £1million. Each club had to make up the deficit, or be financed by a sugar daddy. Financial difficulty would be met with sanctions and points deductions.

You get the picture? The championship is not a happy place, especially when the relegated team coming down from the premiership is given a parachute payment of £1.7million to soften the blow and help them back up again. In the 2010-11 season Worcester enjoyed an income of £2.4million as they also took a dividend from P shares they owned as a founder member of the premiership. Compare that with Esher's £320,000, and given we are a members' club, where no benefactor could own or bankroll the club, we, as the largest community club in the country, have to try and live within our means to the best of our ability. The struggle was unequal, and for a club like Esher a perpetual fight against relegation was always on the cards.

In addition, there were promotion play-offs for the top eight clubs, and relegation play-offs for the bottom four. If you stop to think about that, it meant that the eighth-placed club could actually be promoted to the premiership. In the season of 2010-11, Bristol finished eighth, one point above us. So they could have gone up, and if we had lost the play-offs we would go down to the national leagues, despite finishing fourth from bottom. This was the most nonsensical system ever. There was one reason only for it – more home games to boost revenue, as there was such a shortfall from the RFU which they simply wouldn't acknowledge. Thankfully the championship itself has finally started to put its own house in order by changing some of this, for example the last club goes down, no play off.

However, I had another rugby challenge in front of me in 2011, namely the second Help for Heroes' rugby challenge match. We honestly thought we couldn't possibly do another one, these events tend to be a one-off and unrepeatable, especially as the emotion of the occasion was so heavy that you want to remember it for what it was, an outpouring of support for our wounded soldiers at a time when they were suffering the most.

The reason for the first Twickenham contest was simple – to improve the facilities at Headley Court, the rehabilitation centre based just outside Leatherhead. This time it was different – the plan was to build recovery centres around the country where our wounded soldiers could spend time working out what to do with the rest of their lives. Put bluntly, in twenty years time they would still be without their legs or arms and they would always need our help. Bryn Parry, head of the charity, needed to light the touch paper again; could we do a reprise?

The answer was of course yes, but it had to be different this time. We also had to take on board that the H4H charity was hardly new, and in fact had raised more than £100million. The novelty factor was no longer there, the public at large had dipped their hands deep in their pockets. We had to somehow stimulate the interest to put on another game which would fill Twickenham or at least make a good dent in its capacity.

We dreamed of getting a number of World Cup stars to turn up, and as a consequence of packing out the ground. So we came up with the idea of a northern v southern hemisphere confrontation, surely an intoxicating prospect for a crowd which had gorged on the Rugby World Cup and wanted more. So we set about the task with great enthusiasm, hiring the Twickenham stadium again (this time at a much higher cost, but in these commercial days hardly surprising) and searching for a major sponsor if we cold find one.

More or less the same team of people gathered together for this next effort, and it made sense as we knew the ropes this time. Jeff Blackett in the chair, Jolyon Armstrong and Janice Ashby doing the lion's share of the organising and a squad of faithful RFU and military personnel prepared to do their bit. Very fortunately, we also secured a large sponsor, one of my previous clients, JP Morgan Bank. This was a major development, and it meant we had a serious head start on the financial front.

Rugby legends made themselves available on an even grander scale than before: Sean Fitzpatrick and Michael Lynagh put themselves forward to manage the southern hemisphere, Lawrence Dallaglio, Ieuan Evans and Jason Leonard the northern team. What a set of names, but there was better yet to come: Nick Mallett, the all-conquering South Africa coach, Wayne Smith the All Blacks' World Cup-Winning coach stepped up to take care of coaching the south, while the north had Dean Ryan, an England coaching hopeful and John Kirwan, the former All Black wing and ex-Italy and Japan coach. Ironically, all four of them were hot candidates to assume the vacant England job, which the media picked up on as the Help For Heroes game approached. In fact it became their quiet obsession, with the game becoming somewhat incidental at times as a result. Last but not least Bart Campbell, the CEO of Essentially, the sports marketing group, was a key part of the team. Not only did his organisation reach out all round the world for players, but his events company worked tirelessly to make the pre-match dinner a stunning success, as well as lending a hand in the marketing of the match itself as the big day approached. Bart is a straight-talking Kiwi, who was such an important influence over the months, advising on realistic player opportunities, particularly from the southern hemisphere.

Our biggest problem was on the pitch, as it was proving nigh-on impossible to get the returning World Cup players to commit. This bothered the sponsors as the size of the eventual crowd would be likely determined by the availability of the likes of Brian O'Driscoll the Ireland captain and Sam Warburton, his Wales counterpart. In reality it was a pipe-dream, and I reconciled myself to this very early on in the planning. But of course to the outside world we always had some top players in the pipeline, such as Richie McCaw, and even Dan Carter. We all thought we would persuade Jonny Wilkinson to make himself available, but whatever people's individual feelings about the charity, there was the small matter of professional contracts which meant they could not be released by their clubs or their countries.

I seemed to spend most of my evenings through the autumn on the phone to New Zealand or Australia, negotiating with agents, players and coaches for their players, big names or potential stars. Not for money, because this was a week's experience in England representing a top cause. Southern hemisphere servicemen and women were also being killed and wounded out in Iraq and Afghanistan, and we had decided to allocate some of the funds raised to their own charities. So there was every reason for these players to head north for the match. I threw myself almost obsessively into the teams' recruitment, and indeed, into all aspects of the game.

At the same time, in the second week of October, I was hit with a hammer blow event.

Some six months after I returned to the UK, Charlotte and I had found each other again. It was not without a lot of soul-searching on both sides. Bottom line we had decided we wanted to be together long-term, and for the following twelve months we were happily reunited but knew that the biggest call was just round the corner.

Choices, choices… five years on from the first time we met, we had become so much part of each other's life, but there were some big decisions for us to make now. If it wasn't to happen then we had nowhere left to go. We both felt that we were meant to be together, but somehow the pressure built on us from within, when there was now so little coming from outside. Ironic in a way, as if we had done the hard bit and were falling at the last hurdle… I did not drive the decision but I couldn't fight it either, and we finally broke up.

The sense of loss was overwhelming – when there has been a love so unconditional despite all the challenges we faced, there is no filling the hole that is left. The only way I could even start to deal with it was to fill up every waking hour with the challenging project that this had become. The first Help for Heroes match had coincided with the Lehman collapse and the implosion of my business career, it seemed uncanny that the second one was simultaneous with another trauma, this time in my personal life. At some level I suppose that I succeeded.

In a way, although we raised half the money than before, the effort this time was much more rewarding. Eventually we had gathered almost 1,500 international caps from all around the world, and they all enjoyed an incredible week, visiting the wounded troops, playing golf with them, taking part in a trip to No 10 Downing Street, as well as participating in a thoroughly entertaining rugby match. One of the New Zealand military players, a naval rating, had never been to England before, and for him this was an experience of a lifetime, and all to help out his fellow servicemen.

The pre match dinner was a great success, full of emotion, because a film about the wounded soldiers was shown, and some of those filmed came along to the dinner, which definitely focused the mind. It was clear that the Southern Hemisphere team was bonding exceptionally well, with their mix of New Zealand, Australia, South Africa and South Sea Islanders. I will never forget their post-match debrief at the hotel, when each player had to stand up and recount the most memorable piece of their week, nor will I forget the 5. 0am sing-song by both teams in the bar. I thought that American Pie was more for people of my era, but it's obviously timeless.

General Sir Richard Dannatt, President of Help for Heroes, Constable of the Tower of London (a role dating from the 11th Century) and former Head of the Armed Forces, made a speech at the dinner which I will never forget, and in a weird way I became part of history. "Let me remind you Gentlemen," he said, "that many years ago the Duke of Wellington emptied the Moat of the Tower of London, and here we are hundreds of years later and Simon Halliday has filled it up again." That will be the first and last time I will ever be mentioned in the same breath as the Iron Duke!

Another moment was very special for the management and coaching teams. The night before the match Lawrence Dallaglio organised a dinner at Riva, the well known restaurant in Barnes. What a table it was, Michael Lynagh, Sean Fitzpatrick, Nick Mallett, Jason Leonard, John Kirwan, Ieuan Evans, Dean Ryan, as well as myself and Bart Campbell. We bantered and told great rugby stories, fuelled by bottle after bottle of Italian wine. It was the only expense that this glorious band of ex-players charged for their time. In a professional era, it was special.

The whole match was beamed live to Helmand Province, where hundreds of troops were watching, and more than 150 wounded soldiers were at Twickenham – many more than last time for obvious reasons. This time there was no Prince Charles, and fewer dignitaries from the top echelons of the armed forces, but no matter. We had once again lit a touch paper, and this time the global rugby family had shown its support for the members of our military forces, who put themselves in harm's way. It made us proud, and more than a little humble, to be part of such an occasion. The match itself was free flowing and one of the tries even featured on Sky's top tries of the season!

I had one post-match conversation, which undoubtedly caught my attention. Nick Mallett, the southern hemisphere coach, came up and started to talk about the England coaching job. It was an open secret that he had been offered the role by the RFU following the departure of Martin Johnson and his team. But Nick had himself just returned from the World Cup as coach of Italy, and he wanted some time at home with his family, so he had suggested he would throw his hand in at the end of the Six Nations. This would obviously give someone else a chance to impress – I myself had suggested that this would have to be Stuart Lancaster. He was the cheap option for a start, but the Saxons' coach knew all the players and had their respect. This was a word that had got lost in translation during the World Cup fiasco, both on and off the field. It felt as if the players and management had lost respect for themselves as well.

As Nick spoke, it was clear that he had also spent some time talking to Wayne Smith about his willingness to take on a position with England. Nick's question to me was direct – would I be prepared to be the England team manager? This was almost a déjà vu, since Andy Robinson had asked me the exact same question all those years ago in 2004. On that occasion Francis Baron had blocked my appointment, but there seemed to be no issues this time around. I was the ideal counterpart to the Mallett-Smith axis, given my 'Englishness' and capability with the media, the union and the whole administration process. As a former international I would have empathy with the players, but have enough distance to command their respect and reinforce issues such as personal discipline. What is more, I rather liked the idea of a three-year run at the RWC 2015 with two of the best coaches in the world, and Graham Rowntree as well no doubt.

We parted with a promise to stay in touch, but I agreed that I would allow my name to go forward when it came to the interview with the panel. It was an unexpected end to the rugby adventure with the Help For Heroes. At the end of the process I had been part of a three-year commitment by our great game to come to the aid of an unmatchable charity, and we had helped to raise £2.25million, with many thousands of supporters going away to help 'do their bit' as Bryn Parry, head of the charity would say.

December came and went, and Christmas passed peacefully with Sophie, Alexander and the rest of my family, but being without Charlotte was very tough. We spoke on Christmas Day, and did our best not to allow the emotion to take over too much. I had already decided to go to South Africa for the New Year, which felt like a good place to return to, as I had spent three happy months there in 2009-10. I caught up with so many good friends, it also allowed me to take my mind off the pain that I was feeling. I also dropped in to see Nick Mallett in Knysna, where he was staying with his family. We discussed his vision for the England set-up, and I came away even more convinced that he was the man to return the World Cup to England in 2015.

However, the Six Nations' tournament saw a massive resurgence in English nationalism, as Lancaster called on the Red Rose to revive the sense of patriotism that seemed to have gone missing. There was no real sign of a strategy to be fair, but there was plenty of passion. England could easily have lost their first two matches, but didn't. After a plucky performance against Wales, but a match they never looked like winning, this was enough for the country. Add in a counter-attack win against a lacklustre French team, and a demolition up front of Ireland, and it was impossible really to deny Lancaster his chance.

However I would like to make a counterpoint. People seemed to forget that the brief was to find a world class coaching team, and if there had been a way to include all the main protagonists then perhaps it could have been a dream outcome. There was no doubt however that it was either Lancaster or Mallett. When I spoke to Nick after his series of interviews he felt they could not have gone better. But with the panel in question, Ian McGeechan, Rob Andrew, Conor O'Shea and a newly arrived CEO, it would have been a high-risk call to have gone against the Englishman and the whole rugby world understood the decision.

The importance of Wayne Smith in particular was exemplified by Lancaster's trip to South Africa to persuade him to come on board. I think the reality was that the respect Smith had for Stuart was a personal rather than a rugby one, and in any case he had declared his allegiances, and wasn't going to consider alternatives. Thus the best backs coach in the world was not available to England, but these are the decisions that get made, and only hindsight can play a part in confirming the overall choice made by CEO Ian Ritchie and his selection panel.

And so it came to pass that the Lancaster Era came into being, with his assistant Andy Farrell initially unavailable, so the only person he had with him was Graham Rowntree. Since then though he has brought Mike Catt on board and the team is finally in place. As a patriotic Englishman, no one wants England to succeed more than I. In a funny way, the Lancaster position isn't that different to that of Martin Johnson. He isn't the head coach at all, and has more or less accepted that. He is really a glorified manager, and you can tell he covets the Woodward mantle. Well, let's wait and see, the attacking strategy is, for me, the real differentiator between England as a top five nation, or as top of the world. It's as simple as that. What I do know is that England, as always, has the resources to win the next World Cup and there is now comparative harmony off the field. It feels that for the first time since 2003 there is unity of purpose between administrators, players and coaches, as well as a refreshing lack of ego, which raises the level of excitement and expectation even a full two years away. Let us hope it is enough.

Meanwhile, in April 2012 I took my place in my third London Marathon, running for my other charity Cardiac Risk in the Young, CRY. This was my other mission, which I allowed to dominate many hours, both evenings and weekends in the weeks leading up to the marathon. There are no compromises if you want to get round a twenty-six-mile course in a respectable time, particularly with a fused ankle, courtesy of an operation to sort out the problems with the joint from my injury sustained all those years ago.

My first effort at long-distance running had started in 2006, when I asked a number of fellow retired internationals to run the Bath Half Marathon for this amazing charity. Ever since the twin deaths of Howard and Sebastian English, I had in my mind something special to raise funds. Even though they hadn't died because of rugby, both tragic accidents happened on a rugby pitch. Famous names including Will Carling, Jason Leonard, Mike Teague, Paul Ackford, Richard Hill, Jonathan Webb and many others rallied to the cause. In all some seventy CRY runners took part, we commandeered Bath rugby clubhouse and had a huge reunion afterwards. Eventually we raised £240,000, which went towards a cardiac specialist unit at the Royal Brompton Hospital. We all felt as if we had done something useful. Extending my ambitions to the full marathon seemed obvious, albeit scary.

My first effort in the 2009 London Marathon was five hours forty-six minutes, a truly amazing, but ultimately disappointing, experience because of the time. The second attempt in 2010 was five minutes past the five-hour mark, which was much better, although tantalisingly close to the target I had set myself, which was to run it inside five hours. To this end I became obsessed with this goal, as I prepared for my third London Marathon having been inspired to run it by the death of a sixteen-year-old female hockey international.

Mark Jackson, Paul Ackford, Will Carling, Jason Leonard, Dave Egerton. The Bath Half Marathon (2006) raised £250k for a heart screening centre for CRY (Cardiac Risk in the Young), and marked my return to some sort of fitness after my ankle fusion. Mark may not have been an international but he was fit that day!

The terrible statistic published by the charity of eight young people dying very week in the UK had increased to twelve, mostly because of awareness and more disclosure. But it is such an unacceptable situation and so I felt I had to run again, and CRY was delighted that I was taking part as a patron of the charity. That year more than 100 runners wore CRY vests, a wonderful effort.

Missing my target by only two minutes was upsetting, but nonetheless it was yet another inspirational experience. Sadly a young lady died of a sudden heart attack during the run, again reminding us of the terrible statistics. Football had had its own wake-up call a few weeks earlier with the collapse of Fabrice Muamba during a Bolton-Tottenham match, and he was lucky to escape with his life. It remains a fact that we can prevent these tragedies happening through screening and by constantly raising public awareness. It is regrettable that this charity even has to exist, but I am proud and very humbled to be a patron of such an organisation which does such great work.

Epilogue

And so, what of the future?

Rugby will always be my great passion, after all it defined me as a person and represents values that everyone would respect. So while England progress towards a home World Cup, I shall always have a view, especially as far as midfield backs play is concerned!

On the financials front, the ramifications of the Lehman collapse continue to reverberate throughout the world markets even five years on, the business and personal costs have been long-lasting, and it's not over yet. I still remain connected to financial markets, but other things matter so much more.

My personal take on life has changed forever. Outside finance, it's been all about Esher rugby, Help for Heroes, CRY and Oxford University Sporting Alumni. If I can help companies and people benefit from my experiences then I will, that is the essence of Hallers Consulting, the company I formed a couple of years ago, but which has not yet been awoken into life.

My private life is exactly that, but there are of course some very special people who matter so much. I was blessed with a long marriage and two wonderful children whom Suzanne and I cherish very much. Our beautiful twenty-four year old daughter Sophie has finished her final medical exams, and deserves to be successful after so many years of hard work. She also manages to combine a very serious vocation with a sense of fun and love of life. Meantime our twenty-year old son Alexander has flown through his A levels and started a university course at Newcastle, I can only hope he has as much fun as I did when at university. He is a fine all-round sportsman, and enjoys a wonderful perspective with his sport, work and social life. They are both genuine friends, who have had to accept some tough situations, but I hope that they have always felt my love and support, even in difficult times.

Charlotte, who became the love of my life, is out there somewhere, cheeky smile to the fore no doubt, and a complete one off as one of her closest friends described her. She has been a real life-changer for me and if for whatever reason we haven't been able to find a way forward, what I do know is that Charlotte and I experienced an unjudging and unconditional love. That is irreplaceable and for me will never fade.

Importantly, amidst all my experiences I have been asked to be a patron of the Help for Heroes charity and it is the greatest honour I could possibly wish for. Everything else pales into insignificance, perhaps it is what my life has been leading towards, and my rehab at Headley Court all those years ago was prescient – without their help, I would never have played for England, how great to be able to say thank you in a small way by offering what help I can. Our ongoing support of wounded servicemen and women is critical. Lighting the touchpaper, rather like the rugby match at Twickenham those five years ago, is what it's all about. The tragic murder of Drummer Lee Rigby caused an outpouring of emotion and the public support for our wounded and sick grows stronger. Long may it continue.

As I have realised, I am defined by my emotions and the people I love. They know who they are, and it is to them that I dedicate this collection of thoughts and memories. When I played my last competitive game of rugby in 1992, in some ways it merely turned a page and heralded a new beginning. In my life, I have been unbelievably lucky to meet truly great people and enjoy valuable friendships. Let me never take them for granted. In a world where pain is only just around the corner, we all should be thankful for the good moments and not only deal with the adversity when it comes, but smile in its face.

As the great Nelson Mandela said: "It is not whether you fail, but how you respond when you do."

Finally, I have tried not to judge – though I will certainly be judged myself, and that's the way it should be.

Appendix 1: A very special Christmas message

I received this from Wayne Smith following the Northern/Southern Hemisphere match in 2011. Despite the fact that the All Blacks had just won the Rugby World Cup and his leading role in it, he stated that his week in England coaching the Southern Hemisphere team was one of the most rewarding and fulfilling he had ever spent – great words indeed. He was then sent this poem, which I forwarded to both teams. We both felt that it hit the mark, especially given the time of year. Enough said.

T'was the night before Christmas,
He lived all alone,
In a one bedroom house,
Made of plaster and stone.

I had come down the chimney,
With presents to give,
And to see just who,
In this home, did live.

I looked all about,
A strange sight I did see,
No tinsel, no presents,
Not even a tree.

No stocking by mantle,
Just boots filled with sand,
On the wall hung pictures,
Of far distant lands.

With medals and badges,
Awards of all kinds,
A sober thought,
Came through my mind.

For this house was different,
It was dark and dreary,
I found the home of a soldier,
Once I could see clearly.

The soldier lay sleeping,
Silent, alone,
Curled up on the floor,
In this one bedroom home.

The face was so gentle,
The room in disorder,
Not how I pictured,
a true british soldier.

Was this the hero,
Of whom I'd just read?
Curled up on a poncho,
The floor for a bed?
I realised the families,
That I saw this night,
Owed their lives to these soldiers,
Who were willing to fight.

259

SIMON HALLIDAY

Soon round the world,
The children would play,
And grownups would celebrate,
A bright christmas day.

They all enjoyed freedom,
Each month of the year,
Because of the soldiers,
Like the one lying here.

I couldn't help wonder,
How many lay alone,
On a cold christmas eve,
In a land far from home.

The very thought brought,
A tear to my eye,
I dropped to my knees,
And started to cry.

The soldier awakened,
And I heard a rough voice,
"Santa don't cry,
This life is my choice;

I fight for freedom,
I don't ask for more,

My life is my god,
My country, my corps.."

The soldier rolled over,
And drifted to sleep,
I couldn't control it,
I continued to weep.

I kept watch for hours,
So silent and still,
And we both shivered,
From the cold night's chill.
I did not want to leave,
On that cold, dark, night,
This guardian of honor,
So willing to fight.

Then the soldier rolled over,
With a voice soft and pure,
Whispered, "carry on santa,
It's christmas day, all is secure."

One look at my watch,
And i knew he was right.
"Merry christmas my friend,
And to all a good   night."

This poem was written by a Peacekeeping soldier stationed overseas. The following is his request. I think it is reasonable:

PLEASE. Would you do me the kind favour of sending this to as many people as you can? Christmas will be coming soon and some credit is due to all of the service men and women for our being able to celebrate these festivities. Let's try in this small way to pay a tiny bit of what we owe. Make people stop and think of our heroes, living and dead, who sacrificed themselves for us. Please, do your small part to plant this small seed.

Appendix 2

My unsuccessful Application for CEO post at the RFU. However, it does sum up what I feel is important.

I am very excited that this opportunity has arisen at such an important time for Rugby in England. I believe that I am well equipped to deliver on the wide ranging agenda that faces the sport. I am passionate in my commitment to re-establish England at the top of World Rugby as well as continuing to attract growth within England. I would welcome the opportunity to demonstrate that I am the right person to take the game forward, relying on the following key considerations:

1. Rugby Knowledge
   I have been involved in rugby as a player, coach, manager and administrator for over 30 years at all levels of the Game and have significant experience of, and insight into, the different challenges facing the professional and community games. I also understand both sides of the club v country disputes of the past am confident that I could maintain harmony which would be to the mutual benefit of both in the future.

2. Importance of the Community Game
   I am well versed on the challenges facing the Community Game having spent eight years on the RFU Council. I have also gained practical experience of grassroots rugby as VP of Esher RFC during the club's rise from level 5, former coach of KCS Minis and lead sponsor of the Men and Women's Varsity matches. The CEO must demonstrate his commitment to a strong Community Game and he must be visible to the many junior clubs around the country. I completely endorse this concept.

3. Respect in the Game
   I have significant credibility within the Game as an ex-international and through my other posts and would start from a position of strength in developing relationships with and respect of the Game at all levels.

4. Key Rugby Relationships
   I already know, and have good working relationships, with most of the personalities in PRL, RPA the RFU Council and Management Board. Many of the Club owners and Directors of Rugby are also well known to me. I maintain trusted contacts in the rugby media through whom I will be able to build the RFU's profile.

5. England as a pre-eminent Rugby power – I believe, given the resource base, that England must continuously hold a top-3 position in global rugby rankings. My success in club and international rugby is testament to this ambition in my blood. The structural issues which need to be confronted include topics such as the number of foreign players in the English game, competition structures, future management of the academies, health and safety of players and developing the laws of the Game to enhance its attractiveness while not losing any of its core values. These issues require the long term commitment which I would give.

6. Global Perspective
   The RFU has to show leadership in rugby on a global scale but without appearing arrogant and patronising. It is important that we take the rest of the rugby world with us rather than alienating other countries. I have considerable experience as a successful negotiator both inside and outside of Rugby, and of dealing with different cultures and personalities.

7. Rugby as a Sport for All
   My experience as Head of Disability has taught me to underestimate peoples' potential at my peril. I am committed that the RFU should support initiatives across all spectrums (women, disabled, disadvantaged, inner city, gay and lesbian etc) as well as mainstream for all shapes, sizes and ages.

8. Leadership skills

My business career has afforded me many opportunities to lead teams of people, often in extremely high pressure circumstances. My style is to combine encouragement with a clear message of accountability and responsibility through regular communication with the work force. Tactical and strategic decision making has been my day to day responsibility. The ongoing challenges for Rugby in England are very demanding and will require strong and decisive leadership combined with empathy for all stakeholders. I have the experience and skill set to deliver.

9. Teamwork

More than in any other business the CEO must consult all parts of the Game to ensure every stakeholder feels he has a voice. The professional staff in the RFU contain many high quality individuals who should be empowered through responsible delegation. I am experienced in engendering a team ethic not just from my experience in rugby but also in my professional life where consultation and networking is essential, not least on the bank trading floor where there may be 700 people.

10. Commercial and Financial Capability

The RFU has achieved an enviable position in both commercial and financial terms over the last number of years for which Francis Baron takes much credit. I have the ability to continue that success – for example, I have a significant number of corporate contacts across many business lines which I will be able to leverage. I have a good understanding of the need to market a product in which much has been invested, and to maximise the value of a brand. This is effectively what I have done every day for many years in Investment Banking. Moreover, I have throughout my career had to operate to aggressive and demanding budgets, justifying investment through revenue outlook as well as being prepared to cut costs where necessary. In my business people are the major cost (outside technology) and I have often had to take tough decisions to reduce those costs while treating people fairly.

11. Passion and Commitment

When I voluntarily left Nomura in September 2009, I decided to travel abroad for a few months. I left with a guaranteed appointment in the City on my return, but have resisted attempts to entice me back because I want to be available for the role of CEO of the RFU. I want to devote the next best years of my working life to this job. I have demonstrated my capacity and commitment to be involved in Rugby throughout my City career, combining a 60-hour week with many more hours on rugby matters. Rugby has been my life for many years and I have a passion for it and for England success. At the same time I am very aware, having been the Managing Director of four major Global Investment banks, of the need to be objective as befits an executive in any business. I believe that it is the combination of my passion for the sport and business background which makes me a strong contender for the post.

Index

Ackford, Paul: called up out of retirement by Harlequins for 1992 Pilkington Cup final, *4*.

Andrew, Rob: driving force behind clubs' demand for compensation for release of England players, *180*; appointed as replacement for Chris Spice, *183*; support for Robinson lukewarm at best, *183*; on Elite Players Group,*188*.

Angel, John (ankle specialist): ankle op changes Halliday's life, *87*.

Armstrong, Jolyon: appointed Help for Heroes' rugby administrator *209*; takes on same role for second H4H match, *251*.

Ashby, Janice: invited on to committee for inaugural H4H match *209*; similar organisational role in second H4H match, *251*.

Bailey, Mark: lures Halliday into drinking contest, *31*.

Balshaw, Ian Lions criticism *174*.

Bardner, Julie, *83*.

Barkley, Olly: at end of contract *222*; thinking of leaving Bath, *223*

Barnes, Stuart: drop goal in 1992 Pilkington Cup final, *4*; with Nick Mallett at Vincents Dinner, *23*; England U23 in Italy, *36*; commits to England, *47*; switches from Bristol to Bath in 1985, *47*; resigns from England in disgust, *66*; speech in Pump Rooms about impending retirement of Halliday, *107*.

Baron, Francis: negotiations with clubs, *179*; refuses to appoint another England manager and another performance director, *182*; warns Robinson that he has to get on with Spice, *182*; achievements listed *186*; insists that Halliday and Souster swear affidavit testifying to the events, but they refuse, *192*; resigns from RFU after more than twelve years in charge, *240*; Halliday admires achievements of, *240*.

Bath: Pilkington Cup final 1992, Pilkington Cup record *1*; History, *38;* Leicester defeat sparks twenty-three-game unbeaten run, *45*; Barnes joins from Bristol in 1985, *47*; suffer shock defeat to Moseley in John Player Cup, *50*; the ill-advised 'fly-on-the-wall' TV documentary, *110*; Halliday appointed non-executive director, *218*; win European Challenge Trophy, *225*; Halliday decides club needs COO *225*; scandal after Stevens fails drug test, *227*; further scandal of five players accused of cocaine abuse, *228*; treatment of Stevens and then later of the five players in cocaine case, *228*.

Beazer, Cyril: funds half of student tour, *32*; dies, *33*.

Beckwith Brothers: accept invitation to invest in Harlequins, *163*; unprepared to underwrite club with bankers, *164*.

winery for lunch by Johann Rupert, *194*; persuaded by Rupert to stay on in South Africa for a couple more days, *194-195*; family meets Mandela, *195-196*; Mark Souster suggests fund-raising match at Twickenham for injured servicemen, *206*; date set for charity match, *207*; invites ex-soldier Adam 'Cocksy' Cocks to get involved in H4H match, *207*; appoints His Honour Judge Jeff Blackett as chairman of organising committee, *208*; Jolyon Armstrong in charge of administration, marketing, sponsorship, media etc, *209*; traumatised at start of final week before H4H match by collapse of Lehman Brothers, *213*; meets Charlotte and falls in love, *231*; relationship ends, *232*; decides to travel to Hong Kong, New Zealand and South Africa after leaving Nomura, *234*; to meet Adam Cocks in New Zealand, *237*; itinerary takes on Hong Kong, Vietnam, Singapore then New Zealand, *237*; spends time with Sophie and Alexander before leaving, *237*; last meeting with Charlotte, *237*; receives text from Jeff Blackett informing Halliday of Baron's resignation from RFU, *239*; admits admiration for Baron's achievements, *240*; hosts Sophie's twenty-first birthday party, *243*; traumatic reunion with Charlotte, *243*; tackles preparations for a second H4H match, this time northern hemisphere v southern hemisphere, *250*; J P Morgan come in as sponsors, *251*; Charlotte relationship ends, *252*; after three years working to raise money for H4H Halliday involved in amassing £2.25million, *254*; takes part in third London Marathon running for CRY having begun long distance running with a Bath half marathon in 2006, *255*; London Marathon, *256*; invited to become a patron of Help For Heroes, *Epilogue*.

Rugby playing career: final rugby match, which is against former club Bath, *1*; rugby prepared him for life, *5*; saved from a thumping by referee, a former teacher Mike Thomas *9-10*; Varsity rugby match in 1979, *14*; fly-half and fullback position, *14*; registers for freshers' team, *17*; wins rugby Blue in second year with Eddie Q-A, celebrates victory and salutes the late Dom James, *19-20*; influence of Nick Mallett, *21-22*; sitting between Mallett and Barnes at Vincents Dinner, *23*; touring to France, *27 & 29*; plays against Serge Blanco, *28*; Blanco all-time first choice fullback in Halliday World XV, *28*; touring Hong Kong and Japan with England Students, *30*; lured into drinking contest with Mark Bailey in Japan, *31*; is persuaded by Derek Wyatt to give Bath a second chance, *32*; England U23 tour to Italy 1982 and Romania 1983, *33-34*; Lloyds Insurance tour to California, *34*; England U23 tour to Romania, *35-36*; the Bath phenomenon, *39*; commutes from London to Bath and trains with Dorking, *44*; psychs out his friend Jonathan Webb in Cup semi-final and takes him out, *46*; pays tribute to John Horton, *46-47*; tribute to Tom Hudson, *48-49*; loses temper with Rowell after Southwest defeat against London, *53*; first selection for England v Canada, a non-cap game, *57*;

injury robs Halliday of chance to face the New Zealand All Blacks, *58*; unable to take part in inaugural Rugby World Cup because of work commitments, *66-67*; makes England comeback partnering Will Carling in 1988, *68*; goes on tour of Australia in 1988, *68*; ankle, baby daughter and business persuade him to be unavailable for 1989 Lions' Tour to Australia, *70*; approached by mysterious South African to take part in 1989 'rebel' tour, *71*; Dudley Wood warns that England career would be in jeopardy if he participates in rebel tour, *72*; turns down chance to go on 'rebel' tour, *72*; importance of physical fitness and conditioning,*79*; lecture from Geoff Cooke over alcohol before important Five Nations' match against France in Paris in 1992, *80*; comes close to pulling out of 1992 clash with France through hamstring injury *85*; first plays against a young Carling, *89*; Cooke unhappy with general fitness of, *89*; hamstring forces onto sidelines, *89*; clinches England return with hard match against Leicester, *90*; scores a rare try against Australia under captaincy debut of Carling, *91*; dropped for Guscott, *97*; assessment of Carling the captain and the player, *97-101*; focus on 1990 Grand Slam showdown and defeat by Scotland, *103-106*; decides to leave Bath and join Harlequins, *112*; reflections and analysis of Bath, *112-113*; kicked in eye by team-mate Carling in grudge match v Bath *113*; enjoys 1991 Grand Slam, *116*; pre-Rugby World Cup tour of Australia and Fiji in 1991, *117*; stamped on in Australia, *118*; on bench for start of 1991 Rugby World Cup, *119*; selected on wing against Scotland, *119*; reflections on reaction to 2003 Rugby World Cup win, *120*; reflections on 1991 Rugby World Cup final defeat v Australia, including the 'change of tactics', *120-122*; back-to-back Grand Slam in 1992, *127*; turns down chance to carry on into 1993 after invitation by Cooke, *129*; reflections on own Lions non-career, *169*; memories of Carling TV commentary remarking on Halliday hairstyle v Romania, *170-171*; memories of Guscott wonder try for Lions in 1989, *171*; ankle finally giving out, operation post career, turns to agreement made with RFU medics for op at RFU's expense *176*; receives a letter from Dudley Wood saying that RFU could not create a precedent of funding treatment for ex-players, *176*; eventually undergoes four operations on ankle, *176-177*; recalls run-in with drug-testers after England complete back-top-back Grand Slams, *229*.

Rugby coaching: visits to schools as a guest coach, 7; persuaded to become Esher coach, *154*; meets Esher team manager John Inverdale, *154*; introduces twice-a-week training at Esher, *155*; Esher win the treble of league, Surrey Cup and Junior Team of Year, *155*; bumps into Tom Hudson, now director of sports at Surrey University, *156*; tips off John Kingston, the Richmond coach about Chapman at Harlequins, *157*; retires from coaching Esher in 1995 and moves to

Harlequins as backs coach, *162*; gives up in 1996 after stating that Will Greenwood was most talented midfielder in country, *162*.

Rugby administration: invited to become a trustee of Harlequins, *163*; Best is subjected to vote of no confidence and departs, *163*; possibility of having to sell the golden share to Beckwith Brothers, *164*; confesses Harlequin plight to corporate colleague David Wilson, who suggests speaking to Australian Duncan Savile, *165*; Savile agrees to come to England on next available plane, *165*; bows out of Harlequins, *166*; invited to be a selector for 2001 British and Irish Lions, with special brief to look at English three-quarters *167*; admits he pushed for Jason Robinson and Rob Henderson, but was against Scott Gibbs touring, *170*; co-selectors Derek Quinnell and John O'Driscoll, *172*; anachronism of amateur Lions in professional era, *174*; anger at Balshaw comments about 2001 Lions tour, *174*; selected for RFU committee to identify stars of the future, *176*; resigns from committee after refusal by RFU of financial help for ankle op, *176*; sits on Barbarians' committee, *177*; invited by Fran Cotton to join Club England to help administer the newly professional game in 1998, *177*; discovers, too late, that role involves becoming a member of RFU Council, *177*; amusing allusion to fact that he was now one of Will Carling's '57 old farts', *177*; discovers the tortuous processes in RFU to get decisions made, *177-78*; agrees with Judge Jeff Blackett proposal to reduce size of RFU Council, but is unsurprised when members vote three-year moratorium, *178*; immediate tasks of Club England, *178*; shares Woodward views on the game and the future, *178*; made part of group to establish amount of compensation that RFU should pay clubs for release of their England players, *180*; clash with Baron over agreed amount *180*; Andy Robinson credentials *182*; advises Robinson to resign immediately when Baron refuses to appoint a manager and a performance director *182*; charged by RFU Council to approach Rowell regarding the position of RFU Chairman following Cattermole resignation *183*; anger at Rowell campaign depicted as being in support of élitist end of game,*185*; Thomas suggests a deal whereby he would step down from campaign in exchange for deputy chairmanship, *185*; meeting held to agree to proposal, *185*; Thomas changes mind after being told that he looked like winning the AGM vote, *185*; criticises The Way Ahead report, *186-187*; asked by John Spencer to set up Elite Players' Group, *188*; EPG involved Andrew, McCafferty, Phil Winstanley and Damien Hopley and after half a dozen meetings come up with agreement which is accepted by RFU Council, *188*; admits outspokenness counts against him and is excluded from Professional Game Board, *189*; called by Bath owner Andrew Brownsword and offered position of non-executive director, *217*; disappointment that he did not become chairman of Professional Game

O'Driscoll, John: Lions selector, *172*.

Offiah, Martin: agrees to play in first H4H charity match, *211*.

Ojomoh, Steve: tackled by Halliday in 1992 Pilkington Cup final, *3*.

Ormrod, Mark: Afghanistan veteran features in moving DVD shown on big screen in Twickenham before first H4H match, *215*.

O'Sullivan, Eddie: agrees to help coach International XV in first H4H charity match, *210*.

Ottey, Merlene: meets up with England squad in Lanzarote, leotard stolen and worn by a prop, *96*.

Pilkington Cup: 1992 final, premier domestic club competition,*1*.

Palmer, John: 'most talented centre Halliday played with or against', *39*; finally gets England call-up on 1984 South Africa tour, *Chap 8*.

Quinnell, Derek: Lions selector, brief assessment and appreciation of by Halliday, focus on his pass in famous Barbarians try in 1973 v New Zealand All Blacks, *173-4*.

Quist-Arcton, Edward: conversation with is defining moment in Halliday's rugby career, persuades Halliday to attend Blues training session and register for freshers' team, *17*; dedicates, with Halliday, Blues selection to Dom James, *20*.

RAF Headley Court: *See Headley Court.*

Reason, John: questions Halliday's temperament after outburst at Rowell, *53*.

Redman, Nigel: neutralised by Ackford, but wins line-out ball to set up Bath Pilkington Cup final victory, *3*; leans against shower button during team talk by Spurrell, *43*; agrees to help coach first H4H team in charity match, *210*.

Redundancy: injustice of, *136-38*.

Regan, Mark 'Ronnie': agrees to play in first H4H charity match, *210*.

Rhodes Scholars: importance of in Oxford sport and answer to Cambridge Land Economy, *23*.

Robben Island: visited by Halliday family, *192*.

Robinson, Andy: admired as a player and as a rugby thinker, Halliday acknowledges his ability when he is appointed England coach, then as Lions' assistant coach, Robinson's commitment as coach of England, so Fran Cotton calls on Halliday as a selector, *171*; credit for contribution to England's 2003 Rugby World Cup success,*181*; appointed England head coach and suggests Halliday become team manager,*182*; ignores Halliday advice to step down when Baron refused to appoint a team manager and a different performance director, Baron warns Robinson,*182*; selections are questioned,*183*; Halliday concludes that Robinson was set up to fail, *183*.

Vaughan, Pete: former Blackheath No8 a big influence in turnaround of Esher fortunes, *155*.

Vessey, Rupert: calls up Halliday as emergency cover against Perpignan and Agen, *29*.

Volley, Paul: agrees to play in first H4H charity match, *210*.

Watkinson, Tony: Oxford Rugby captain,*18*; perfect passer and wise man, *30*.

Watson, Alan (sports doctor): Halliday introduced to by Bath and England scrum-half Richard Hill, treats top sports people in Britain, sorts out Halliday hamstring in time for 1992 England v France match,*84-85*.

Watts, Hugh: joint head of Moor Park, product of Downside,*8-9*.

Way Ahead, The: report into future of RFU, Halliday critical, estimated cost of setting up report process estimated at £1million,*185*.

Webb, Jonathan:1992 Pilkington Cup final, *3*; upset by Halliday smashing into him at first high ball in cup semi-final between Bath and Bristol,*46*.

Wilson, David: introduces Australian millionaire Duncan Savile to Harlequins,*165*.

Winstanley, Phil (secretary of Premier Rugby Ltd): brought onto Elite Player Group,*188*.

Winterbottom, Peter: scores try in 1992 Pilkington Cup final, *3;* invited to become a trustee of Harlequins with Halliday, *166*.

Wiseman, Luke: becomes creative director of research at UBS after confrontation with Sants; involved in horrific accident,*130-31*.

Wood, Dudley: warns Halliday of England career threat if he takes part in 'rebel' tour, *72*; writes letter to Halliday explaining that the RFU cannot pay for ankle surgery as would set a precedent of funding treatment for ex-players,*176*.

Woodward, Sir Clive: Foreword; felt he should have been put in charge of 2001 Lions,*173*; argues strongly for better facilities for England squad, fails to understand how 2003 Rugby World Cup victory did not result in significant change of attitude regarding availability of top players for national team, anger at failure to persuade clubs to release England players more often to prepare for 2004 Six Nations,*178-80*; resigns as England manager following thrashing Down Under and poor 2004 Six Nations, assessment of achievements for England and English Rugby,*180-82*.

Wyatt, Derek: persuades Halliday to give Bath another chance, *32*.